The Galatians

The Galatians

Celtic Invaders of Greece and Asia Minor

John D Grainger

First published in Great Britain in 2020 by
Pen & Sword History
An imprint of
Pen & Sword Books Ltd
Yorkshire – Philadelphia

Copyright © John D Grainger 2019

ISBN 978 1 52677 068 4

The right of John D Grainger to be identified as Author
of this work has been asserted by him in accordance with
the Copyright, Designs and Patents Act 1988.

A CIP catalogue record for this book is
available from the British Library.

All rights reserved. No part of this book may be reproduced or
transmitted in any form or by any means, electronic or mechanical
including photocopying, recording or by any information storage and
retrieval system, without permission from the Publisher in writing.

Typeset by Mac Style
Printed and bound in the UK by TJ International Ltd,
Padstow, Cornwall.

Pen & Sword Books Limited incorporates the imprints of Atlas,
Archaeology, Aviation, Discovery, Family History, Fiction, History,
Maritime, Military, Military Classics, Politics, Select, Transport,
True Crime, Air World, Frontline Publishing, Leo Cooper, Remember
When, Seaforth Publishing, The Praetorian Press, Wharncliffe
Local History, Wharncliffe Transport, Wharncliffe True Crime
and White Owl.

For a complete list of Pen & Sword titles please contact

PEN & SWORD BOOKS LIMITED
47 Church Street, Barnsley, South Yorkshire, S70 2AS, England
E-mail: enquiries@pen-and-sword.co.uk
Website: www.pen-and-sword.co.uk

Or

PEN AND SWORD BOOKS
1950 Lawrence Rd, Havertown, PA 19083, USA
E-mail: Uspen-and-sword@casematepublishers.com
Website: www.penandswordbooks.com

Contents

Introduction		vi
Maps		xi
Chapter 1	The Approach to Macedon	1
Chapter 2	The Raids into Macedon	19
Chapter 3	The Raids into Greece	40
Chapter 4	Two New Galatian States	55
Chapter 5	Galatians into Asia	80
Chapter 6	Mercenaries	107
Chapter 7	Galatia and its Wars	124
Chapter 8	Galatia Facing Pergamon and Rome	148
Chapter 9	Collapse and Recovery	166
Chapter 10	The End of the Scordisci	181
Chapter 11	The Kingdom of Galatia	198
Chapter 12	A Roman Province	216
Appendix: Three Roman Emperors from Galatia		220
Notes and References		224
Bibliography		239
Index		242

Introduction

'Galatian' is the Greek term for the people who invaded the Greek and Asian lands in the third century BC, settling, many of them, in 'Galatia' in central Asia Minor. They were notorious among the Greeks as the barbarian raiders who sacked Delphi, and who attacked many of the Greek cities in Greek Asia. They founded several states in the Balkans and Asia Minor which lasted for several centuries; the Romans used a more descriptive term 'Gallograeci'.

The immediate origin of the invaders was in the northern Balkans, north of the Danube River. But these people, or at least their immediate ancestors, had themselves arrived from further west relatively recently. The original home of the Gauls (which was the Western European, or Roman, term for them) was in all probability a wide stretch of land north of the Alps, where the settlements are associated in particular with the La Tène period in archaeology, but developing out of the preceding Hallstatt period, extended from northern France, through southern Germany, and into Bohemia.[1] They began expanding at more or less the same time as the Greeks began their colonizing activities, in the eighth/seventh centuries BC, and about the same time that Rome claimed to have been founded. However, not being literate, their colonizations have not been as well recorded as those of the Greeks and Romans.

Despite this lack of literacy, they were one of the great peoples of the classical world, eventually occupying an enormous territory, from Spain to Poland and Romania, and into the Ukraine and Asia Minor. As such they had a greater extent of territory than either the Greeks (before Alexander, at least) or Rome (before its later imperial expansion in the first century BC). But, like the Greeks in their independent cities, they were much divided, into 'tribes' rather than cities, though both were independent, and their history is, because most of them did not write, more of an archaeological problem than a historical, based on the records of their enemies.

They were, above all, feared by the Mediterranean peoples because of their warlike prowess, though this was something they shared, of course, with every other people of the region. This, and their proclivity to invade their neighbours, resulted in widespread conquests. They came early into the occupation of all Gaul – to use the Roman name – then spread east along the upper Danube and into the Balkans. In the late-fifth century BC bands of them successively invaded Italy, spreading through the Po Valley and subjugating its inhabitants. In the process of their raids, they captured and sacked Rome early in the fourth century.[2]

These Italian conquests converted northern Italy into 'Cisalpine Gaul' – 'Gaul this side of the Alps' – and the result helps explain related conquests in the east. They may have invaded as a single people, though it is more likely that they came in successive waves, and when they settled into their conquests they did so as a series of tribal groups. These 'tribes' often bore the names of similar tribes in other lands. For example, there were Boii in northern Italy and in Bohemia, and there were Senones in Italy and in northern France. The implication is that the parent tribes dispatched fragments of themselves as raiders searching for loot and aiming to acquire a new homeland; they were quite likely to coordinate arrangements with other Gallic tribes in the same situation. That 'situation' was probably overpopulation at home.[3] The same solution to that same problem was adopted by Italian tribes such as the Samnites, where those born at a certain time were selected for dispatch, an action known to Rome as the '*ver sacrum*' – the 'sacred spring';[4] how voluntary this was is unclear, but the process among the Gauls was clearly successful, judging by their wide geographical spread.

Rome itself had experienced that population difficulty and had also solved it by conquest, but they did so in the near vicinity of their own city, and held on to their colonists by organizing them to form detached parts of itself – *coloniae* – a small-scale version of the Gallic response.[5] Rome thus became a compact conquest empire, while the Gauls remained fragmented and later on were subjected to Roman conquest. And yet the Romans, the Greeks, and the Gauls were all in effect colonizing in very similar ways, and using very similar methods. As it happens, the Roman method, enforced by the relatively narrow land that they were operating in, turned out to be the most powerful, but from several centres the

Greeks, then the Gauls, expanded most successfully. The sheer scale and extent of the Gallic expansion, however, would have made it impossible to retain any sort of unity, even if they had been united in their original homes. There never was any suggestion of a Gallic empire.

Gauls from northern Italy harried Romans and other Italians for the next generation, after the sack of Rome (c.390 BC), and meanwhile they firmly established themselves in the north of the peninsula, where they maintained their independence for the next two centuries. Another route of expansion took more Gauls into Spain, and still more went eastwards. This expansion was undoubtedly a process of conquest, but, despite the Gallic reputation for savage warfare, it was not necessarily a process involving the extermination of the conquered. In Spain the invaders appear to have blended with little difficulty with the natives, forming a group of tribes called the Celtiberians, who occupied much of the centre of the peninsula.[6] This process of assimilation was no doubt also the effect of the Gallic conquest elsewhere, so that their rapid progress in expanding was in part due to their propensity to assimilate conquered peoples. If the expelled Gauls, driven from their homelands, and forming, at least at first, warbands often comprised mainly of men, then assimilation would be relatively easy by intermarriage. The Gauls seem in most cases to have established themselves as a ruling group, without too much continuing disturbance to the existing inhabitants.

The recognition of the presence of Gauls in any particular place or region, in the absence of detailed written sources, depends largely on archaeology, a subject contaminated in some areas by modern political-historical and racial theories. (There are some written materials to help out, but they are either Greek or Roman, and are as contaminated by enmity as the modern theories by racist prejudices; both have to be used with care.) The archaeological evidence is also by no means easy to interpret. It depends on discerning a set of characteristics in excavations – burial customs, pottery shapes, types of metalwork, evidence of chariots and horses, hill forts, all of which are intricate and subject to dispute and alternative explanations. This evidence, however, has produced an agreed interpretation that the Gallic expansion into the Balkans reached the Danube by the early fourth century, at about the same time that the Gauls were sacking Rome and settling in Cisalpine Gaul.[7]

Precision in detail, however, is less easy than making wide assumptions, and the dating of many of the finds is difficult. Widespread claims for the conquest of modern Romania or substantial inroads into the Ukraine or Poland cannot be easily sustained, though the evidence is suggestive.[8] In the Balkans, the real concentration of the Gallic settlements – now that they are within the Greek area, they can be called 'Galatians' – appears to be in the area of the confluence of the Tisza, the Drava and the Save rivers with the Danube. This is an area called the Banat in Ottoman times, centred particularly on Belgrade, which had the Keltic name of Singidunum. It is a wide inland area, fertile, well-watered, and with usable routes leading in all directions – an ideal base from which to mount raids and expand conquests – and trade. (It was the centre of Ottoman power for several centuries, as it had been a Roman legionary base and a Byzantine power centre before the Ottomans.) Whoever lived in the area before the Galatians arrived were clearly subjugated by them, and the Galatian tribe called the Scordisci emerged in control; at least one group, the Hylli, seem to be the product of Gallic-Illyrian intermarriage, and it is probable that a large part of the Scordisci were in fact of Illyrian descent, which becomes clear in the study of the names of the latest inhabitants.[9]

The Scordisci appear to be an amalgamation of parts of the Gallic tribes of the Boii and the Taurisci, plus the aboriginal Illyrians and some Thracians. Another part of the Boii was a tribe settled in Bohemia, and the Taurisci were also in modern Austria (where they formed one of the constituents of the later Gallic kingdom of Noricum). The two tribes appear to have collaborated in sending out contingents south-eastwards, and these contingents conquered their new homeland and, in the process, eventually amalgamated, becoming the Scordisci.[10] This was the tribe in control of the Belgrade/Banat area in the first half of the fourth century, and was the source of the greatest Gallic invasions of all.

Note on names

As already pointed out the people who are the subject of this book have several names: Gauls to the Romans, but Galatians to the Greeks. They may also be more generally referred to as Kelts. Here the term 'Gauls' is restricted to those in Gaul and Italy: 'Galatians' refers to those in the Balkans and Asia Minor. Where it is necessary to refer to all these collectively, the term Kelts can be used. There is an issue in historical/archaeological studies with the term 'Kelts'; my use of the term here has no relevance to such a dispute; it is only one of convenience. The spelling 'Keltic' is used in this book to distinguish the people of the ancient world from the romanticised Celts of folklore, football, and modern mythology. The idea of a Celtic world is also under increasing discussion by archaeologists and ancient historians, though no consensus has yet emerged. The use of 'Keltic' here also distinguishes our Galatians of this book from that discussion.

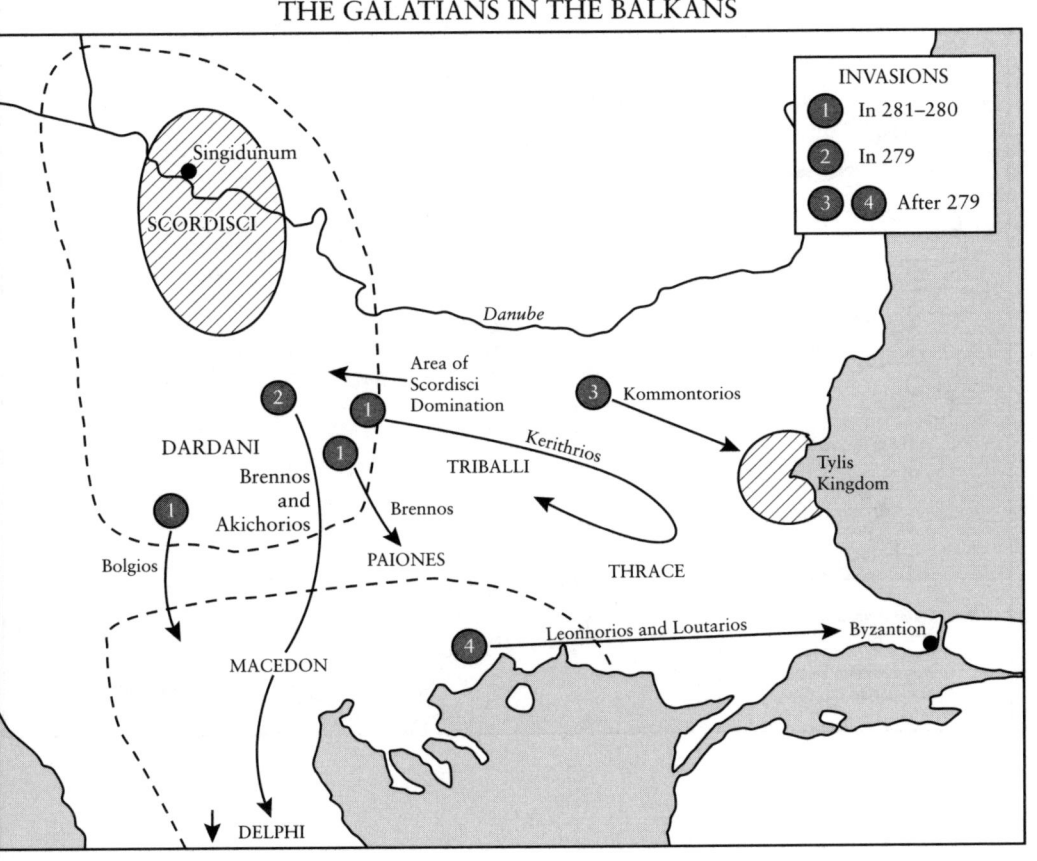

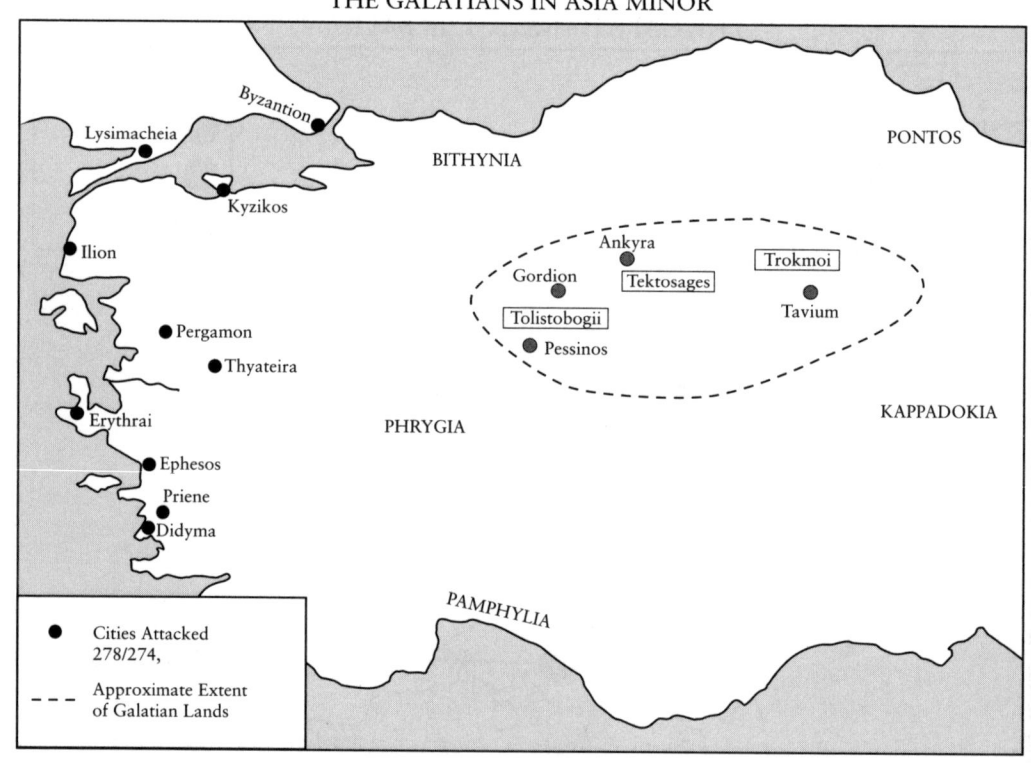

Chapter 1

The Approach to Macedon

Philip II, king of the Macedonians from 359 to 336 BC, campaigned several times into Thrace, the lands to the north and east of his kingdom, and over the period of his reign he succeeded in conquering large areas of it. He failed to conquer several cities on the Propontis (the Sea of Marmara), where Perinthos and Byzantion failed to succumb to his attacks, but in the Thracian interior he was able to gain control of the land as far as the Haemos Mountains (i.e. the Balkan Mountains), and was able to establish a couple of Macedonian colonies and several forts in that territory to maintain his control.[1]

The Macedonian control which was thus established over much of Thrace was less than firm, and it may better be characterized as superficial. It appears to have consisted of a few major garrisons at such places as Philippopolis and Kabyle, where colonists were established; these were linked by smaller posts or forts which were spread along the connecting roads, though as a means of maintaining control this was unlikely to have been successful for very long.[2] A number of the local Thracian chiefs had survived by submitting formally to Macedonian authority; several of these were members of the Odrysian royal family which had ruled in the area for the previous two centuries, still active. Such submissions were only good for the lifetime of Philip and his interlocutor, however; further trouble would ensue when one of them died.

The Thracian mode of succession was to divide the kingdom among all males with a claim, which made for weakness, especially in the face of the new Macedonian aggressiveness. The Greek cities on the coasts of the Aegean, the Propontis and on the Black Sea were largely under Philip's control or were friendly towards him, but this was in part the result of Thracian hostility, and holding both the cities and Thrace in the same regime would be difficult. Such arrangements as Philip made for the government of the conquests relied more on the threat of retaliation if trouble arose than on conciliation and protection. No governor for the conquered region was appointed by Philip, as far as we know; Alexander did appoint one when he was about to set off on his campaign in Asia Minor, which emphasized the explicitly personal nature of Philip's conquests.

Beyond the Haemos Mountains Philip had made diplomatic contacts with other tribes and rulers, and had conducted some raids, especially along the Black Sea coastal area, and even across the Danube, but no permanent conquests had been made.[3] His northern boundary was thus the Haemos range. On the other hand, those raids into the north had been clear messages to the inhabitants north of the mountains that conquest might well come at any time, and Philip's diplomacy was always aggressive, seeking submissions. To the kings and chiefs of the land between the Haemos Mountains and the Danube River, it will have been obvious that they were likely to be the next on Philip's target list, though, as it happened, the next were the Persians. The whole scheme of conquests and colonization in the north had a highly provisional look to it; if Philip was serious about holding this land, he would need to deploy time and troops, and to find good reasons to do so – but he was after other prey.

Under the circumstances it is a little surprising that the murder of Philip in 336 was not followed by an instant Thracian rebellion. There were still a number of members of the old Thracian royal houses of the Odrysai alive and active who could have led such a rising, but their recent submissions will have restrained them.

In the event the trouble when it came was a war with the Triballi, who were located north of the Haemos range and west of the conquered region, between those mountains and the Danube. This people had refrained from becoming involved in Philip's conquests, but had watched carefully for the opportunity to snatch some advantage from the wreckage he was making of other areas; in 339, they had intercepted a baggage train of loot and captives gathered by Philip in a raid on the Skythians – '20,000' captives and '20,000' horses and other still more portable loot, according to the sources, which probably reflected Macedonian annoyance. Philip had not reacted, even though he himself was wounded in the fight.[4]

Possibly his wound immobilized him for a time, but he had several competent generals who could have administered punishment. No doubt the Triballi were marked in his mind for future punishment. No doubt also this success will have whetted Triballian appetites.

The new Macedonian king, Alexander III, having swiftly dealt with the usual Illyrian raids which always followed on the death of a Macedonian king, and having dealt similarly with stirrings of troubles in Greece, turned to attack the Triballi. He was opposed at the pass through the Haemos and broke through; the Triballians evacuated their families to an island in the Danube, and stood to fight in defence of their lands and people. Alexander approached in battle formation, and sent ships along the Danube as a threat to the island. The Triballi were again defeated. Both battles are said to have cost only fifty Macedonian casualties between them, but about 5,000 Triballi died; these figures may even be correct, at least approximately.

The second defeat brought the submission of the Triballian king, Syrmos, and a peace agreement was made. Arrian reports that other Thracian tribes also now submitted; these were presumably Thracians who had originally submitted to Philip; renewing their submissions to Alexander would establish Macedonian control for the rest of Alexander's own lifetime.

Alexander captured the major Danubian crossing point at the modern town of Zimnicea (the later Roman town of Novae, or Ad Novas), during that Triballian war, though the town was burnt in the process. Beyond the river he now encountered his first Galatians. Like the Triballi, when Philip was campaigning in Thrace the Galatians had been watching events south of the river with interest, and now joined in the peace talks, sending an embassy to make contact with Alexander.[5]

This embassy implies that the envoys represented a fairly well-organized polity. Just as Syrmos negotiated on behalf of the kingdom of the Triballi, so the envoys of the Galatians were speaking on behalf of an organized state. It is customary to speak of these peoples, Galatians and Triballi, as tribes, but it is clear that Syrmos had a powerful authority over his people, and so must be counted as their king. The Galatian embassy was sent by some similar tribal-wide authority, a king or, more likely, a ruling aristocracy, probably from the nearest organized Galatian community, and therefore the one most concerned. The envoys had come from a considerable distance, for Strabo claims they represented 'Kelts who lived about the Adriatic',[6] suggesting that he did not really know where they came from, though it was clearly from a considerable distance, and from north of the Danube.

The Galatian state was, in fact, presumably that of the Scordisci, located in the Banat region. This was a new-minted tribe which was confected from groups detached from the Taurisci and Boii to the north. The reference to the Adriatic suggests that some of these Galatians at least were also, or were later, on the Adriatic coast. This means, however, that the Galatians who were living by the Danube were part of the same state as the envoys. They had been in that area for perhaps seventy years, which is plenty of time for the invaders to organize themselves as a Galatian tribe; the rulers were the leaders of the invasion and their genetic successors. The name Scordisci may not yet have been adopted, but may be used here for convenience.

There had evidently been time for the Galatians north of the Danube to report on Alexander's Triballian campaign – they will no doubt have noted Philip's campaign as well – and then for the envoys to travel from the Banat to the neighbourhood of Zimnicea in time to attend the peace conference. Alexander's campaign had evidently taken some time, for he had to arrange for his ships to sail from the Propontis (or even from the Aegean) to the Danube and then up the river, which would have taken perhaps two or three weeks to accomplish. The Kelts' embassy could have been organized and dispatched to arrive well in time to watch the burning of the bridge-town after the final Triballian defeat. There would be no reason for them to be on the spot earlier; it was only as a response to Alexander's campaign against the Triballi that they came so far from the centre of Galatian power. Had Alexander, as Philip before him, continued his work of conquest in the Balkans as far as the Danube, he would have clearly met and probably fought the Scordisci fairly soon. For the moment he was some distance away, and his destruction of the town and the river crossing implied that he had no intention of campaigning further; but from the town to the Banat was not very far.

The Galatians asked for Alexander's friendship, or so Arrian puts it, but then adds that 'they exchanged pledges'. This was therefore an agreement between equals, not a submission of the Galatians to Alexander. The two sides were agreeing not to go to war with each other, so that both sides could get on with their own particular plans without fear of an attack from the rear by the other. This clearly suited Alexander, since his intention was to take up his father's plan and campaign against the Persian Empire; it obviously also suited the Galatians, though we can only guess at their plans from what happened later. It is a confirmation of the Galatians' assumption of political equality with Alexander that their reply when he asked them what the Galatians feared most, fairly obviously expecting to be nominated himself, was to instance their fear of the sky falling on them, or the earth opening up to swallow them, or the sea overwhelming them. That is, they feared the gods, not men. There was also a threat buried in that reply, as well as a more obvious assertion of equality. The agreement they had made was, that is, to be regarded as only a temporary arrangement, which might be denounced by either side if necessary; in the way of such agreements it would last only until one party to it died – it therefore expired in 323, on the death of Alexander.[7]

As it was, of course, both of the Macedonian kings had their eyes fixed on richer game. Philip had begun an invasion of the Persian Empire in the year before he died, and, as soon as Alexander had dealt with his various European and Macedonian problems in the same superficial way as his father in Thrace, he set off to conquer the east. The Galatians, having made a first contact with Alexander and the Macedonians, renewed that contact when the king returned from his Indian adventure to Babylon, being one of numerous sets of envoys who were no doubt principally anxious to discover what Alexander's plans were.[8] It has been suggested that the agreement they had made at the Danube meeting was that the Galatians would protect the Macedonian frontier on the Danube side while Alexander was off campaigning,[9] but there is no actual evidence for this other than that the peace they had made endured during Alexander's lifetime in accordance with normal diplomatic practice, and indeed if they made a peace agreement ('exchanged pledges') there would be no need for anything more detailed. Certainly the Galatians did not interfere when there was a major Thracian revolt in 331, nor again after a major Macedonian defeat north of the Danube near the Black Sea coast in 325. The best interpretation for the envoys' visit to Babylon in 325/324 is that they were there to congratulate the king, like almost everybody else in the crowd of envoys, and to try to discover his plans for the Balkans; a renewal of their former peace agreement was perhaps their main intention as a means of fending off a possible attack. They could fully appreciate the difference made by Alexander's extensive conquests in terms of his ability to exercise his power. We may note that, like all the other envoys, they had been fully aware of Alexander's progress, and duly understood that his return to Babylon suggested a further campaign in the Mediterranean area. The publication of Alexander's plans after his death can only have partly reassured them.[10]

It may be better to see the issue from the Galatian point of view, in so far as we can discern it. The arrival of the Galatians in the Balkan region was fairly recent, beginning, it appears, about 400 BC. One must assume that a relatively small set of settlers arrived first, possibly preceded by raiders, or at least men who explored the region, gaining some idea of its geography and people. The eventual invasion brought in a larger Galatian force, including families, who spread widely in search of land on which to settle. The precise events in the Balkans are not known, but those in Italy, which had happened a generation earlier, may suggest the outline of the process.

The movement into Italy began, it seems, with the infiltration of individuals and small groups, some of them merchants seeking to purchase well-made Italian goods for export to the north; this took place over perhaps two centuries, before a mass movement began. As knowledge of the wealth of Italy spread, probably in the Etruscan region in particular, larger movements of whole 'tribes' began to arrive. The first was apparently the Insubres, from Gaul, and the Boii, from Bohemia. Other groups arrived later, and took up lands around these two. The process began c. 400 BC. The earliest arrivals settled in the north and the later groups passed them to settle next along. Seven or eight distinct groups – 'tribes' – are attested, some arriving from Gaul, others from Germany. Between them they occupied much of the Po Valley; resistance came from the Veneti north of the Adriatic, and from the Etruscans (and eventually, the Romans) in the peninsula.[11]

The movement into the Balkans was partly on this pattern, but the result was different. The Keltic homeland was wide, from the Atlantic coast as far east as Bohemia, but it was, it seems, fully occupied, and overpopulation is the favoured explanation of the migrations among the ancient historians. In some cases the migrants were parts of an established tribe: one of the tribes which reached Asia Minor, the Tektosages, had branches in Bavaria and in southern Gaul, the Bavarian branch was probably the original, and the other two were probably offshoots.[12] Another group, the Boii, were based originally in Bohemia, and sent out colonizing groups into Italy, and into the northern Balkans.[13]

The migrant groups were well organized for their move. Their purpose was to acquire land; if that land was occupied, they were most likely to establish themselves as a ruling aristocracy rather than drive out the earlier inhabitants – they wanted subjects, as well as land. The migration, however, was obviously unsettling both for the victims and for the Kelts themselves, so that one result was a restlessness among them which might emerge as raiding parties. Those who settled, however, organized themselves on the pattern of their original society, as a 'tribe'. They may have been a cohesive offshoot of an original tribe in the homeland, as the Italian Boii evidently were, or they may have been a mixed group from several different tribes who joined together and constituted themselves into a new tribe, with a new name. Some of the names of the new tribes suggest that the migrant groups were half of one sort, with established names – Senones, Lingones, Boii – and half of the other, with new names – Ananes, Libici, Insubres. The latter group no doubt either chose a new name for themselves when they formed their union, or adopted one fastened on them by others.

The Italian tribes, when faced with opposition from the Veneti or the Romans or the Etruscans, were able to recruit Gaesatae, bands of warriors who would join the migrant groups and so reinforce their military capability.[14] It was not a large step from such mercenary groups to autonomous raiding parties, and then perhaps to becoming the spearheads of the migration; that seems to have been the stage to which the Balkan migrations had developed, and when their decisive movement into the southern Balkans began.

The Kelts appear to have been in occupation of modern Hungary about the time that Philip II became the Macedonian king, *c.* 360 BC, no doubt after preliminary infiltration.[15] This was probably a migration in which the invaders established their power over the original inhabitants, though there were perhaps also larger-scale movements, as certainly happened in Italy. Once past the narrow gap between the mountains which is the site of the modern city of Bratislava, a wide low-lying country lay before the migrants, stretching as far as the Carpathian Mountains, which marked the western border of ancient Dacia, and with the Danube flowing through it. This territory appears to have become dominated by the migrating Kelts by, at latest, the mid-fourth century BC.[16]

This was as unsettling a movement as was that into Italy. There is no sign that contingents of Gaesatae were needed to enforce the conquest – but then we have fewer sources other than archaeology, so this cannot be taken as definitive. Certainly the flat nature of the Hungarian Plain would allow rapid conquest, especially by mounted forces. There were, no doubt, some who were keen to seek out vulnerable victims, but they were all also surely conscious of the rising power of Macedon to the south. We must assume that the conquest was quickly succeeded by a movement among the migrants to consolidate themselves into a state, and to establish their authority over their conquered subjects. The envoys of 335 BC to Alexander presuppose they represented an organized government formed by the united tribes. On the pattern of the homeland and the work of the Kelts in Italy, this political system took the form of distinct populations, described as tribes, which occupied clear territories. Of these the one which will concern this study most is that of the Scordisci, the southernmost group of those inhabiting the Hungarian Plain, established around the fort town of Singidunum, at the junction of the Danube and the Sava River. The name of any other tribes have apparently vanished, along with their territories, as a result of later subject rebellions and Roman conquest. This, of course, implies strongly that the Keltic presence was limited to achieving rule over non-Keltic subjects. Archaeology suggests that they concentrated along the Danube particularly.[17]

The settlement of this Scordisci group placed them on the frontier of Keltic territory, and so no doubt they will have had to keep their swords sharp, and this Keltic state will have been most concerned at the advances being made by Macedonian forces to their south, advances which had been headed northwards as the Kelts arrived.

It is, probably, therefore from the Scordisci that the recorded embassies of the Kelts came to see Alexander on the Danube, and later in Babylon in 335 and 324, and it seems clear that by that time the Scordiscian state was fully organized – that is, that the component parts of the invaders had coalesced successfully. It is not a name known from other parts of the Keltic region, so we may assume it was not originally a Keltic population from a particular original tribe; it was therefore a new tribal name adopted for the amalgam of several Keltic groups, presumably derived from Mount Scordus nearby.

This state was sufficiently alert to send out envoys who could make agreements on behalf of the whole, as with Alexander in 335. It is, however, not evident that the Scordiscian state was as yet notably powerful. If, as must also be assumed, its arrival had involved the conquest of the indigenous inhabitants, Illyrian and Thracian, the state would be as subject to rebellion and outside interferences as were Macedon's conquests in the southern Balkans. An armed encounter with Alexander would obviously be dangerous, and we may credit the Galatian rulers with sufficient sense of self-preservation to understand that they needed to avoid a collision with such a power. The peace they had agreed at the Danube was, therefore, of the mutually hands-off type, letting both sides get on with their more immediate concerns without interference. It may seem therefore that their boastfulness to Alexander was in the nature of a bluff; that he heard it and retired to the south may have suggested to the Galatians that their bluff had succeeded.

For the Scordisci therefore the half-century from the time of their meeting with Alexander in 335 was a time of consolidation, settlement, conquest of their immediate neighbours, and increasing their population. This latter aim was accomplished in part by the immigration of further Galatians from the north, by their own natural increase, by the assimilation of conquered Illyrians and Thracians and others, and by the conversion of these new subjects into Galatians – intermarriage would help in this, as would the recruitment of these natives as foot soldiers on the promise of loot. When the invasion of Macedon came, it is noted by one historian that it was by Galatians and Thracians together, and that the Galatians were unexpectedly numerous.[18] We hear of a woman, Onomaris, who is supposed to have led them in the conquest of the

Autariatai, an Illyrian people, whose territory was in the western Balkans – away from any possible clash with the Macedonians in Thrace.[19] There are clear indications of conquests of other Illyrians – the group called Hylli is supposed to be a mixture of Galatians and Illyrians[20] – and it seems that attacks were made on the Dacians, their neighbours beyond the Carpathian Mountains.

The Dacians proved to be very resistant. There is some evidence from archaeology of the adoption of certain Keltic manufacturing techniques by the Dacians, but little sign of much Keltic settlement in the area, other than perhaps by valued craftsmen. The evidence for the Galatian presence is the findings of Keltic-type metalwork, some of which was clearly manufactured in Dacia, but this should not be expanded to imply, or suggest, or state, that Keltic settlement was extensive.[21] This is an issue which will recur in this study.

The later Dacian kingdom proved to be very hostile towards the Scordiscian state, which was so damaged in the conflict that the Romans later accomplished a relatively easy conquest. The Keltic-style metalwork, so prominent in the evidence, may have been imported in trade, or it may have been made by Keltic smiths who were settled among the Dacians. In neither case can it be concluded that there were more than a few Kelts in Dacia.[22]

Other Galatian groups seem to have bypassed Dacia altogether, moving to the north of the Carpathians, to settle in the upper Dniestr region, where half a dozen 'settlements' are known. Still other groups went on to settle along the lower Dniepr Valley in the Ukraine, sending either raids or traders, or settlements into the Crimea, though it has to be said again that this is the result of archaeological discoveries of Galatian-type metalwork, which may equally have been acquired by trade. A significant concentration of finds and burials has been located in the Kyiv area. The evidence is therefore mixed: a scatter of metalwork, as in Dacia, which might be no more than the evidence of trade, but several regions where a combination of finds implies some Keltic settlement. There are Keltic-type burials (with La Tène contents), widely but thinly spread, but these are individuals only and are hardly evidence of widespread settlement, unlike the concentration in the Kyiv area.[23] The Dacians themselves were evidently always too tough to be tackled.

Elsewhere the Scordisci Galatians destroyed the Autariatai and sent raiding parties through the Illyrian territories from their centre in the Banat and to the Adriatic coast – whence no doubt the comments by Arrian and Strabo (from King Ptolemy's memoirs) that they came from that region.[24] The raids forced a large group of Autariatai out of their homes. They were intercepted by Kassandros, the Macedonian king, who settled them on his frontier.[25] The actual result does not seem to have involved extensive conquests by the Kelts in this area, but more the reduction in power of the Kelts' potential enemies, no doubt by being well-raided and looted, and subsequently in decline politically and militarily. Much of this is certainly assumption, though enmity between Galatians and Autariatai is certain.[26] It will be noted that these raids carefully kept clear of Macedon and its unstable conquests.

The Scordiscian regime's aggressiveness – though its existence is, I repeat, only an assumption at this point for the fourth century BC – replicated the problem which had led to the foundation of the Scordiscian state in the first place. The wider their conquests the greater their population, and this increase in population soon passed beyond the resources of the area, and probably beyond the ability of whatever central authority had been developed to exercise full control. It was part of the recent pattern of Galatian history for groups to split off and act independently. This was the source of the movement of the original population which formed the Scordisci, and of the raids which might precede the actual expansion settlement.[27] There is no reason to suppose that this sequence of raids and migrations was unwelcome to the Kelts. It was no different in essence from the Greek colonial efforts of two or three centuries before, or of contemporary Roman colonizations. The traditional Galatian solution to overpopulation was to send out selected fragments of the people to establish a new home for themselves elsewhere, or simply to let the groups go. The Scordisci, by 300 BC, had been in occupation of their northern Balkan lands for up to a century, and perhaps in a few cases longer.

By this time the various original sections, Kelts and Illyrians, would seem to have become fairly well integrated, but by then any further expansion towards the west was hardly possible. Their fellow Kelts occupied all Europe from the north Balkans to the Atlantic Ocean, so expansion towards the north and west was now barred. In Italy the Romans had organized the population of the peninsula in a powerful defence against Gallic raids from Cisalpine Gaul, and had successfully defeated the most advanced Gallic tribes – the Senones were conquered in 283. There was now no possibility of expansion there, and over the next two centuries every attempt failed. Gaul, Spain, Germany and Bohemia were also all similarly out of the question because Gauls had conquered or occupied most of those lands; the Dacians were evidently as resistant to Keltic raids or conquest as the Romans. The lands to the south and south-east of the Scordisci were the only possible directions in which expansion could take place, but there also the prospect was daunting. To the south the Macedonian kingdom and the cities of Greece were well organized for defence – a siege of a city was not the preferred Galatian form of warfare – and the kingdoms which had been founded out of his empire after Alexander's death were rich and powerful.

The precise stages of Galatian developments in the north Balkans are not known. Archaeologists have identified two elements, however, which suggest that the Danube was by no means a serious frontier line separating the Galatians from the Macedonian and Thracian territories. In that area south of the Danube, the area the Romans later called Lower Moesia, between the Danube and the Haemos Mountains, a considerable quantity of artefacts of Keltic origin have been found throughout the lands of the Triballi. This has been taken to mean that Galatian settlement took place in that territory, but this is likely to be going too far, as it is also in Dacia, for the presence of artefacts made in the Galatian style cannot be assumed to mark the presence of Galatians themselves.[28] To provide a contrary example, there are finds in the Balkan region of many coins which were minted in Macedon in the reigns of Philip and Alexander, but there is no suggestion that this means a settlement of Macedonians in these areas; instead this is interpreted as a sign of tribute paid by those kings to keep the Galatians at bay, or the pay of returning mercenaries.[29] Neither of these interpretations is necessary. The Galatians and Alexander had concluded a peace agreement, which both kept to; there was no need for tribute payments to keep the peace – not that there is any evidence for them. The returning soldiers, if any did return, are likely to have had many other than Macedonian coins in their backpacks – there would be

Persian coins, Persian treasures, Indian items, and so on, none of which are present. For neither tribute payments nor Galatian mercenaries is there any other evidence than the finds of the Macedonian artefacts themselves.

For both there is a more plausible explanation than inventing explanations out of thin air. Trade was a vigorous practice among all the peoples of the Balkans, Galatian or not, and it is by far the most likely reason for the movement of these items in both directions. The coins moving north of the Danube out of Macedonia fit neatly with the artefacts in the south to support a balance of trade in the Galatians' and others' favour – supplemented, of course, by the products of the Galatians' raids and conquests.

The Thracians, between the Haemos and the Danube, had no doubt been considerably weakened by their defeats at the hands of the Macedonians. The Triballi, for instance, are no more in evidence after about 290 BC. Extermination is not necessarily to be assumed, but repeated defeats would no doubt break up the tribe into its component sections, some groups fleeing elsewhere, some joining the raiders, some removed to the slave markets – and many dying, of course. It was the tribal structure which disappeared, not necessarily the people. Further weakening, particularly in the military sense, was produced by Alexander's recruitment of Thracians into his army, of which several thousands of young men accompanied him in the great campaigns. There was rather more of them than those who had been killed in their war, and of these very few will ever have returned to Thrace.[30] The campaign in Persia had also reduced Macedonian manpower at home. Alexander's regent in Macedon, Antipater, had to supervise Greece as well as guard the northern frontier; further, he had to dispatch reinforcements to Alexander all over Asia almost every year.[31] He was in a sense fortunate that the peace agreement with the Scordisci held. In Thrace there is evidence, largely in the form of the local manufacture of coins in the names of non-Macedonian rulers,[32] that Macedonian authority was less than strong, and by no means pervasive; in particular one of the surviving members of the Odrysian royal family, Seuthes III, was developing a local power base in the northern part of the Macedonian conquests, sheltered by a section of the Haemos range.[33]

The Galatians meanwhile were expanding their power over their neighbours, particularly to the west in Illyria, by their domination of the Autariatai. The expansion of the Scordisci was clearly a further threat to those neighbours, and south of the Danube the divided and weakened Thracians were a tempting target. The Galatians' victims in the period after Alexander included the Illyrians and the Dardani, as well as the Autariatai – though the Dardani perhaps only feared attack rather than suffered it, while the former two had certainly both suffered severely. It does not seem that the Thracians were directly bothered, but a branch of that people were later included in the Scordiscian state, described as those east of the Morava River.[34] That is, these were Scordiscian subjects, but were still recognizably Thracian.

The break-up of Alexander's empire proceeded slowly but inexorably, and in Macedon Antipater's death in 319 was soon followed by the seizure of local power by his son Kassandros. He was firmly allied for the next twenty years with his neighbour, the new satrap of Thrace, Lysimachos, each reinforcing the independence of the other, which went some way to resist the local disintegration. The extent of Lysimachos' authority in Thrace is not known precisely, and it may well have varied over time, but he was a formidable campaigner. He collided with Seuthes in a drawn battle; subsequent intermarriages of the two men with each other's daughters seems to have persuaded both men, together with their drawn battle, to avoid further disputes.[35] The whole region was clearly much disturbed. Archaeological evidence of burnt towns at Vetren, at the headwaters of the Axios River, for example, and at Pernik at the head of the Strymon Valley, is dated to this time. These two places are not far apart, and are at the western end of the great central plain of Thrace. They are also at the heads of valleys which lead into Macedon from Thrace; they were border towns of the Macedonian-controlled area, and as such were no doubt both vulnerable and obvious targets. Who burned the places, however, and exactly when, is wholly unknown; it is also uncertain who inhabited them, though it is perhaps most likely to be Macedonians.[36]

It is tempting always, when evidence of destruction appears in an excavation, to seek to attribute it to some known event or war or conqueror or king, and such destruction has naturally been assigned by various interpreters to all possible agencies, including, in these cases, the

Galatians from the north. The attribution to any particular case cannot be accepted without better evidence than archaeology alone can supply. If it was the result of a Galatian raid, for example, this would imply there had been a considerable intrusion of Galatians into Thrace, whereas it is clear that the Galatians' main attention at the time was devoted towards the lands to the west and south-west, into Illyria or towards their south into the lands north of the Haemos (Lower Moesia). They were not particularly numerous, and were still keeping clear of the Macedonians. There was so much fighting in the Thracian region as a whole at the end of the fourth century that any of the candidates could be responsible for the damage – or, of course, none of them.

In these circumstances it is very probable that, by moving south from the Banat area around Singidunum as well as expanding westwards, Galatian control was, by 300 BC, being imposed on the western and north-western parts of Thrace and along the Morava Valley. Seuthes' kingdom was to the east of this, north of Lysimachos' territory. This latter appears to have included the city of Philippopolis and the original Thracian territory conquered by Philip, but not the Haemos foothills and valleys to the north, or the Valley of the Roses in which Seuthes' new city of Seuthopolis was being built. But west of that area and north of the Haemos Mountains it seems that at the time there was no authority of any size or power. This was exactly the sort of unorganized and divided territory of small clans and villages which had resulted from the elimination of Thracian and Triballian higher authorities. It was into such a fragmented social situation that the restless philo-migrating Galatians would choose to raid and then take over to establish control. They were not apparently seeking opposition and a fight but land, and a weak region would clearly inevitably attract them.

In 298 Kassandros, king of Macedon, evicted one band of Galatians who had reached the Haemos. Their leader was Kambaules, and his exploit is judged by Pausanias, rather implausibly, to have been the inspiration for the great Keltic invasions of Macedon two decades later, though Kambaules did not penetrate very far into Macedonian territory.[37] For the moment, however, Kassandros had driven them out, or perhaps stopped them getting in. Their presence in the Haemos would suggest that there were now Galatians in some numbers in the area to the north-west, towards Singidunum. The collision, however, cannot be made to imply an intention by Kambaules to invade Macedon, though Thrace was a possible target. Kassandros' reaction suggests that it was his own intention to enforce his power in Thrace. Kambaules therefore did not fail in an aim to invade Macedon, but the Galatians of the Banat were duly warned that Macedon, and Kassandros, were alert.

The date and place of this Galatian intrusion – it was hardly an invasion – are significant. In 301 King Antigonos I had been defeated and killed at the Battle of Ipsos in Asia Minor. Four rival kings – rivals of Antigonos and rivals of each other – had cooperated in the victory, and had promptly disagreed over the division of Antigonos' territories. The only two of the victors whose alliance continued firm were Kassandros and Lysimachos, largely, it seems, because Kassandros had no wish to claim any of the major spoils, at least not for himself, while Lysimachos, whose individual contribution to the victory had been the greatest, took over most of Asia Minor as far as the Taurus Mountains, becoming at once the most powerful of the rival kings.[38]

From then on Lysimachos' main interest lay in Asia Minor; he retained control of part of Thrace, but does not seem to have concerned himself with it for some time, and his territory was reduced in all probability to little more than the Thracian Chersonese (the Gallipoli Peninsula) and the coast of the Black Sea.[39] This meant that Seuthes could flourish in independence in his new city and kingdom. Kassandros in Macedon was constantly occupied with his distracting and disturbing neighbours, in Greece and beyond his northern and western boundaries, and by 298 he was probably dying – he died the next year, of some disease assumed to have been akin to tuberculosis. In that year also he led an expeditionary force westwards to campaign in the Ionian Islands, ending with an attempt to besiege the city of Kerkyra off the Adriatic coast, which it was an old ambition of his to control; he was driven off by a rival expedition from Sicily of Agathokles, the Syracusan king – a Greek army defeating a Macedonian, to the glee of the former.[40]

In 298, therefore, neither Kassandros nor Lysimachos were present in the Balkan region when Kambaules began his raid, and the Macedonian king was ill as well as absent. This was precisely the sort of political situation which would attract a Galatian (or any other) adventurer such as

Kambaules. It probably explains why he then made his attempt, whatever it was aimed at, though Kassandros was still sufficiently active and swift in response to thwart him. The death of Kassandros next year, and the rapid succession of his three sons in turn, the death of two of them, and the murder of their mother, was not, it seems, disturbing enough after Kambaules' defeat to invite Galatian attention, particularly since three of the greatest warlords of the time, Lysimachos, Demetrios the son of Antigonos, and Pyrrhos the Epeirote king, were also meddling in Macedonian affairs. Any one of these could deliver as swift a defeat as Kassandros. The actual result in Macedon, by 294, was that Demetrios had taken over control, and at once he set about a massive recruitment and armament programme. Lysimachos meanwhile campaigned again in Thrace, and against the Getai north of the Danube, though, as usual, with mixed results. The Galatians were not involved. They had apparently learned, partly from Kambaules' experience, partly from mere observation, that a powerful warlike king in Macedon was not to be challenged.

Neither Kassandros nor Lysimachos had made any attempt to contest the expansion of the Galatians from their Banat base. Blocking the intrusion of Kambaules' raid was the only contact either king had apparently made with them, and it could be dismissed as a maverick episode. Lysimachos' campaign in 295 or so against the Getai king Dromichaites may possibly have been a reaction to Kambaules' raid, or to some instability connected to the continuing succession crisis in Macedon, but it may equally have been nothing of the sort. Lysimachos was sufficiently pragmatic to ignore, or accept, Demetrios' seizure of Macedon in 294, though he did give shelter to the surviving son of Kassandros, a former king whom Demetrios had driven out, so providing himself with the possible excuse to intervene later. The main attention of all the kings during Demetrios' reign was on his extensive and threatening military and naval preparations, which were clearly aimed at attempting to recover his father's or Alexander's lost kingdom. In the circumstances neither he nor Lysimachos had much time to devote to the Galatians. This is not to say that the Galatians ignored the lands to the south; quite the contrary.

By the 280s, therefore, the Kelts of the Balkans had been in place for eighty years, and at least one powerful state had developed, the Scordisci, which had established some sort of domination over a good part of the Balkan region to its south. In that time the Kelts had expanded their population, by receiving Keltic immigrants and by integrating the native populations into their state. There had therefore emerged, for the first time, a relatively stable and powerful state north of Macedon, and one which, though it had not made any overtly hostile move, except perhaps that by Kambaules, had, nevertheless, to be now regarded as a major threat to the Macedonian kingdom. Its expanding population and its political integration gave it the human resources to invade, if it chose, and its warlike methods posed a clear and major threat. There is no indication that any of the various Macedonian rulers in the 280s noticed that threat.

The half-century since Alexander had first encountered the Galatians on the Danube had brought the Macedonian kingdom and the Scordisci closer to each other, but only geographically. This was due to the political expansion of the Scordisci over the lands north of Macedon. The Macedonian kings cannot have been unaware of this, though they were generally kept busy holding on to their thrones and power in the face of competition from their Macedonian peers. The insidiousness of the Galatian advance is evident, but, apart from Kambaules' raid, they had evidently been careful to avoid any direct challenge to Macedonian power. But they were also evidently expansionist, and extending their authority in such a way as to bring into their state considerable numbers of non-Galatians. The overall result, however, was a growth in Galatian power, and a clear diminution in Macedonian. And any Macedonian king was isolated amongst his fellows.

Chapter 2

The Raids into Macedon

The retreat of Kambaules' people in the face of Kassandros' force in 298 was not followed up by either side; Kassandros was no doubt quite satisfied with driving them away. Kambaules was probably acting independently. Lysimachos does not seem to have been involved. The defeat of the raid, however, may have sufficiently annoyed its participants to lead them to hanker after a new attempt. It is suggested by Pausanias that the reason was their wish for 'the loot and rape of the world',[1] though this is merely reporting the general reputation which the Galatians have in the sources and is probably simply Pausanias' own unsupported assumption. It cannot be taken as a record of their motivation.

For, despite this suggested impatience, the next Galatian attack did not come for nearly two decades. The involvement of Lysimachos and Demetrios in Macedonian affairs, both of them notable warriors with large armies, was even more deterring to invaders than Kassandros' activities in successfully defending his kingdom. Indeed, the net result of the intrigues between 297 and 284 over who should rule Macedon was that Demetrios ruled for the next six years, then, when the Macedonians were driven to expel him, Lysimachos secured control of the whole kingdom in two stages, so constructing a powerful kingdom stretching from the Pindus to the Taurus Mountains in eastern Asia Minor – an even more deterring polity.[2]

In that same period, though this is largely an assumption once more, it seems that the Galatians in the Balkans were increasing in number and ambition. This had been linked with the decisive Roman victory over a coalition of enemies, including Gauls from northern Italy, at the Battle of Sentinum in 295,[3] which put a severe check on the possibilities of further Gallic conquests in Italy, and deterred raids as well. Ten years later the most advanced of the Gallic groups in Italy, the Senones, were conquered.[4] Occasional raids into the peninsula did occur, down to the great invasion of 225, and even later with the campaigns of the Cimbri and Teutoni, but the victory at Sentinum marks the decisive shift in the balance of power away from the Gauls in northern Italy.

The assumption is that those Italian Gauls who could not stomach a life without indulging in raiding turned to the Balkans after the Roman victories, for it was there that such action was still possible.[5] This reaction seems likely enough, and some Boii are noted as moving there, and it is certain that by the late-280s the Galatians in the Balkans were much more powerful and active and presumably more numerous than they had been ten or twenty years before; more importantly they were organized and led competently. Being numerous the internal pressures were compelling them to look for yet another new homeland.

The Roman reply to the Gallic attacks had the result that the city's position as the most powerful and militarily-effective polity in Italy had been decisively consolidated. This had taken a century to achieve (from the sack of Rome in 390 or 387), and for the next century after the reduction of the Senones in 283 the city intermittently defended Italy against occasional Gallic attacks and raids, and in doing so it conquered the Gallic territories in the north of Italy. Its instruments were a large and efficient military organization and the practice of planting citizen colonies in the conquered lands through which to enforce Roman control. That is, the Gallic invasions and raids and conquests had had the effect in Italy of forcing the growth of Roman power and the expansion of its territory.

The same effect may be seen in the Balkans and later in Asia Minor. The first region to which this new more powerful Galatian punch was administered was Macedon; this was followed by another punch directed into Greece. The defeat of these attacks was followed by similar raids into Asia Minor. In all cases the effect was powerful, and the reaction of both sides was interesting, and in places decisive for the future. Macedon and the Aitolian League emerged strengthened and with increased confidence from the attacks; other Greeks were less involved and less pleased with themselves, with good reason. In Asia, the Seleukid kingdom was successful in containing the invaders, but there it was the Attalid kingdom which eventually emerged with the greatest increase in its reputation, though this was as much due to skilful propaganda as it was to actual military achievements. Many of the Greek cities in Asia showed powerful reactions of various types. All over the Balkans and Asia, the Galatian invaders settled into these lands for the next two centuries, in some cases as extortionary states, in others as accepted members in what is now curiously called the 'international community'.

For the period after Kassandros, the solidity of royal control in Macedon, under whatever king – Kassandros, Demetrios, or Lysimachos – was such that no raids, still less any invasions, were able to penetrate Macedonian defences, and in fact there is no record of any such attempts. On the other hand, the Galatians did have access to all the lands north of the Macedonian frontier from the Adriatic to the Black Sea, and they appear to have continued to expand their control over parts of those lands, or at least they exerted their domination over the areas from which they could exact tribute or gather loot, as well as increasing their population by conquering and by immigration.

The opening which allowed the Galatians to penetrate the Macedonian defences came in and after 281. In that year Lysimachos was attacked by King Seleukos, who ruled from Syria to the Indian borders. He prepared the ground well for his war, so that Lysimachos' regime disintegrated even before the final battle. Lysimachos' family life had descended into intrigue, killing and general unpleasantness, and his popularity and acceptability in Asia Minor was fading fast. Seleukos had been approached by more than one member of Lysimachos' own family, and by other groups, officials and individuals, asking him to come north from Syria to intervene, and to free them from Lysimachos' increasingly autocratic and erratic rule. Having ensured that there was no possibility of being attacked by Ptolemy from Egypt, he marched north. Lysimachos stood to fight at Korupedion in the west of Asia Minor, and, like Antigonos before him, went down to defeat and death in the battle.[6] As usual, the victory only began another set of disputes over the division of the kingdom.

Seleukos began to take control of Lysimachos' territories, and looked forward to becoming king in Macedon, his old homeland. The land in Asia Minor was relatively easy to secure, since he was already in control of much of it even before the battle, but it still took time to organize. Securing the European territories was rather more difficult. He spent several months dealing with problems and difficulties in Asia Minor before he moved on to Europe. Besides Seleukos, there were at least three other men, perhaps four, who could lay a fairly convincing claim to the kingship of Macedon, as opposed to taking over all Lysimachos' kingdom; they could all instance a hereditary claim of sorts, so their claims were on the grounds of their ancestry. Antigonos the son of Demetrios was heir to his father, who had been king from 294 to 288; Pyrrhos, king of Epeiros, had a certain popularity among the Macedonians for his warrior skills, and had been king of part of Western Macedon until driven out by Lysimachos, but he was now developing other ambitions; Lysimachos' widow, Arsinoe II, daughter of Ptolemy I, brought three of her sons by Lysimachos to the Macedonian city of Kassandreia, and could claim the kingship for her eldest, a teenaged boy called Ptolemy.

Two other men had claims; Seleukos by right of conquest, and there was one more, another Ptolemy, the eldest son of King Ptolemy I of Egypt. He had been denied the succession to his father's Egyptian kingship in favour of his younger half-brother Ptolemy II, who had inherited from his father a year before. Ptolemy the claimant, who was nicknamed 'Keraunos' ('Thunderbolt'), from his impetuosity and violent temperament, had left the Egyptian court as a result, for his life was clearly in danger if he had stayed. He had taken refuge at first with Lysimachos and Arsinoe, nursing his grudge. He felt entitled to be a king, and if it was not to be of Egypt, then another place would do, preferably, in the circumstances, Macedon. With Lysimachos' death – he had fought in Lysimachos' army – he shifted his allegiance for the moment to the victor, and Seleukos may have made some half-promise to set Ptolemy up as a king somewhere, but then Seleukos showed his determination to make himself king in Macedon by crossing the Hellespont into the Thracian Chersonese. He had taken over Lysimachos' army, and had sent most of his own troops home to Syria, where most of his soldiers lived. Ptolemy accompanied him, along with a group of officers apparently mainly from Lysimachos' forces. He decoyed the king away from these other followers to see, he claimed, a curious altar, and there killed him. Returning to those followers, whose allegiance had apparently been secured beforehand, Ptolemy was proclaimed king in Macedon.[7]

The situation was, of course, confused. Keraunos successfully established himself as king, first at Lysimacheia in the Chersonese, then in central Macedon, and to reinforce his claim he married his half-sister, Lysimachos' widow, Arsinoe II. He was especially concerned to eliminate all rivals, so to strengthen his position he killed two of Arsinoe's sons, apparently directly after the wedding; however, the eldest son, another Ptolemy, had stayed away from the ceremony, sensibly suspicious of his new stepfather's intentions from the start. Arsinoe immediately fled for refuge to the island of Samothrace.

This killing, however, only disposed of Keraunos' internal opponents.[8] He was attacked by Antigonos, who controlled Athens and parts of Greece and had held on to a part of Demetrios' fleet, but defeated him in a naval battle.[9] Pyrrhos had developed an ambition to campaign in Italy, and he was bought off by being provided with contingents of troops, ships, elephants and money by Keraunos and by all the other kings, for he was a constantly-disturbing element, and they were only too pleased to get rid of him.[10] Arsinoe's eldest son, Ptolemy son of Lysimachos, went to Illyria and recruited an army with the aid of the Illyrian King Monunios, with which he invaded Macedon, but he was defeated by Keraunos, though he then escaped again.[11] It seemed that, after his murder of Seleukos and the defeat of his rivals, Keraunos' unscrupulousness and ferocity had succeeded in establishing his rule in Macedon, but in the process he had accumulated a formidable list of powerful enemies. The defeat of an Illyrian invasion, a traditional event at the accession of any new Macedonian king, but this time one led by the pretender Ptolemy, must have persuaded many Macedonians that Keraunos was acceptable as their king, despite his violence and murderousness.

The political confusion in Macedon lasted for much of 280, and it attracted Galatian attention, hardly surprisingly. It was clearly a much more deep-seated condition than the earlier crises, as under the sons of Kassandros, or when Lysimachos died. They could see that Keraunos, though he was apparently well set, was in fact holding on very precariously, unpopular, murderous, the killer of his stepchildren, Seleukos, and then guilty of complacency brought on by his success. Further, it was clear that he was politically isolated. He had no international friends. There was no possibility of help for him coming from any of the other kings – his half-brother Ptolemy II was king in Egypt, and even though Keraunos had formally repudiated any claim to the Egyptian kingship, he was still his bitter rival; Pyrrhos set off for Italy during 280, and stayed there for five years; Seleukos' son Antiochos was establishing himself in his father's huge empire, and was keen to gain revenge for his father's murder; Antigonos, son of Demetrios, was already an open and active enemy.

In addition, the army which Seleukos had been intending to use in Macedon, the former army of Lysimachos, had ceased to exist. Seleukos' own original army had probably returned to Syria, where the men had been living for the past twenty or thirty years, and where the younger men had been born and had grown up. The men of the army of Lysimachos were similarly domiciled in Asia and Thrace, with more in Macedon, but only those living in Europe were available, since, like the Syrians, those living in Asia had no doubt returned home, and were now Antiochos' subjects. So Keraunos was limited in his military power to the men of the army of Macedon, which had been much depleted by the previous fifty years of near-continuous fighting. Many of the men undoubtedly disliked their new king. To the Galatians it was clear that the moment had arrived: for the first time in thirty years Macedon was vulnerable. And in that time their own numbers had greatly increased.[12]

One source for the subsequent events, Pausanias, claims that the leaders of the attack were survivors of the raid led by Kambaules.[13] This may be true, or it may be that his exploit had only inspired them – they would be twenty years older by the time this new attack was being planned. Kambaules himself was not involved. They had clearly learned a good deal about the lands of Thrace, Macedon and Greece in that time, and had laid their plans for the attack accordingly. A very large force, partly cavalry but mainly infantry, was gathered,[14] and four commanders are named by Pausanias at the start: Kerithrios, Brennos, Akichorios and Bolgios. The numbers quoted are scarcely believable, but were clearly very large; it seems probable that the army was gathered from a large part of the Keltic lands, not just the advanced post in the Banat and the nearby lands. The whole invasion was clearly well planned, and the gathering of the invasion force was one element of that planning.

The size of the force is stated to be so large that it is highly unlikely that it was composed purely of Galatians, and in fact one source says it included, and was always accompanied by, Thracians and Illyrians, to whom such an invasion would have seemed quite natural. The infantry – the number of men is claimed to be 150,000 – was probably made up of men of the subjugated peoples whom the Scordiscian Galatians had been conquering and dominating for the previous fifty years. The cavalry, said to be 20,000, is also unlikely to have been recruited only from men domiciled in the Scordisci country. Later information implies that recruits had also been gathered from other Gallic regions, in the upper Danube valley and from Germany and Noricum, and perhaps Italy. There was certainly a full population of Galatians still in the Scordisci country even after the raiders had left – their base was clearly not to be endangered. So the invading horde was a complex mixture of Galatians from the Scordisci, Galatians from other tribes, and infantry gathered, perhaps by force, from the subjects of the Scordisci – though it would not take much persuasion to get the Balkan peoples to participate in a raid on Macedon and Greece.

At this point it is necessary to consider what the aims of the commanders were. We know what they actually did, and what the ancient sources assume they meant to do, which was to search out loot, but this was not necessarily what they intended at the start. Loot was certainly part of their aims, but that was probably not their only intention. At least one group quickly settled down to form a new kingdom in Thrace, which suggests an original intention to do just that, and other groups involved went on into Asia Minor with the deliberate aim to found other states. It seems probable therefore that, from the beginning, some at least of the Galatians had the aim of acquiring territory, certainly in Thrace, and possibly in Macedon or Greece; it was these men who were accompanied by their families and their possessions. Others clearly aimed merely at gathering loot and slaves, and perhaps then returning with their winnings to a homeland in the northern Balkans or elsewhere.

This invasion force was clearly very much larger than any other mounted by the Galatians or the Gauls, except perhaps that which invaded Italy in 225 to be defeated at the Battle of Telamon. That force was also accompanied by women and children, but it also included groups of deliberately-recruited bands of warriors, called Gaesatae, coming in from other parts of Gaul. It seems likely that the Macedonian invasion force was similarly reinforced. The sheer size of the army also implies that the Galatians knew that they were tackling a very difficult task.

Then there is the question of how they set about their campaign, which was, it is clear, aimed initially only at Macedon. They determined on a preliminary three-pronged attack, no doubt in part because their large forces would be feeding themselves from captured or looted supplies, so that by advancing along separate routes they would spread the load; it would also perhaps divide their opponents, and possibly limit the potentiality for quarrels between their leaders. At the same time, the three forces also deliberately aimed at different targets. Kerithrios led his force eastwards into Thrace and later attacked the remnants of the Triballi.[15] If it was the Macedonian kingdom which was the main target, this suggests that Ptolemy Keraunos had inherited the whole of Lysimachos' European territories, including the Thracian lands, though he does not seem to have been involved in defending Thrace. It is more likely that the Galatian leaders simply had varied personal aims.

The other two Galatian armies attacked different sectors of the Macedonian northern frontier. The immediate intention surely was twofold: first, to disperse and divide the defending forces, but second, to launch an invasion of Macedon. Since this is what the Galatians actually did, it seems reasonable to assume that this was their original intention. Needless to say, as in all military operations, the plans did not work out.

Of the three armies, Kerithrios' force attacked Thrace and the Triballi;[16] if these targets are named in the order they were dealt with, this implies that the first target was Thrace, and that the Triballi were attacked later. The relationship between the Galatians and the Triballi is not known, but the latter had been badly weakened by their past disasters at the hands of the Macedonians and were presumably by this time largely under Scordiscian Galatian domination. Geographically they lay to the west of Kerithrios' route into Thrace, and would be likely ignored in the first charge. If that is so, then Kerithrios' subsequent reverse movement out of Thrace suggests that he had to deal with some sort of trouble from the Triballi, possibly a 'rebellion', which developed when it was seen that the main Galatian armed strength was deployed and fully occupied elsewhere.

One of the victims of Kerithrios' campaign seems to have been Seuthopolis, the new city of King Seuthes III in the Valley of the Roses, to the north of the lands ruled by the Macedonians. His kingdom was in fact effectively independent, certainly now that Lysimachos, with whom he had had a peace agreement, was dead. Seuthes himself died *c.*300 BC, and the date of the death of his son Kotys II is placed at *c.*280.[17] The city was destroyed and (bearing in mind the initial temptation to link archaeological evidence of destruction to known historical evidence of a disaster) it must be presumed that it was attacked and taken by Kerithrios' Galatians, who also no doubt accounted for King Kotys. Then from Thrace Kerithrios' force presumably turned back to the west to deal with the Triballi. This Galatian army was thus very busy, certainly doing quite enough to occupy the campaigning season of 280; it was clearly unable to participate in any direct invasion of Macedon.

The army under Brennos and Akichorios attacked the Paiones, inhabitants of the Rhodope Mountains north of Macedon. It is the result of this fighting which is so persuasive about Galatian plans when considered alongside the behaviour of the force commanded by Bolgios. For in this first attempt to penetrate the Macedonian frontier they apparently could not get through the defence put up by the Paionians, and who apparently put up a most effective resistance. (It may also have been on this occasion that the towns at Vetren and Pernik, discussed in the previous chapter, were taken and severely damaged: they were in positions, at the heads of the Axios and Strymon valleys, which were clearly on the routes that the Galatians would take if they were aiming to invade Macedon.) The fighting, however, was sufficiently costly to the Paionians that they were very badly damaged, and the following year could not resist further. If the target of this Galatian force was Macedon, it failed to get through; on the other hand, it was able to do so in the next year's campaign without too much difficulty; it seems probable that the Paionians made peace with the invaders rather than endure another invasion.

Bolgios' force moved west and then south through Illyria. In fact, it may be that raiding through the Illyrian valleys was their ultimate intention on this occasion, though that land had been well scourged by Galatian raids already. The final population group between the Galatians in the north and Illyria and Macedon was the Dardani, who clearly knew what they were in for. The Dardanian king contacted Keraunos, offering an alliance and '20,000' men, presumably in exchange for a forward movement by Keraunos to help defend the Dardanian lands.[18]

Keraunos' self-regard had been boosted by his successes – his murder of Seleukos; his seizure of power; the capture and driving out of Arsinoe; the defeat of her eldest son Ptolemy, with his Illyrian allies; and his naval victory over Antigonos. He clearly understood what the Dardanian king feared, and evidently knew that the Galatians were approaching, though probably he did not understand their numbers or their ferocity. By the time he was meeting the Dardanian king, probably very late in 280, he will have known that Kerithrios' force had turned back from its Thracian campaign to deal with the Triballi, and probably that the Brennos/Akichorios force had not managed to finally break through the Paionians. He therefore would have to deal with only a part of the Galatian strength.

The timing is only an assumption here; it is probable that Bolgios arrived first, before the other Galatian forces attempted to invade Macedon; in that case Keraunos moved to meet the first invader. Keraunos may have calculated that a fight between the Galatians and the Dardanians, especially in the winter, was likely to inflict severe damage on both forces. He consulted his self-confidence and refused the alliance, explaining that it would not be honourable for a people who had conquered Asia to rely on help from a barbarian warband. This does imply, however, that he had no real idea of the greatly weakened state into which Macedon had slipped after fifty years of warfare and the repeated dispatches of its people overseas to other men's wars; of the cost of Kassandros' and Demetrios' wars; nor of his own unpopularity with the Macedonians because of his murderousness.

Not unnaturally the Dardanian king departed, no doubt thoroughly annoyed at Keraunos' insulting characterization of himself and his people. Perhaps he made the same calculations as Keraunos may have done – it would be a fairly obvious process. So, when the Galatians approached he agreed to let them pass through his territory.[19] Perhaps he paid tribute; perhaps the right of way was in place of any tribute payment; maybe his people joined in the invasion of Macedon – this was, after all, a traditional activity of such tribes as the Dardanians. The result was that Bolgios' force arrived in Macedon before Keraunos' force was ready.

This invasion was the only one of the three Galatian attacks to reach Macedon in the first attempt, and this is the clue to the timing of all. The Galatians moved to attack during 280, and Bolgios' force penetrated into Macedon thanks to the passage granted by the Dardanian king. Bolgios therefore had a clear passage, while the others had to fight, and failed. When he was victorious, Bolgios retreated. Bolgios' retirement can only have been due either to the fact that the collection of loot was satisfactory, or that he was nervous of being the only successful invader and so retired because he feared a counter-attack by the Macedonians. There followed a winter's delay (280/279). The other two invasions therefore had failed, that by Kerithrios because of the Triballian 'rebellion', and that of Brennos and Akichorios because of Paionian resistance. Hence the main invasion would be in 279, the next year.

The description of the first contact of Bolgios and Keraunos is probably a repetition of the earlier contact between Bolgios and the Dardanian king – which clearly must have taken place – but with a different outcome. Galatian envoys reached Keraunos from Bolgios, once the Galatian army was at or close to the Macedonian frontier in the north-west. They attempted to levy blackmail, demanding to be bought off, or else. Whereas the Dardanian king made an agreement, perhaps allowing the Galatians through his territory as part of such a payment, Keraunos refused.

He had, of course, sound reasons for doing so, since such a demand is normally only the first, and having given in once he would be much more likely to have to continue paying in the face of other demands. (This was the situation in which the city of Byzantion later found itself in its relations with Galatian Tylis.) Keraunos certainly could have paid, and there were Macedonian precedents for this – Philip II had paid such blackmail at the start of his reign, but only as a temporary measure, and he denounced the agreement as soon as he was free to do so. The situation was closely parallel, and both men having gained their thrones in a time of conflict, neither man's claim on the kingship was at all secure; both men were beset on all sides, both men were being threatened before they had gathered their forces for defence, and in such circumstances gaining time for a breathing space in a fraught time was a reasonable political tactic. Or, as Keraunos' entourage urged, he could have prevaricated and delayed the envoys, while collecting his full army together, and while Bolgios' men became restless and their Dardanian hosts began to regret their agreement. Instead, hot-headedly, he refused to delay – no doubt the Galatians were busily ravaging the countryside and collecting loot while he considered. Perhaps he replied with even more stinging insults than those directed at the Dardanians; instead, he proposed his own terms, by which the Galatians would provide hostages and hand over their armaments. These terms were laughed at by the Galatians, and were clearly seen as insulting.[20]

The army of Bolgios was nearby; Keraunos advanced to drive it out, without waiting for the full levy of the Macedonians. This was yet another mistake, attributable particularly to over-confidence, and perhaps to ignorance. Had he waited he would probably have been able to field an army equal or greater in numbers to that of Bolgios, and would have had a good chance of winning;[21] as it was, the battle which took place was still a hard one. The Macedonians had long memories of combating similar barbarian invasions, beginning quite recently with the Illyrian army led by Ptolemy son of Lysimachos. In the face of a new barbarian invasion they would have flooded to Keraunos' banner, no matter how he was personally disliked, if he had stood forth again as the defender of Macedon against barbarians. When he had won the battle, he would have been firmly seated in power as Macedonian king. Not for nothing is he regarded as thoughtless and impulsive.

Instead, with his outnumbered army, he was comprehensively defeated. We do not have a description of the battle, but at a guess his relatively small force was surrounded, so that the phalanx could be attacked in flank and penetrated, and then the Galatians with their longer swords could set about the Macedonian infantry, reversing the advantage of the long Macedonian *sarissa* which had won Alexander's wars; the Macedonian cavalry had no doubt already been driven away by the more numerous Galatian horse. Keraunos himself was wounded several times in the fighting, then captured, then beheaded, and his head paraded on a pike; this broke the Macedonians. The soldiers were scattered or killed.[22]

The battle may have been lost by the Macedonians, and their king killed, but the reaction of the population of Macedon was automatic. Amid the mourning for the dead and the anxiety for the prisoners, defensive measures were quickly taken. Some soldiers who escaped from the battlefield, probably mainly horsemen, spread the word of the defeat quickly. Prayers were said, people in the country took refuge in the cities, city gates were closed, and the walls were manned.[23] As it happened, either because he had made his point by his victory, and no doubt had gathered some loot – and the demand for blackmail payment rather suggests that loot had been Bolgios' main aim at this stage in the campaign – or because the Galatian casualties had been heavy (though there is no indication in the sources of these), or because he was not supported by the other Galatian forces, who were busy elsewhere – or for all of these reasons – Bolgios called off further operations and retired northwards.[24] The prospect of attempting to capture a long series of walled Macedonian cities was no doubt daunting.

But it is probable that the main reason is that the overall plan had not worked. The other invasion armies had failed to break through the defences and Bolgios, after a hard fight, had no support. The plan had perhaps been to break down Macedon's defences in preparation for a full invasion next year. Keraunos' decision to fight had not been so reckless after all, only premature, but his defeat ensured that another attack would certainly come next year.

There followed a breathing space of some months. Kerithrios' operations in Thrace and those of Bolgios in western Macedon were perhaps contemporaneous, beginning in the summer of 280, but, in Bolgios' case, extending into January or February of 279, which was the time of Keraunos' death; and Kerithrios' force had had plenty to do in Thrace; by having to turn back to deal with the Triballi, he had to do rather more than had been planned. But both of these operations were well separated geographically, and both had had plenty of fighting. The army of Brennos and Akichorios had not penetrated the mountains and the Paionian defensive barrier; that is, they had been defeated. In that time gap, from early 279 to the time of the full Galatian invasion in the summer of that year, the Macedonians searched for a new king.

The precise dating of all this is not wholly clear, but a reasonable estimate can be made. Keraunos is allotted a reign of one year and five months by the chronographer Eusebios, and it is clear from the evidence of the Babylonian Astronomical Diaries that Seleukos was murdered in late summer (August/September) of 281.[25] This would bring the death of Keraunos to January or February 279. A winter campaign by the Galatian army in the Illyrian Mountains is not easy to accept – though it would help to explain why Brennos' force did not get through the Rhodope Mountains, and why Bolgios' force did not make it through Illyria and Dardania until the start of 279 – and, of course, this is yet another reason why Bolgios' force turned back, since by that time of year supplies would be impossible to find, especially as the Macedonians had taken refuge in their cities. These events are often dated to 281, but that is unlikely. Certainly there was a hiatus in Macedon after Lysimachos' death in February or March 281, but this was only the absence of a king, and first Seleukos then Keraunos quickly filled that gap; Seleukos until August/September, and Keraunos from September. There was no breakdown of government and order in that short period. It is only with the shredding away of the Seleukid/Lysimachean army after Seleukos' death, and the appearance as king of the rash, impulsive, and unpopular Keraunos, who was challenged by his half-sister, by her son, and by Antigonos, that the kingdom was revealed as obviously open to attack.

One must see the mustering of the Galatian forces in the spring of 280, and the invasion by Kerithrios' and Bolgios' forces as beginning in the summer of that year, once the harvest was in. Bolgios' force, despite the unlikelihood of a winter campaign, clearly did indulge in one, delayed perhaps by their preliminary raids into Illyria, and by the negotiations with the Dardanian king. (Brennos' force in the Rhodope Mountains will have similarly faced difficult conditions.) As added evidence there is the note in Plutarch that Pyrrhos in Italy heard the news of Keraunos' death in the summer of 279, news which will probably not have been carried across the Adriatic until the beginning of the 279 sailing season.[26]

Had the Galatians restricted their ambitions to territorial acquisition and restrained their thirst for loot and portable wealth, the kingdom of Macedon might have fallen out of Macedonian control and become a Greek Galatia. In the aftermath of Bolgios' retirement and Keraunos' death, and in the shadow of the likely renewal of the invasion, which was clearly being prepared in the spring and early summer of 279 in the lands to the north, the Macedonians struggled to recover their balance and revive their kingdom. This required, first of all, a king to be found who was acceptable to the Macedonians generally. There were several candidates, most of whom were tried and found wanting.

In the preceding ten years, there had been kings from three of the major Macedonian royal families, and candidates from all of them were present in Macedon in this crisis. In all these attempts to find a new king, a hereditary connection to one of the preceding dynasties was evidently required. The problem was, as in all hereditary systems, ability was thereby often ignored – or rather their lack of ability was ignored – but they eventually learned the lesson.

The dead Ptolemy Keraunos was therefore succeeded by his brother Meleagros, who was apparently present in Macedon during all of his brother's reign. The Macedonians elected him as their king – or possibly he simply made himself king by hereditary right – in place of his brother;[27] there is no indication that Keraunos himself had gone through the usual Macedonian process of election by the army, so presumably Meleagros did not see the need either. He was unsuccessful as king, hardly surprisingly in the circumstances, since by choosing him – or rather, perhaps, accepting his succession – the Macedonians may well have been expecting him to bring help from abroad, from Ptolemy II in Egypt, or perhaps he was expected to have some of his brother's military ability, if, perhaps, less of his impetuosity. But events in Macedon were moving too quickly, and within two months Meleagros was judged to be not competent to rule. He was deposed, and Antipater son of Philip was chosen as the new king.

Meleagros had lasted for two months, and Antipater lasted for only forty-five days. He was the son of Philip, the brother of Kassandros, and so the grandson of the great regent Antipater; he had taken refuge at Lysimachos' court when Demetrios seized Macedon in 294.[28] He apparently stayed there quietly while Demetrios ruled, and he also survived throughout Lysimachos' and Keraunos' times as kings in Macedon, presumably living in the kingdom.

The life of Antipater thus suggests that he showed little or no interest in seeking any sort of power. We may assume he had his place at the upper end of the social scale in Macedon under Kassandros and his sons, and under Lysimachos. He was, after all, a member of the royal family, and brother-in-law to King Lysimachos (one of whose many wives was Antipater's sister Nikaia). To survive under Lysimachos in his last years implies a complete lack of any ambition, nor even any suspicion of an ambition. He was left alone, which in the circumstances argues an obvious, serious, and long-standing refusal to be politically involved in Macedonian affairs. It is perhaps still more remarkable, and a testimony of his withdrawn and unambitious nature, that he survived again under Keraunos, who was even more murderous than Lysimachos, and actually sought out competitors to kill them. And, of course, he survived under Meleagros as well.

Yet, after all this, and despite his withdrawn nature, he was almost the last representative of a distinguished Macedonian dynasty, the nephew of Kassandros, and the grandson of the great Antipater, as elevated a line of descent as anyone in Macedon, since the extinction of the Argead kings during the wars of Alexander's successors. When Ptolemy and Meleagros had failed, he had been the obvious choice to succeed them; no doubt his origin and his ancestry were assumed to be sufficient to instil ability, or at least respect. But he lasted as king only forty-five days. He earned the nickname 'Etesias' from the length of his reign, this being about the same length of time as the hot summer 'Etesian' winds – his brief reign was probably over before the winds came, but it may have overlapped that season. (Keraunos died in February, Meleagros lasted two months, Antipater for 45 days – this takes us to early June, at least.) Probably elected because of his ancestry, his long-standing reluctance to wield power was nevertheless surely well known. Perhaps it was expected he would rise to the occasion.[29] Bolgios and his men, having killed Ptolemy and perhaps forced the succession of Meleagros, had returned northwards, carrying their plunder, during the latter's reign. He had thus been king while the kingdom was being ransacked. Antipater's reign was thus a moment of relative peace between invasions, for the second attack, commanded by Brennos, came only sometime after Bolgios' retirement northwards.

It is not to be expected that the reigns of these brief Macedonian kings followed upon one another immediately; there were probably gaps between them, in which discussions, elections, and travelling took place. The death of Keraunos and the choice of Meleagros may well have been separated by a gap of at least several days. The deposition of Meleagros in March/April 279, after his reign of two months, was certainly quickly followed by the elevation of Antipater, who was perhaps with the army at the time as part of the general mobilization in face of the invasions, but one must still allow a few days between these events. (A refusal to wield political power did not also mean a refusal to fight in defence of the kingdom; as a Macedonian gentleman Antipater will have had the normal military training.) Antipater's reign, therefore, probably began in April and may not have ended until June of 279.

During this time Brennos was collecting his forces, and recruiting those of Bolgios' and Kerithrios' men who wanted another crack at Macedon. This time he will have made sure that the path south through the mountains was clear. If the Paionians still resisted it was not for long – possibly the survivors were bribed, but more likely the prospect of facing the full strength of the Galatians rather than just a third of them, would induce them to step aside after the casualties they had already suffered. The Galatians' preparations and their progress will have been known to the Macedonians by their scouts, and perhaps by warnings from the Paionians. The news of their enemies' approach, probably in June, again after the harvest, will have been one of the main reasons for the deposition of Antipater. He was not militarily competent enough to be trusted to command in the face of a new invasion.

Antipater, however, was a king who operated well enough in peace; he would have been a competent king had there not been a war to fight, and especially not a Galatian war. He received at least one foreign embassy during his reign, when the Athenian Demochares, son of Laches, and a nephew of the orator Demosthenes, arrived to negotiate changes to the Macedonian position in Attica. Demochares had been in exile during Demetrios' reign, and had returned home to Athens in 286, when Demetrios fell. He had already been sent on embassies to Lysimachos and to Ptolemy, soliciting friendship and money to fund the revival of the city and its democratic constitution. The friendship of the kings was at first to be a safeguard against the return of Demetrios, but from 285 he was a prisoner of Seleukos and was never going to be released. The funds which Demochares was collecting were now being used to re-fortify the city, including the walls of Peiraios. He had already secured the return of Eleusis to the city's authority.[30]

The third king Demochares visited was Antipater, though both the date and the precise person are disputed. The deposed King Antipater, son of Kassander, may be dismissed, for he had been a hostage/prisoner of Lysimachos, and it is unlikely that he would be able to provide the twenty talents which Demochares came away with; and anyway the embassy to Lysimachos made a separate contact with that Antipater pointless; he obviously, as a prisoner and now cut loose from his dependence, did not have the resources Demochares needed. The only other King Antipater at that time was the man briefly reigning in Macedon in 279, Antipater Etesias. From Athens it perhaps seemed that Bolgios' invasion and withdrawal was the end of the matter, and that the new king, being of such a distinguished and useful ancestry, was now fairly seated in office. Demochares' embassy was well timed, therefore, and he came away with his twenty talents of Macedonian money. At the same time, he will have become aware that any conclusions based on Bolgios' withdrawal were wrong, that a new Galatian invasion was likely, and this news he will have taken back with him to Athens with his present.

The failure of these kings to measure up to the military crisis was the obvious cause of their deposition. Meanwhile an officer, Sosthenes, was gathering forces into a renewed Macedonian army. He was possibly doing this under the orders of the kings, but it is more likely that it was on his own initiative. He had probably been one of Lysimachos' officers, but he was clearly seen as experienced and competent and well-known, and this was why he was chosen as *strategos*. He refused the title of king because he was not of royal descent, thereby demonstrating the necessity of that quality for a new king – but he was clearly a capable military officer.[31]

It is probable that during Sosthenes' period the two remaining kings of this confused period were elected successively as successors to Meleagros and Antipater: Ptolemy son of Lysimachos was the survivor of Keraunos' homicidal accession and his campaign against his internal rivals, he had already attempted to seize the kingship once. His royal descent (from both Ptolemy I and Lysimachos, and from Antipater through his mother), his common sense (he had deliberately avoided Keraunos, and so had survived), and his obvious determination, were presumably the qualities which counted for him, but he was still only a teenager. He did not last very long as king, perhaps because he attempted to gain control of the army from Sosthenes. Sosthenes himself clearly had strong support among the soldiers; his election as *strategos* was by the army, separate from any election of any of the kings. This gave him an authority which was independent of any king. Given Ptolemy's youth, and his history of contact with the Illyrians, as king he could only be a figurehead, and his deposition, if he ever exercised any royal authority, cannot have been a surprise. (He survived, however, as did Antipater, and probably Meleagros; Ptolemy was later given a small principality in Asia Minor by Ptolemy II.)

The last of these kings was Arrhidaios, and he is the most obscure of them all. He is actually named as 'Alexander' by one source, and so he might then have been a son of Lysimachos (who had a son of that name, whom he had murdered), but the name Arrhidaios is just as well attested; he may be a scion of one of the upland local kings in western Macedon. Either way, like all the rest, he did not hold the royal office for very long.[32] The effective master of the kingdom all through this last period was evidently Sosthenes, the elected commander of the army, who is credited with an authority lasting for two years, until 277. It seems possible that there was a clear gap in the succession for some time after Arrhidaios. None of these brief kings was killed, and at least three of them, Antipater, Ptolemy, and Arrhidaios, may have continued to exercise some authority in parts of the country, possibly even by agreement with Sosthenes; no doubt they also fought the Galatians when they arrived.[33] In the looming emergency, the election of another king was presumably seen as a distraction; after the collection of hopeless kings already discarded this would seem a reasonable reaction.

It was therefore an army commanded by Sosthenes which confronted Brennos' invading force. Brennos had gathered a much bigger army than Bolgios had commanded, and this time it was the only one to campaign; dividing their forces had been unsuccessful. This army probably included men from both the other forces, men who scented greater profits by a new invasion, as well, again presumably, as the majority of the army Brennos and Akichorios had commanded the year before. Neither Bolgios nor Kerithrios appears to have participated, though Akichorios was again Brennos' colleague.

Brennos persuaded his men to march against a different target, Greece itself, rather than Macedon, which had perhaps provided less booty than expected, particularly given that the cities had been locked up tight against Bolgios' men. It appears that loot rather than conquest was still the Galatians' main target.

Brennos brought his army south through the mountains in the late summer of 279. According to Pausanias, he had had to argue hard to persuade his fellows to mount another attack, which again suggests that Keraunos' battle, and perhaps that of Brennos' bold force against the Paionians, had caused plenty of Galatian casualties. He played on their cupidity, emphasizing the wealth to be found in the sanctuaries and cities in Greece, but also pointing to the weakness of the Greeks who had suffered under the domination of the Macedonians for the last half-century, and their extreme division into relatively small states. His army, even if the numbers quoted by Pausanias are wildly exaggerated, was clearly very large.[34]

The route they travelled is generally assumed to have been by way of the Axios Valley, and so therefore through Paionia, the community which had been battered by Brennos the year before;[35] alternatively, another suggestion is that they came by Bolgios' former route through Illyria and Dardania and into western Macedon.[36] Whichever way they came, they were met by Sosthenes' army, which was defeated; its survivors immediately withdrew into the cities, no doubt by prearrangement.[37] The Galatians began pillaging the countryside, but it is likely that they found this activity little to their liking. The harvest had long been gathered in by the time they invaded, and any valuables will have been collected and stored in the cities. Brennos, true to his plan and his promise, now directed then into a campaign southward into Greece.

It is also likely that the reception the Galatians received from the revived Macedonian army was more fierce and determined than they had expected. Keraunos' resistance, and that of the Paionians, had been bad enough, but now they were fighting against the same men but under a better commander. And the withdrawal into the well-stocked and well-defended cities was a move clearly planned in advance; the Macedonians were no panicked and defeated enemy. So this was another reason for the Galatians to move on. They left Macedon battered still more, and with at least three alive and active but deposed former kings still present. The kingdom's agony was set to continue.

Chapter 3

The Raids into Greece

Brennos and his men moved on south from Macedon, first into Thessaly, and then into central Greece. This may have been their plan from the start of the campaign, but they will have known that they would have to fight a battle to get through Macedon – the Macedonians, especially under their new general, were not going to be as amenable as the Dardanians and allow them a clear passage. Having won the victory, the Galatians naturally looked for loot and supplies, but it does not seem likely that they had stayed around in Macedon for very long; no doubt both those items were in short supply, given that the Macedonians had had fair warning of the enemy's approach. Brennos did suggest that the temples might provide useful loot – unless this is a Greek invention, to emphasize the Galatians' irreligion. The lack of loot propelled the Galatians to go further south into Greece.

In Thessaly they are said to have committed 'outrages', which might be anything from massacres to stealing food and valuables, or even just being present.[1] Thessalian society was of the feudal type, lords and serfs; it is likely that the lords holed up in their castles and cities, leaving the peasantry to suffer from the outrages. In a sign that some of the Greeks were actually not that different from the Dardanians and Illyrians in their attitude to the Galatians, some Thessalians joined them in their march, either by treaty or by compulsion, but certainly in the search for loot at the expense of other Greeks.[2] It was one more element in the ethnic mix of the invaders. South of Thessaly they approached the Greek defensive army.

The news of the renewed invasion had galvanized some of the Greeks into a moment of unaccustomed cooperation; possibly it was the Demochares who spread the alarm.[3] All the peoples from Phokis to the Isthmus sent contingents to block the pass at Thermopylai, and, since Brennos and his people took their time about looting Macedon and

Thessaly, the Greek forces managed to reach the pass first, while the Galatians were still in the Phthiotis and Magnesia, to the south and west of Thessaly. The Boiotians and the Aitolians were the most numerous contingents in the Greek array, for they, with the Phokians, would be the most immediately threatened once the invaders came further south; it is evident that Delphi was seen to be the most likely target.

Between the Phokians and Thessaly, and so between the Greek force which concentrated at Thermopylai and the approaching Galatians, there were the small communities about the Malian Gulf and in the valley of the Spercheios River – the Malians and the Ainianians. They were left outside the Greek defended region, and so had no choice but to submit to the invaders if they were to survive. Like some of the Thessalians, they were compelled to submit and then to participate. Also directly threatened was the Aitolian country, which stretched right across the Greek peninsula as far as Herakleia Trachineia on the south coast of the Malian Gulf, but north of Thermopylai, and therefore also vulnerable and outside the Greeks' defence line. The league produced 7000 hoplite infantry, 790 light infantry, and some cavalry for the defence. Athens, which under the domination of King Antigonos had been largely disarmed, produced 1000 hoplites and 500 cavalry under the command of Kallippos son of Moirokles of Eleusis, a noted contemporary politician. At this point we come up against Pausanias' tendency to distortion. He interpreted the Galatian invasion as a sort of repetition of that of the Persians, and used the events of that time as his template for the fight against the Galatians. He therefore exaggerated the Athenian participation, inventing, it seems, an Athenian warship squadron, and assigning the command over the whole allied force to Kallippos, even though the contingent he brought was one of the smallest. In fact, it was probably an Aitolian, if anyone, who was in overall command, though it may be that the commanders of the larger contingents were unwilling to serve under each other. In the event whoever exercised the overall command could not control the several contingents.

An appeal had gone out also to the kings. Antigonos contributed 500 mercenary infantry. He was, of course, in control of Peiraios, and if any ships were involved they were probably his; possibly Pausanias transferred Antigonos' ships to Athens, but in fact there was really no role for warships in the events. Pausanias says that Antigonos' troops were from Macedon, but Antigonos was not yet in control there, so they were his own troops, from the garrison at Peiraios, or perhaps from his city of Demetrias in Magnesia, but almost entirely mercenaries. King Antiochos also sent 500 mercenaries.[4] Neither of these contingents was generous, but all the kings had other, and more serious, concerns – one of which was the situation in Macedon, which certainly excited their cupidity.

The self-centredness of all Greek states was only superficially surrendered by the gathering of this defending force. One reason for the joint army being formed is that it was meeting at Thermopylai, which had a distinct historical resonance (and was perhaps Pausanias point of reference in his reinterpretation), but more to the point it was a narrow pass, between the sea and the mountains, in which the Greek spearmen could concentrate and fight most effectively. Refugees and reporters will have already explained the Galatian techniques of warfare, which much resembled the 'Highland charge' of the Scottish clans in the seventeenth and eighteenth centuries. This was effective in open country, and against poorly disciplined or outnumbered enemies, but against a well-disciplined army without flanks to turn, it generally failed (as it did at Culloden). But, as more than one Greek army at Thermopylai has discovered, flanks there can usually be turned.

The Greeks had assembled in the pass well before the Galatians came near it. They were thus able to send out a force of cavalry and light infantry to block the crossings of the Spercheios, and to break the bridges over the river. This certainly delayed the invaders, but not for very long. A selected force of Galatian swimmers crossed the river and got through the marshes at the estuary, while others floated over on their large oval shields (made of wood and hide), whilst still more found the water shallow enough to let them wade across. This was all sufficiently unexpected to drive off the Greek reconnaissance force. Presumably the fact that the Greeks tended to wear heavy armour prevented them exercising their military imagination – swimming and floating across were surely obvious expedients.

The Greeks retreated back to the camp in the pass, no doubt by prearrangement, for they could not have expected to block the huge Galatian army for very long at the river with such a small force. The

Malians hastily repaired the bridges, so as to make sure that the invaders would move away out of their territory. Once across this river the Galatians were in Aitolian territory. This was an area, Oitia and the city of Herakleia, which had been incorporated in the league only a year or so before, perhaps in the knowledge that the Galatians were coming. The land was ravaged, but Herakleia was defended with vigour. This seems to have surprised the Greeks, an emotion which is evident in Pausanias' account,[5] but the city had joined the Aitolian League only the year before: the Aitolian defenders were on their mettle. In fact, the Galatian attack on the city was less than determined. Brennos knew that it was not a major objective, and most of his force simply went past the city to attack the Greeks in the pass.

Brennos had been informed about the Greek position by deserters from the Greek army, perhaps by men captured from the advanced force at the Spercheios, or by the Ainianians or the Malians, but any Greek will have known where the army would assemble, and it would not take a long reconnaissance for the Galatians to find them. It was here that the Galatian method of war, a reckless charge, was less than sensible. The Greeks, with the mountains on their left held by light infantry, and the sea on their right (with or without ships present), were irremovable. His men having suffered serious casualties, Brennos withdrew them back to the Spercheios valley.[6]

Brennos gave his men a week's rest while investigating the possibilities. He clearly appreciated the fragility of the Greek coalition. The willingness of the Thessalians and the Ainianians to join him, and of the Malians to assist him in moving the Galatians out of their territory, made it clear that the Greeks were fundamentally divided, that their loyalty was primarily, even exclusively, to their own city, and that a threat to the homeland of one of the group could compel its contingent in the pass to head for home. The obvious victim must be Aitolia, which lay mainly to the west, whereas the rest of the contingents of the allied army came from cities to the south, out of reach behind the pass. The Aitolians had contributed one of the largest contingents to the joint army and so their removal would significantly weaken the whole force. He attempted first to get a contingent over Mount Oitia, from where it would be able to attack Doris and then reached Amphissa and so Delphi, but the sanctuary of

Athene above the town of Trachis was held by a force commanded by Telesarchos, the commander of the Seleukid contingent which had been sent by King Antiochos. They successfully defended the temple, and therefore continued to block the route south, though Telesarchos himself was killed.[7]

Once again the talent for Greek particularism came to Brennos' aid. His army had spread up the Spercheios valley, into the country of the Ainianians. Their leaders, and the Thessalians, urged him onward, showing him another route into Aitolia further west – neither the Ainianians nor the Thessalians had any liking for the Aitolians. This time the invading force was large (as opposed to the apparently small force at Trachis). Commanded by two of the Galatian chiefs, Orestorios and Komboutis, an army of '40,000' infantry and 800 cavalry – Greek calculations as usual are not to be believed – climbed out of the Spercheios valley and came down onto the Aitolian city of Kallion.

The city and the league were taken by surprise – another failure of military imagination; since at Oitia the enemy had tried one outflanking move, and since Thermopylai was notorious for such a possibility, one would have expected a guard, or at least a picquet, would be placed to cover all possible outflanking routes. The Galatians took the city, then behaved with revolting cruelty, or so the Aitolians claimed, and burnt the city. This was all Aitolian territory, the land of the Apodotoi, though the people are referred to as Kallians, a sign perhaps of the recent urbanization of the area. They resisted, of course, and as word spread of the Galatian atrocities, or perhaps simply of the invasion of their land, the whole Aitolian population, old and young, men and women, set out to punish the invaders, in a quite remarkable display of fury and resolution. This included the Aitolian contingent at Thermopylai, which decamped at once to assist their people as soon as they heard the news. So far, therefore, Brennos' strategy of outflanking and deliberately provocative destruction was working.

In fact, the Galatians, under attack, turned to retreat by the way they had come. On the way they met and defeated a detachment of Achaian hoplites from Patrai, who were separated from the main force, or perhaps were still on their way to Thermopylai. This fight, however, delayed the Galatians – which supports the view that this Galatian detachment was not really all that large after all, and certainly not anywhere near as large as Pausanias claimed – who may have been using a self-glorifying Aitolian account, or an Achaian.[8] The Aitolians occupied the hills, as they had done in earlier crises of invasion (by the Macedonians), and rained stones, boulders, javelins, and arrows down on the retreating enemy. They harassed them so ferociously on that retreat that the invaders lost, so it is said, half their number, though one must assume that the losses fell disproportionately on the infantry.[9]

The Greeks at Thermopylai, though weakened by the withdrawal of the Aitolians, still blocked the route through the pass. But Brennos' strategy of evasion, misdirection, and seeking out alternative routes, had worked once, and he convinced some Ainianians to reveal the old route to the hills which the Persians had found two centuries before. It was guarded by a Phokian contingent, but they were unsighted by a mist, outnumbered, and defeated. They did manage to warn the main army down in the pass, however, that the way had been left open, and the main army broke up, each contingent retreating to its home territory.

Brennos had sent Akichorios and his force to preoccupy the main Greek army, and see if and when it disintegrated, while he took a large part of the Galatians first against the Phokians and then towards Delphi. He was clearly aware that the Aitolians had been thoroughly aroused by the attack on Kallion, but his strategy of compelling the enemy army to break up had clearly succeeded. Once the main Greek force left the pass, Akichorios was free to follow Brennos' force, but at the same time it is clear that not only had the Greeks broken their formation, so had the Galatians.

The temple at Delphi was defended by a force from Phokis, 400 hoplites from Amphissa, some available Aitolians, and the Delphians themselves, and these had sufficient warning of the attack to get into a defensive position. Akichorios' army, probably the largest of the Galatian divisions, approached only slowly. It was harassed on its march by the main Aitolian force from Thermopylai, which had been unable to defend Kallion, but now turned about to face the larger enemy; meanwhile the Kallian attackers were being harassed by the Aitolian defensive forces. The same tactics of harassment were now employed against Akichorios, whose advance, already perhaps cautious, was clearly slowed drastically. He was also concerned to protect the baggage and the accumulated looted treasure which belonged to the whole army; this would slow him still further.

Brennos had marched his men at speed – they were not hampered by the baggage as was Akichorios' force – and they were weary and hungry as they approached Delphi. He was advised to attack at once, while the local forces were surprised and weak, but he chose to give his men a night's rest. The march was so badly organized that the men had to find their own supplies from the farms and villages, and these included plenty of wine, which the Galatians fell on with glee. (Later it was claimed that the Delphian oracle had suggested leaving the wine to be found, one of those cases, no doubt, where the oracle claimed retrospective credit.) As a result, not only was the night spent in carousing, but the attack in the morning was then delayed even further by the unreadiness of the army. Meanwhile about 1200 more Aitolians under Philomelos arrived to boost the defence.

The weather turned nasty, with snow, and thunder and lightning. The Greeks also recorded earthquakes, not surprising in that area, which dislodged boulders from the hillsides so that the Galatians felt they were coming under divine attack (or so it was claimed), a sentiment no doubt encouraged by the Greeks, who felt that their god was on their side. The Galatians, after their troubled and sleepless night of snow and falling rocks, were driven back, partly by a frontal assault by the hoplite phalanx, and partly by the harassing flanking fire from the hills on either side, both human and divine. The next night – their troops having been fighting or under fire for two days and a night, after their carousing night with little sleep, the Galatians panicked at the slightest sound. No doubt their fears were assisted by more Greek harassment, and by their own superstitious fears of attacking a noted sanctuary.

Greeks remembered – or imagined – visions of interference by ancient heroes, and by an epiphany of the god of the sanctuary, reported by a group of priests who charged into the midst of the army in their robes, hair flying. Apollo was, they claimed, seen to be assisting in the defence.[10] This was a great encouragement to the Delphians, who could appreciate as well as anyone the value of the sanctuary, not to mention the further value of a new legend by which the gods were credited with defending themselves and their temple.

The panic in the Galatian camp led to them fighting each other in the dark, not an unknown reaction in other armies. The defenders harassed them into retreating day by day, which prevented any foraging. The news went to the Boiotians, who were still in arms after their retirement from Thermopylai, and they set about harassing the army of Akichorios, joined with some of the Athenians who was still present.[11]

Brennos was mortally wounded during the fighting. He had been a remarkably inventive commander, willing to change course and shift targets when blocked, and capable of inspiring his men to considerable feats of marching. None of the other Galatian commanders were in his league, and those of whom we do know generally suffered defeat. He is said to have given final orders that the only way the Galatians could escape was to kill their wounded and then march away. He himself, being wounded, committed suicide. None of this can have helped the morale of the surviving Galatians.[12]

It has to be said that there was a tradition in Greek histories that the sanctuary actually fell to the invaders and was looted; certainly the Galatians retarded plenty of loot, though it is clear, from contemporary evidence, the sanctuary itself was not taken.[13] Given the heightened emotions involved together with the rivalries and enmities among the Greeks, especially towards the Aitolians, and the recriminations which followed, this alternative account is not surprising, and it is quite possible that the temple was untroubled, while treasures were looted, though it seems less convincing than the account given above. Similarly, the Aitolians used to claim the credit for the defence, not unjustly, but they did have a tendency to write out the contributions of others, and they were vociferous in their own claims.

Command of the Galatian forces devolved on to Akichorios, who brought the army to the Spercheios River, crossing once again. He may have assumed that at their boundary the Aitolians would cease their pursuit. If so, he was correct, but he then found that the Malians and the Thessalians, who had joined the Galatians earlier, were now hostile once more, and the harassment continued.[14] The story has no room for the women and children who travelled with the invaders. They clearly did not take part in the fighting at Thermopylai and Delphi, so they were possibly left under guard in the Spercheios valley. They will have been collected during the retreat.

It was said, by the Greeks, that none of the Celts escaped,[15] though this is clearly untrue. The Galatian force was in fact said to have been annihilated at least three times: at the Spercheios crossing, according to Pausanias; in Thessaly, according to Justin; and by the Dardanians in Diodoros' account. No doubt there are more specious claims made to disguise less valiant conduct. All this is not necessarily contradictory, since there were several Galatian bands, and for them to split up for greater speed would make a certain sense.[16] What is clear is that the invaders suffered very badly in their retreat.

The Thessalians are more likely to have harassed them out of Thessaly rather than to have forced them to stand and endure a do-or-die fight. They were plainly leaving, and to hinder the desperate and angry force was not sensible; it was the same reasoning which had operated to convince some Thessalians to assist the original southward movement of the invaders – to get rid of them. One source, indeed, connects this band with the formation of the later Keltic state of the Scordisci, on the Danube;[17] annihilation is not believable.

The Aitolians came out of the whole affair as the heroes, not least in their own eyes. In the future they would exploit the reputation this gave them to the full. The comparison with the Persian invasion, which is so persistent a feature of Pausanias' account, but which was an inevitable consequence of the stand made by the Greeks at Thermopylai, enabled the Aitolians to still claim credit a century later, but not wholly without complaint and opposition.[18] The Aitolians used their reputation to take over the Soteria celebration at Delphi, originally instituted to celebrate the securing of the sanctuary from Persian attack, and to develop it into one giving thanks for defeating the Galatians, simultaneously therefore glorifying the Aitolians. The story of the assistance provided by the god spread rapidly, and was clearly widely believed. Within a year the Koans, who, so far as we know, were not involved directly in any of these events, resolved to make an offering to Apollo, Zeus the Saviour, and Nike (that is, Victory), recording on the inscription the god's involvement.[19]

When the record is closely examined, however, it is clear that the Aitolians had really acted wholly in their own interest, as they always had, and as did every other Greek state. That is to say, the Aitolians' policy with regard to the Galatians was to defend their own territory, and they scarcely stepped outside of their boundaries at any point in the fighting. When the Galatians retreated, the Aitolians pursued and harassed them as far as the Spercheios River, their northern boundary,[20] but there they stopped; in the same way they had only begun to fight the Kelts once they had crossed the Spercheios on the way south. They were acting, of course, in the same way that all Greek states did; the joint army at Thermopylai was composed mainly of forces from central Greece whose homelands would be the next to be ravaged if the invaders had got through the pass. There were no contingents, apart from the small Achaian force from Patrai, from south of the Isthmus, but if the invaders broke through at Thermopylai, no doubt a Peloponnesian joint army would have quickly gathered at Corinth or Megara to block the Isthmus. The concept of the joint defence of all Greece was alien to all the Greek states.

The Aitolians capitalized on their success with equally successful propaganda, claiming to be the saviours of Greece, for which they certainly had an arguable case, though one that was neither indisputable nor exclusive, and of Delphi, about which there was just as much argument. The temple was adorned with Aitolian trophies of the war, statues of gods, statues of Aitolian commanders, a statue of the personification of Aitolia as a woman, armed and seated on a heap of Keltic shields – actual captured Keltic shields – in a display which was a conscious and deliberate imitation of the display of Persian shields which the Athenians had taken at Marathon.[21] The message was that the Aitolians were the new Athenians, the new saviours of Greece, where the Macedonians – the inveterate enemies of the Aitolians – had failed in their historic mission of blocking the way from the north. Aitolian coins vigorously publicized these deeds for the next century and a half.[22] At least one other community, Thespiai of Boiotia, was grateful enough to the Aitolians to dedicate a statue at Olympia, probably of the Aitolian commander Plaistainos son of Eurydamos, where he stood amongst kings.[23] Athens put up a portrait of their own commander Kallippos beside that of Leosthenes, the heroic commander against the Macedonians in the Lamian War fifty years earlier.[24] The message here is that Athens defended Greece against the barbarians wherever they came from.

After the Galatian attack, others, not directly involved, came to check on what had happened, and to hear the elaborating stories, and to sacrifice and give thanks for the shrine's preservation, as did the envoys from Kos.[25] In the process the work of the Boiotians, the Phokians, the unfortunate Achaian detachment, the Athenians, and the mercenaries of Antigonos and Antiochos, were all side-lined.

Also less than clear is the activity of the Galatians at Delphi. The implication of the stories is that the temple was spared, though the Galatians may have got into the city. Some looting evidently did take place, since some pieces from Delphi were deposited in the sanctuary at Tolosa in Gaul, perhaps by some participating Tektosages.[26] The Koan inscription makes it clear that the temple, though attacked, was not seriously pillaged.

It is characteristic of the Greek accounts that once the Galatians were driven north of the Spercheios details fail us. We hear nothing of their journey through Thessaly other than that the Thessalians harassed them; nothing about their route, their numbers, or any new outrages in which, in their defeat and in a rich country, they surely indulged. The surviving Galatians certainly got through as far as Macedon as an organized warband. By this time it was early in 277, but still winter. They now had to fight again, against the Macedonians once more. Sosthenes was still in command of the army, possibly now without any king to hamper him, though it is certain that some of the deposed kings were still around.

Sosthenes, therefore, had to fight the retreating survivors of the invaders once again. Quite likely, once he understood that they had no intention of staying, he would be quite as willing to let them leave as the commanders to the south. But not all of them left, and some bands hung around and had to be rooted out.

The retreating force, probably still commanded by Akichorios, broke up when in Macedon, a factor which tends to suggest that they were not then under any sort of attack. Some of them went on northwards to become, as Justin says, the founders of the Scordisci state.[27] A second group, or rather two groups travelling together, commanded by Leonnorios and Loutarios, separated from the home going group, and turned eastwards. They moved along the Thracian coast, which took them out of the reach of the Macedonians, as was perhaps their initial intention. By the middle of 277 they were in the Thracian Chersonese, possibly having captured and plundered the city of Lysimacheia on the way.[28] (Their activities from there on are discussed in chapter 5.)

At some time in this period, for which the sources are absent or excessively fragmentary, Sosthenes died, or was killed, perhaps in June of 277. If any of the deposed kings made any attempt to re-seize power after he was gone they were unsuccessful, and no such attempt is recorded. But one of the events in this period was an odd little naval war which was waged between Antiochos I and Antigonos Gonatas.[29] Antigonos, probably in pursuit of this war, brought his army to the Chersonese, and there he encountered a band of Galatians, whom he enticed into a trap and then massacred.[30]

Antigonos then played his masterstroke by enlisting Galatians into his forces as (relatively cheap) mercenaries. This rescued numbers of Galatians from probable early death at Greek or Macedonian hands (or Antigonos'), removed them from marauding in Greece and Macedon, and provided Antigonos himself with a useful and easily expendable force of soldiers. It was with this mercenary army that he succeeded in establishing control over Macedon at some time during 277 after Sosthenes' death.

Antigonos made careful use of his Greek mercenaries and the enlisted Galatians, and succeeded in driving out the invaders; he also succeeded in driving out his competitors.[31] He had done most of this by late 277, but it took him another ten months to gain control of Kassandreia, which had been seized first by Eurydike, the former wife of Ptolemy I and the mother of Keraunos, but she was then succeeded, perhaps by means of a *coup d'état*, by a tyrant, Apollodoros, who held control of the city for the next ten months, using increasingly-extreme social and political policies to maintain his control.

Two of the rejected kings, Ptolemy son of Lysimachos and Antipater son of Philip, fled for refuge to Egypt, though when this removal took place – whether during the post-Galatian anarchy which seems to have followed Sosthenes' death, or in the face of Antigonos' success – is not known. Ptolemy II gave them shelter, no doubt regarding them as useful cards which he might play in the continuing international competition. They turned out, as might have been expected from their origins, very differently useful. Ptolemy son of Lysimachos (the son of Arsinoe II, who became the new wife of Ptolemy II, her brother, a factor which clearly affected his fate) was soon placed in a little principality of his own at Telmessos in Lykia.[32] This planted a son of Lysimachos on the borders of Seleukos' conquest in Asia Minor, now under Antiochos I, as a possible pretender there.

Antipater's lack of ambition returned once he was safe in Egypt. He almost vanished from view. He is mentioned in a single source about twenty years after his flight from Macedon. He was living quietly in Egypt, and had developed, and was constantly indulging, a passion for playing dice.[33]

Both of these men were obviously threats to Antiochos I and Antigonos when they were in the hands of Ptolemy II. A son of Lysimachos planted on the border of his father's former kingdom could not be seen as anything other than a threat. Both men still had claims on the kingship of Macedon, even though they had been rejected by the Macedonians – but stranger things than the restoration of one of them had happened – such as their elevation in the first place. That these threats did not lead to any serious activity aimed at overthrowing the kings does not lessen their intermittent potency. They could clearly be activated by Ptolemy II whenever he wished.

But Antigonos in Macedon had other problems than these distant failed kings. He had gained control of the Macedonian kingdom by the end of 277, and of the city of Kassandreia during 276. To this he added the various cities in Greece which he had inherited from his father. The removal of his rivals included making peace with Antiochos, as a result of which Antigonos married Antiochos' sister Phila. This was a link with the Seleukid kingdom which proved to be both useful and permanent. There was one more claimant to Macedon he had to face, however. Pyrrhos returned from Italy and Sicily in 275 and next year, restless as ever, he invaded Macedon. The old attraction between him and the Macedonian soldiers worked once more, though others might have seen in him a revival of the spirit of Ptolemy Keraunos. Antigonos' Macedonian soldiers changed sides in the battle (though his Galatian mercenaries fought for him to the death). Antigonos was beaten in a fight and was reduced to controlling only the city of Thessaloniki.

And yet Pyrrhos, as the Macedonians should have known by now, was a hopeless king, anywhere but his ancestral Epeirote kingdom. His Galatian mercenaries rifled some of the royal tombs at Aigai, and he made no apology, nor did he punish them. He never finished off his conquest of Macedon – the final details were apparently too tedious for his attention – but instead he went off to fight another war in Greece, leaving Antigonos to intrigue against him from his base at Thessaloniki.[34] In that Greek campaign he was killed when an old woman threw a roof tile at him as he tried to enter the city of Argos on an elephant which got stuck in the city gate, a suitably ignominious death for a careless king; his elimination allowed everyone to breathe a heartfelt sigh of relief.[35]

Antigonos resumed his kingship of Macedon once more. And this time he held on to it. Further, he ruled for another thirty years, at the end of which he had successfully planted his dynasty solidly in power in the country. This was one of the main political results of the Galatian invasions, to bring Macedon back from its fragmentation and weakness and disputed kingship into a condition where it was once again one of the Great Powers of the Macedonian world.

In Greece, on the other hand, the divisions of the region between the city states was confirmed yet again, even emphasized, by the defeat of the invaders. The Macedonians had long memories of barbarian invasions from the north, and when a capable king ruled they could accept him; heredity was perhaps less important there in the end than respecting their customs and traditions, and both were subordinated to a capability of ruling and commanding; the litany of rejected kings from Demetrios I to Pyrrhos is a clear indication of Macedonian preferences. The Galatian experience had been traumatic, probably the worst barbarian invasion Macedon had ever endured, and it could be put down, possibly, to the weakness of the ruling kings. So when a working, sensible, and largely peaceable king came along, all his competitors were swiftly discarded.

In Greece, the barbarian threat had been less than dire, and had affected only a few states. The invaders were defeated by the assembled armies of the Greek cities, so that those cities could congratulate themselves that their political system had worked. They could preen themselves on being able to combine against such a threat when it was necessary, comparing their response to the Galatian invasions with that to the Persian attacks two centuries before, even though the combination in both cases had been fractious, partial, and had broken up all too quickly. In other words, the threat had not been sufficient or prolonged enough to jolt the cities out of their political complacency, and they reverted to their state of division for another century and a half – until an even more brutal conqueror came along.

The Greek winners were clearly the Aitolians, whose league had held together in the crisis, and whose people had demonstrated a powerful unity and determination to drive out the invaders. But they crowed about their success too loudly; they had been unpopular before the Galatian invasions, and they were disliked after it; nevertheless, for the next three generations they were the most powerful Greek state. This was, along with the recovery of Macedon under Antigonos, the single greatest result of the Galatian invasion in Greece.

Chapter 4

Two New Galatian States

It was not only among the established states of the Balkan Peninsula that the Galatian invasions had a profound effect. The Galatians themselves were also affected. Three tribes moved east into Asia, and their fates will be examined in the next chapter – it is surely an extraordinary matter to find a new state of Kelts planted in Asia Minor, in the land of the Hittites and the Phrygians – but there were also established two Galatian states in the Balkans, one a long-standing fixture in the Balkan state system, the other a brief presence, if unpleasant. The effect of these two were as powerful on their neighbours as they had been on their Greek-speaking victims.

The Scordisci

The evacuation of Greece and Macedon took the beaten Galatians formerly commanded by Brennos and now (presumably) by Akichorios, in two directions. One group headed north through the Dardanian country, where the Dardani copied the Thessalians and turned on their former allies.[1] The survivors returned to the Banat country. Some perhaps went onwards further north, if that had been their homes, perhaps as far as Germany, and in one case apparently to Gaul, the clue some of the loot at Tolosa. The second group, as already mentioned, turned east and moved along the Thracian coast into the lands bordering on the Hellespont and the Propontis.[2]

The result of their retirement (if that is not too gentle a word for their defeat) from Greece was eventually the formation in the Balkans of two new Galatian states by the survivors and others, the Scordisci and the Tylis. Neither of these two states is known at all well, the source material being as fragmentary and discontinuous as anything else about Thrace and the Galatians generally. The name of the Scordisci is first noted by

Justin, writing in the second century AD, in relation to the return of one part of the Greek expedition, where he notes that the returnees formed the Scordiscian kingdom on their arrival.[3]

From that it is assumed that the state was founded in 278 or 277, but that is not necessarily to be inferred from Justin's words, though he does say that they 'chose the name of Scordisci for themselves'; this may be his assumption, knowing that they bore that name later, it is not at all certain that it was ever a kingdom, kingship being an institution only two of the Galatian (or Keltic) states had in the ancient world. Perhaps it had a king, though, at the very end, close to the time of Justin's source, Pompeius Trogus, as a state with that name is not referred to in written sources until the beginning of the second century.[4] I have, as will have been noted, used the name for the state which had come into existence in the Banat not long after 400 BC, and whose envoys met Alexander in 335.

Another group which appears to have left the Banat region at about the time that the defeated forces returned, and which moved into Thrace, became the founders of the Tylis kingdom – this is the other Galatian kingdom – while some of those who had defected from the main returning army also contributed to its formation. The kingdom of Tylis is discussed in the latter half of this chapter; the Scordisci may be taken before this, but only after consideration of the situation in Macedon and Thrace in the aftermath of the great retreat.

There was for some years a confused condition of affairs in both Macedon and Thrace after the invasions and the retreat, in the lands on either side of the Haemos mountain range. The invasions had had a decisive effect in Macedon, as noted in the last chapter, in eventually forcing the acceptance of a competent king; and it had hardly less effect on the tribes between the Macedonian frontier and the Danube. To the west the Illyrians had been badly damaged by the Galatian invasions, but had survived, though infiltrated and still often attacked by the invaders, almost as though the Scordisci preserved the Illyrians as prey so that they could practise their raiding techniques on them.

Their effect on Thrace was much greater. The tribal organizations of the Triballi and the Thracians in eastern Thrace had been all-but destroyed in the troubles since the invasion by Philip II. In combination with the invasions of Philip and Alexander between 350 and 335, and then of Alexander's governors, and eventually of Lysimachos, all of whom fought the Thracians with ferocity, the Galatian invaders in 281-277 had probably performed the final social and political destruction to a tribal system which was already reeling towards collapse from the Macedonian attacks. There can have been only broken remnants of the old tribal order left by the time the Galatian movements subsided.

The initial Thracian revival after Alexander's time, which was associated with Seuthes III and his city of Seuthopolis, had been stillborn; the city had been destroyed, either by Lysimachos or more likely by Kerithrios' Galatian raid in 280; that Galatian raid also almost finished off the Triballi. The Macedonian colonies of Philippopolis and Kabyle certainly survived for a time, though it is possible that the former had suffered badly; the two border towns of Vetren and Pernik had been destroyed, though we cannot tell by whom.[5] At Kabyle coins produced there later were in the name of a Thracian, who was either a magistrate or a ruler of some sort, his authority was probably restricted to the town and its immediate environs.[6]

However, a broken political system such as evidently had been the result in Thrace because of the several invasions and passages of armies, does not mean the extermination of the population. Certainly casualties were great – Alexander killed at least 5000, so Arrian claimed,[7] and Philip and Lysimachos were probably even more lethal – but it is effectively impossible to exterminate a whole people without industrial methods, and not even then. Some will always survive. The Triballi, for example, were battered by Alexander, by Lysimachos (probably), and by Kerithrios, yet they were still identifiable as a much-weakened tribal group for some time after all that.[8]

What was destroyed in the fighting, of course, was the elite layer of the population, those whose conspicuous wealth gave them the authority of leading figures in the tribe, and made them the obvious targets for the invaders, both as possessors of portable valuables, which could be looted and stolen, and as the wielders of political and military power within the society. These were the men who had the authority to mobilize the people, either to resist attack, or to persuade them to submit to conquest. They were the glue which held such tribes together, and without such an elite social layer the tribes disintegrated into their component sections, which would have been clans, or even individual families.⁹ The elite were never numerous, and if they kept fighting every invader, they would soon be killed off – and if their wealth was stolen by those same invaders, they could not be replaced. In the place of the former tribal organization there remained the smaller population units, villages, families, clans, out of which eventually a new state might arise, but only after a period of peace and capital accumulation, financial and military; only then could a return be made to a renewed and larger political system.

This new, post-invasion condition was one, therefore, of small, even minuscule, political units. This was what existed in the territory north of Macedon in the period before the Galatian invasions of Macedonia and Greece, and after they had returned, defeated, from Greece and Macedon. It was out of these fragments that new tribes, cities, and kingdoms had to be constructed, two of these being the Scordisci and Tylis states. In these the new elite were the Galatians, some of them became rich from their predatory raids; the rural population whom they subjugated were a mixture of peoples, Illyrians, Thracians, other Galatians, even Greeks and Macedonians. Beyond them, the Dardanians had survived the invasions well, thanks to the devious and successful diplomacy of their king, and they now emerged strengthened; to the west, the Illyrians similarly had survived, and some of them developed a new state which troubled the Romans and the Macedonians during the next century.

Macedon itself slowly recovered during the 270s. Antigonos imposed peace on the kingdom which permitted it to recover. The work took several years, and the detailed recovery very much longer. For the next thirty years he operated to encourage this recovery, taking care that his wars were defensive and limited, even reducing his involvement in the affairs of Greece to a minimum, relying mainly on alliances with local groups (as in Athens) or on supporting local tyrants in other cities, such as Argos.¹⁰

One of the results of this necessary policy of recovery was that Antigonos had to relinquish any conquests to the north of Macedon proper, and give up any hope of recovering the lands which had been gained by the kings from Philip II to Lysimachos. These extensive conquests had always been difficult to hold, and their original conquest had never been more than superficial, and had had to be repeated several times. The people there were still rebellious even after fifty years of Macedonian conquest and rule; with the drastically-reduced resources of Macedon after the conquests in Asia and the Galatian wars, holding such an extensive territory was impossible; Antigonos apparently made no attempt to exert his authority beyond the old Macedonian boundaries.

The northern frontier of Macedon therefore retreated to where it had been at the beginning of Philip II's reign, along an approximate line from the mouth of the Nestos River to the Pindos Mountains, utilizing the convenient mountain ranges as the frontier but holding in some strength the passages through them. This was, as earlier Macedonian experience had shown, a defensible line, one which had very largely held at first against the Galatians. The line was close enough to the centres of Macedonian manpower in the plain to be guarded and to allow Macedonian forces, if an attack was threatened, to arrive in time close to the frontier to drive out any invaders, and in most cases to prevent their penetrating the defensive line in the first place.

This left the land north of that frontier, as far as the Danube, the land still called Thrace, outside any of the organized kingdoms, at least for the moment. It was in this area and out of the fragmented populations which had survived the invasions and conquests that the Galatians crafted their two new states.

There were two kingdoms north of Macedon which had survived the invasions, like Macedon, battered but unbroken. Due north of Macedon were the Paionians, who had been part of the Macedonian family of peoples, with an autonomous dynasty in office from the time of Philip II (and perhaps before) for well over a century. Their fight against Brennos' forces in 279 had no doubt left them weakened, but in the new circumstances it was in Antigonos' interest that the kingdom should survive and continue; from Macedon's viewpoint, Paionia was a most useful buffer state, which could absorb blows from the north – just as it had done at the beginning of the Galatian attacks – and which, moreover, might give good notice of any northern troubles.

The other kingdom which had survived was that of the Dardanians. The king had played a clever game amid the Galatian invasions, first allying with them, then attacking them, and no doubt fleecing them of as much of their Greek and Macedonian loot as he could seize. As a result, the Dardanian kingdom emerged from the invasions both strengthened and powerful, and no doubt it absorbed some of the damaged and smaller neighbours, and so increased its population. It occupied a fairly extensive territory north and west of the Paionians, between them and the Galatian Scordisci, who dominated the Banat and the surrounding lands. So between them these two surviving states covered much of Macedonians' northern frontier; but while the Paionians were friendly, the Dardanians were consistently hostile; it was Dardanian enmity which kept the northern frontier active throughout the third century. To the east of the Paionians was Thrace, which did not recover for some time, partly because of the battering it had received, but also due to the absence of politically-effective leadership.

The Galatian returnees, not surprisingly since their expedition had been composed of voluntary groups who came together for the single occasion, broke up once the dangerous journey seemed over. There emerged at least three, perhaps four, separate groups. The largest became the Scordisci and settled back into the Banat region, many of the participants probably having set out from that area in the first place. A second group, perhaps under a chief called Kommontorios, who actually may not have taken part in the Greek expedition, moved out of the Banat into Thrace, following the route of Kambaules and Kerithrios, and became the founding group of the Tylis kingdom. The third group was that under Leonnorios and Loutarios, which had broken away from the main force while it was still in Macedon, or the Dardanian country, and eventually became the founders of the Asian states of Galatia. It is also possible that a fourth group abandoned the Balkans altogether. These are said to have gone 'home' to Gaul, to the Tektosages of southern Gaul, and to have deposited their stolen Greek treasures in the sacred lake of the temple of Tolosa (Toulouse), whence some of it was re-looted by a Roman expedition in 106 BC. This story is often doubted, but we know from further examples that contact continued to be made between the several branches of the Tektosages, a tribe much given both to dividing and to each section retaining its Tektosagian identity. There were continuing Tektosagian groups in Gaul and Asia and Germany, and the idea of some individuals from the Greek expedition heading to the Gallic homeland to boast of their deeds and display their loot is hardly unbelievable; boasting seems to have been a male Galatian character trait. Justin also notes that this treasure display inspired more of the Tektosages of Gaul to migrate eastwards when they settled in Pannonia. The story of a 'return' to Tolosa may be doubted, but one may not necessarily doubt the mass movement of a group from Gaul to the Hungarian Plain, and the second to a degree depends on accepting the first.[11] A Tectosagian group was certainly present in the Greek invasion force, and followed the other two into Asia.

Despite this disclaimer, there is little doubt that the Scordiscian state was organized and established in the distinctive geographical situation in the Banat area well before the return of the defeated refugees from Greece. The wealth acquired by the participants became the social basis for the aristocrats who were the rulers. By the time they were returning northwards, having got through the Dardanians' lands, they were under the leadership of a man called Bathanattos.[12] He was a survivor of the Greek expedition: Akichorios was no longer the leader; either he died in one of the various fights during the return, or he was deposed as leader. Bathanattos appears to have been the leader of those who were determined to return to the Danube area and to settle down there, apparently with unpleasant memories of their experiences. The people are said to have refused to use gold in reaction to the ill fortune of the Delphian attack; they were perfectly willing to use silver, however.[13] (This, if it is true, might imply their failure to capture the temple, or simply be a reaction to their defeat and the large number of casualties they had suffered.) No doubt the returnees' arrival caused a good deal of political unrest (they were, after all planning to settle elsewhere), but Bathanattos established some authority, and can be regarded as the re-founder of the state. But since Galatian settlement in the area was by this time a century old, what occurred was the reinforcement of the earlier settlement; Bathanattos emerged as a major figure partly because he had already emerged as the returnees' leader, and partly no doubt because he had held on to a substantial quantity of Greek loot.

In fact, the returnees had little choice as to their destination. Unless they were to go off on their travels again, perhaps following in the tracks of the invaders of Thrace or Asia, the Banat area was as far as they were likely to get. To the north was the Pannonian area, the Hungarian Plain, on both sides of the Danube, which was by this time fully organized and controlled by Keltic groups – from whom the Kelts of the Banat had themselves probably come as part of the continuous migration and conquests during the previous centuries. To the east, the Dacians had received some Keltic immigrants and goods, but were now probably less than welcoming to more, and later became actively hostile.[14] And it must be presumed that, after their homeward retreat over a distance of almost 1000 kilometres, fighting repeatedly, and subdividing more than once, it is unlikely that the survivors were either numerous or were willing to go further. Their repeated battles will have cost them many casualties, and more were suffered by the harassment they received on their return march.

Most of the men probably were from the Banat region in the first place, and those that were not would be from other Keltic areas, especially Pannonia, Italy and Germany. With a determined leader such as Bathanattos, whose name was remembered as much as that of Brennos, it was possible to form a new and defensible – and aggressive – polity. They must also have been conscious that they themselves had been seriously weakened by their casualties, and may have feared a revenge attack from Macedon – but hardly from Greece, with its divisions. All around they could see the weakness of the fragmented and damaged tribes of the Balkans, and as foreigners in the land, the Galatians no doubt fully realized that only in unity would they be likely to survive. This, of course, was hardly new; they had dominated the region before the Greek expeditions, which in fact were clearly anomalous.

The Scordisci are usually referred to as a tribe, or as a tribal state, but they actually formed a typically Keltic state. Bathanattos is not described as a king, but he was clearly a charismatic leader, giving his name to the road they had travelled along in their retreat from Greece, and fathering a noted family of descendants- either that or the term Bathanatti referred to the group of survivors he had led and their descendants.[15]

From the names of Scordiscians recorded in written sources and on inscriptions it is clear that the underlying population of the state south of the Danube, the Galatians' subjects, remained Illyrian or Thracian, with the two being separated by the Morava River, though both were part of the state and the separation was not total.[16] There were perhaps other groups in the territory, and, given that the Keltic element in the population was fairly small, it may well be that it was the heterogeneous nature of the population which ensured the evolution of a more integrated state. The Keltic element will have formed the ruling group, no doubt, though it seems that the integration of the various groups was successful, since Illyrian and Thracian names occur in the later ruling group.[17]

The political status of the Scordisci as a kingdom is not clearly attested until fairly late in its history, and then not certainly. But when the Scordisci were under severe pressure they may have accepted the leadership of one man. This they did in the expeditionary forces of 281–277 under Brennos, then Akichorios, and as did the survivors of that disaster under Bathanattos – but he was not a king. Later, in Asian Galatia, kings emerged, but only under Roman pressure; the Romans wanted a single man that they could hold responsible for order, hence a king. An intermittent kingship is possible, though that may only be the effect of the intermittent nature of the sources. It does not appear, from Athenaios' notice of him, that Bathanattos founded a royal dynasty; later leaders all seem to be mentioned as coping with an emergency, such as, later, the Dacian invasions; that is, they were leaders who emerged for the emergency only. In the place of a fully-established kingship, one must assume an oligarchic system, probably hereditary (and therefore, more correctly, aristocratic), and in the hands of the Keltic elite – though it seems that the several ethnic groups in the state merged so that a good deal of integration took place over the next two centuries.[18] It may be that the aristocracy was internally very competitive, though no internal disputes among the Scordisci are recorded.

The territory they inhabited has been referred to here as the Banat, which is the provincial name of the area around Belgrade in Ottoman times, but which is useful as denominating a clear geographical area. This was centred on the fortress city of Singidunum (a Keltic name), on the site of modern Belgrade, which was at a most advantageous geographical situation. It stands at the junction of the Sava and the Danube rivers, thereby dominating three major river routes, to north, east, and north-west; a little downstream to the east there was the Morava River, along which there was a clear route to the south. Nearly 150 kilometres further north-west, the Drava River joins the Danube, providing still another route, this time into Pannonia. The Sava developed into a major land route towards northern Italy, where for a time in the third and second centuries the Kelts of the Scordisci, and those of Pannonia, had continuing contacts with the Gauls of Cisalpine Gaul. To the north of Italy there also developed the Keltic kingdom of Noricum, which was for a long time a state firmly allied to the Roman Republic.[19] In addition to the Sava and Drava routes to the north-west, the Danube provided routes to the north into Pannonia, the Hungarian Plain, and on towards Germany, and also to the north-east, avoiding Dacia by going north of the Carpathian Mountains, and into the valley of the Borysthenes (Bug) River and so on to the Black Sea, the Dniepr Valley, and the Greco-Skythian Bosporan kingdom in the Crimea. To the north was the Tisza River route, parallel for much of the way to the Danube, but closer to Dacia, and to the north-east were the mountains of Dacia, like Noricum a major source of metals. With such wide access to these lands, resources and trade routes, the fortress town at Singidunum was an obvious centre for trade, and so a source of wealth, and it rapidly developed into the Scordiscian capital. A second urban foundation, Taurunum, lay across the Sava from Singidunum, so that, together these two towns controlled the entrance to that river valley from the Danube, and the Danube route itself.

The state founded in the fourth century BC was initially small, perhaps including no more than the Banat area itself. It is known to have expanded along the Sava River Valley later, and the area later called Pannonia by the Romans to the north was already occupied and dominated by European Kelts, who were separate politically from the Scordisci, but were probably friendly, for it was from this population that the original Galatian population of the Scordisci derived, and to which some of the survivors of the Delphi expedition returned; family relationships are to be expected. Expansion east along the Danube valley would be difficult, for the river flows through difficult gorges for some distance, but equally that would provide a helpful barrier against enemies moving upriver. Similarly, expansion southwards along the Morava River into the region called by the Romans Upper Moesia, proved to be difficult also, but for a different reason. For to the south was the Dardanian kingdom, controlling the Scopje basin and dominating the surrounding lands; the hostility between the Scordiscian Galatians and the Dardanians which had begun during the former's return march northwards, appears to have continued after they were both settled in their new states with new boundaries. The Scordiscian state extended into Illyria, and many Scordiscian names in the first centuries BC and AD were 'Illyrianised'.[20]

One of the reasons for the consolidation of the Galatians in the Banat into an organized state, which was distinct from other Keltic states in the area of central Europe, was that they faced the developing Dardanian hostility, which burst into open warfare between the two in 197, in a war in which Philip V of Macedon and the Scordisci were, if not active allies, both hostile to the Dardani (though these had no doubt had earlier confrontations back to the Greek expedition's return).[21] They were compelled to develop a state system in order to resist the expansionary aims of their surrounding rivals and enemies, and to organize their own expansion. (In the south, it was Dardani who were now the inveterate raiders across the Macedonian frontier.)

This was, of course, a condition of persistent hostility, and hostilities are always one of the main factors in studying the formation of a state out of a group of separate peoples or clans. The kingdom of Noricum was formed from several Keltic and non-Keltic elements in part as a result of the development of local wealth derived from mining and the manufacturing of high quality metal goods. Republican Rome was a prime market for such products, and this was one of the main reasons the two states were politically friendly – one produced the goods, the other bought them.[22] Such wealth stimulated the envy of enemies, which in turn stimulated the development of a stronger governmental system for defence, including the integration of the several elements of the population, who were all equally threatened by enemies.

The position of the Scordisci at a major trading crossroads had the same effect as the metals of the Noricans, and to hold and develop and defend that trading source of wealth a properly organized state was certainly required. The initial expansion of the Scordisci would seem to have been along the Sava River valley to the north-west of the Banat, either exploiting or contriving the trade route along that valley. The major Balkan crisis which we call the Second Romano-Macedonian War (200–197) involved not merely Macedon and Rome, but the Dardanians as well, and the Scordiscian state also. It was a situation in which a series of enmities coalesced – Macedon's enemies were Rome and the Dardani, who were therefore allied; the Dardani and the Scordisci were enemies, and so the latter allied with the Macedonians. It was at this crisis that the Scordisci turned decisively southwards to engage in active warfare against the Dardanians, while Philip V campaigned against them and defeated them in battle at Stobi in Paionia. Once such active fighting began, mutual hostility continued as the Scordisci expanded southwards, partly at Dardanian expense.[23]

Archaeologically, the presence of elements of the 'La Tène' Iron Age culture are taken as indicative of Galatian settlement, and there is a strong concentration of such material in the Banat, especially along the valleys of the Danube and the Sava and Drava rivers, and around their confluences. Beyond, to the east, there is another scatter of such finds, much less concentrated, in what became the Roman province of Lower Moesia, south of the Danube and north of the Haemos Mountains.[24] There is no sign of such evidence in Thrace (which is odd, given the existence there of the Tylis kingdom), or in the Dardanian territories, which may be explained by their mutual hostility. Dacia, on the other hand, received a considerable migration of Kelts, probably as individuals – assuming that the remains indicate the arrival of people, not just goods acquired in trade. They were concentrated into the metal-rich area of the north of Dacia, the territory which later formed the heartland of the Dacian kingdom, which suggests that the Keltic immigrants might have been professional miners and metalworkers – a link between developments in Dacia and Noricum is obviously likely.

The Scordisci, therefore, by the middle of the third century BC, after a century and a half of occupying the Banat and its contributory river valleys, was a serious power in the region, probably the most vigorous and expansionist state in the Balkans, and so one at enmity with all its neighbours, particularly those to the south and the east. This was an expanding Galatian state, willing to accept other ethnic groups into its population as well as any Kelts. It was clearly Keltic in origin, but developed as a multi-ethnic state, and as such settled confidently into the existence as one more of the 'tribal states' of the region. It was, like every contemporary state, willing to seize on the weakness of any neighbour, and to ally with any other state if it brought advantage.

The Kingdom of Tylis

The other new Galatian state in the Balkans, the daughter, in a way, to the Scordisci, was the kingdom of Tylis, established in Thrace. It was founded in the immediate aftermath of the retreat from Greece, beginning with the settlement of a Galatian group under a leader called Kommontorios, referred to as their king,[25] a most unusual distinction amongst the Galatians, though perhaps it meant no more than their commander and leader – and yet it was always referred to as a kingdom in our sources. Part of the group was composed of survivors of the Greek expedition who had broken away from the main group while it was heading for home, and part was another group which had left their Danubian homeland during the return of the defeated army, perhaps aiming originally to take part in the great raid. They had instead moved into Thrace, clearly searching for a new base, and intent on creating a new kingdom, possibly part of the expedition led by Kerithrios, men who had already prospected the possibilities in Thrace.[26] The conditions in Thrace were evidently very confused, and it seems there were other autonomous Galatian warbands at large apart from those of Kommontorios, Leonnorios and Loutarios. One of these bands was defeated and massacred by Antigonos Gonatas in his ambush of a Galatian force at Lysimacheia in 277, an event which no doubt compelled a greater concentration by the rest.[27]

Antigonos recruited as mercenaries other Galatian bands who were present in Macedon; they proved to be more loyal to him than the Macedonians, but then Galatian mercenaries in Macedon must have led precarious lives, while the Macedonians were considering him as the latest candidate as their king, not just their employer. Being employed by the king in establishing a renewed kingdom was much the same work for the mercenaries as the other bands were doing in the Banat with Bathanattos, or Kommontorios' men in Thrace. And, of course, they ceased to be so much of a public danger when under some degree of discipline as part of the royal army, not to mention that Antigonos used them up in his battles, thereby getting rid of them, protecting his own Macedonians, and saving on their pay, all at the same time.

The majority of Kommontorios' men, perhaps under some pressure from their by-now numerous enemies in Thrace, consolidated into a single group with the latecomers from the Danubian area and established themselves as a kingdom which became called Tylis. Antigonos and Kommontorios absorbed or killed off the stray wandering Galatian bands, while others moved off into Asia. And all this happened within at the most a couple of years of the return of the great raid from Greece.

The kingdom of Tylis has been perhaps the most mysterious of the Galatian states founded in this period of the invasions of the East. We know something of its origin, as noted in the last paragraph, and something of its destruction, but little or nothing of its history between these events; nor is its location altogether clear, though it is known to have been in Thrace. As a political entity it lasted only a little over sixty years.[28]

The condition of Thrace in 277 was no doubt both confused and confusing. The native Thracian population had been battered by half a century of warfare against Macedonian rulers, and now had to cope with the wandering Galatian bands. Of the Galatian forces in the region, two groups had separated from the greater raiding force and moved eastwards under the command of Leonnorios and Loutarios. This group was evidently composed of men dissatisfied with the results of the Greek/Macedonian expeditions, and, being accompanied by their families, had always intended to continue raiding and invading new lands until they were able to settle as a community somewhere. The second group, commanded by Kommontorios, seems, at least by their actions, to have intended from the start to secure territory for themselves in Thrace, and perhaps raiding for loot had always been a secondary activity. They arrived and planted themselves without delay, and did not move. This suggests that at least some of the leaders were already familiar with Thrace, and had arrived with a clear plan of action – this, of course, would fit well with the obvious planning by Brennos and his colleagues and by Bathanattos, evidently a Galatian characteristic.

These two groups remained quite separate and evidently had quite different aims. It would, however, be naive to pretend that they did not meet and mingle. It may be assumed that some broke away from each of the groups to join the other, or even completely away from both. They both spent time in eastern Thrace before reaching decisions on their final intentions. Quite probably the firm and early decision of Kommontorios' group to settle in Thrace was made clear to the others, and that the

Leonnorios/Loutarios group was therefore not welcome. There, after a time, it is likely that both suffered defections, and their numbers were reduced.

Several influences and actions contributed to this reduction. There were the inevitable casualties. There may not have been many wounded surviving from the Greek expedition – the Greek sources claim that before leaving central Greece the wounded from the fighting at Thermopylai and Delphi had been killed[29] – but one would suppose that the march along the Thracian coast had not been unopposed, and that further deaths had occurred; there were a series of Greek cities along that coast, but although there is no indication that any fighting took place, that is no guarantee that all was peaceful. The number of people in the Leonnorios/Loutarios group is put at 20,000,[30] and while this is as unacceptable as any number from the ancient world, it may be in the neighbourhood of probability. But whatever the number when the group split from Akichorios' main body, it will have been considerably lower by the time they reached Thrace; 20,000 (which included the families) is probably their approximate number when they crossed into Asia.

In Thrace, further problems chipped away at the size of the forces. The ambush of Antigonos at Lysimacheia is said to have caused the deaths of '18000' Galatians,[31] while Antigonos' subsequent recruiting of Galatian soldiers as mercenaries was probably at the expense, at least partly, of these groups. And finally, the two commanders were recruited, with their whole warband, by the king of Bithynia and transported across the Bosporos into Asia. Altogether it is likely that the whole of the Leonnorios/Loutarios warband can be roughly accounted for by these various actions, moves, treacheries, and calamities – though it is surely probable that some also remained in Thrace, while others will have joined with them. The force which Antigonos massacred was another, it seems, which had broken away from the breakaway forces, and these directionless groups may have been gradually disintegrating ever since they arrived in Thrace. At least one other substantial group was the Tektosages, who followed the Asian groups across the Bosporos; they must have been in Thrace before they moved east, but nothing is known of them at that time

The force under Kommontorios may or may not have joined with that under Leonnorios and Loutarios at some point, but he did not join in the Asian expedition, nor does he seem to have been involved in the Macedonian expedition earlier, nor in the fighting against Antigonos. Instead all the indications are that he immediately established his force in Thrace and organized them as the kingdom of Tylis.

In the immediate aftermath of the failure of the Greek campaign, therefore, apart from the main group retreating north with Bathanattos, there were at least five substantial Keltic forces in Thrace: those led by Leonnorios and Loukarios; the Tektosages; that under Kommontorios, which may have been in two parts; and that in the Chersonese which was caught and destroyed by Antigonos. Within a short time they all either moved away or consolidated into a kingdom – or, of course, died.

We may see Kommontorios, then, as one of those men who saw an opportunity and worked determinedly to realize it. Leonnorios and Loutarios by contrast seem to have been more adventurous, seeking new opportunities to gather loot, and enjoying the excitement of raiding and fighting before searching for their new homes; they may also have been under pressure from their people to continue moving and raiding. Certainly Kommontorios succeeded in establishing his little kingdom, and probably, given the dire condition of Thrace at the time, this took place fairly soon after his force's arrived there.

Where exactly the kingdom was, however, is unclear. It used to be thought to be located in the Haemos Mountains, then it was suggested that it was in the valley of the Thundza River.[32] Both of these are in fact in much the same area as Seuthes III's defunct kingdom (and where Kambaules' raid in 298 came to grief), and would have included the wrecked site of Seuthopolis, where, to be sure, there is some archaeological evidence for a Galatian presence.[33] A more detailed consideration of the distribution of Keltic artefacts in Thrace, combined with some details in the written sources, now suggests that the kingdom was closer to the coast, in the area inland of the Gulf of Burgas, and close to the Greek cities of Apollonia Pontica, Mesambria, and Odessos.[34] It is thought in one theory that the kingdom controlled the former Thracian/Macedonian city of Kabyle at one point, but the evidence is not strong, consisting, as at Seuthopolis, of the finding of a few Keltic-type artefacts, which do not necessarily imply more than trade.[35]

The clue to the kingdom's location lies in appreciating that these Galatians kept themselves aloof from the Thracian population they dominated.[36] In order to do so these Galatians retained to a degree their former predatory habits, modified into a blackmail regime. This was certainly their relationship with the city of Byzantion. Perhaps, however, the other coastal cities did not suffer from the same attentions. Byzantion was some way away from the centre of the Tylis kingdom, whereas the other cities were geographically contiguous to its territory and appear to have had settled into a more or less comfortable relationship based on protection – for which they would pay, of course – and trade; indeed, under the circumstances they had no choice. Byzantion, on the other hand, had to be periodically menaced by expeditions which ravaged its mainland territory as an instance of what the kings could do if denied their reward. Polybios notes that a series of tributary payments were made by the city, beginning with one to Kommontorios in the 270s, amounting to 3000 gold pieces; later demands were for 5000, then 10,000, and finally a demand for an annual payment of eighty talents. The successive rises in the demands, were, of course, the direct result of paying the blackmail in the first place. How many times the demand came in is not known, but the first was in the 270s and the last in the 220s. The final demand, the one for eighty talents annually, was the one which finally brought Byzantion to resist, and appears to have been made in 221 or 220 BC.[37]

The cities closer to, or enveloped by, the kingdom – Apollonia Pontica, Mesambria and Odessos – probably did not need to be blackmailed; they no doubt could simply be taxed regularly – as indeed was Byzantion, in its particular way. The same happened no doubt to the Thracian peasantry in the country around Tylis, which is thought to be the Galatians' own city, or perhaps camp, but has not been located, other than by assuming that it was at one of several places whose modern names might somehow resemble it. The fact that deliberate expeditions had to be made to levy blackmail on Byzantion implies that, unlike Apollonia and the other cities, Byzantion was not close to the Tylis kingdom, and was increasingly reluctant to pay. These considerations, together with some archaeological evidence and some place-name evidence, suggest that the territory of the kingdom was close to the smaller Greek cities, and that it stretched inland from the coast at the Gulf of Burgas for perhaps forty or fifty kilometres, the territory being an approximate semi-circle with its centre perhaps at the head of the bay. The city of Kabyle, which is thought to have formed part of the kingdom for a time, is about fifty kilometres from the coast, and securing control of it may well have been an attempt by one of the kings to extend his power further inland; Byzantion was rather further away, and was a stronger city than any of the others.

This state was therefore different from all other Galatian states in the east. First, it appears from the origin to be ruled by a king. This is, as already noted, highly unusual for a Galatian state, but the evidence seems conclusive, in that when it became involved with a major crisis near the end of its life, the ruler was always described as a king. On the other hand, this may be because the Greek sources we have could not think of any other way to describe the ruler. But the state was also run on different lines from others: it does not seem to have integrated its Galatian and Thracian populations, but to have kept them separate, the Thracians, of course, being subordinate. It kept its predatory habit, to the extent that it prayed regularly on the local Greek cities. All this – king, racial separation, predation – makes it out as a singular and distinctly different state and society.

These characteristics made Tylis an insufferable neighbour and ruler, and its methods will have built up considerable resentment both in the Thracians who were in effect it serfs (and probably subject to enslavement and sale) and among the Greek cities. If Byzantion's experience is typical, the taxation regime applied to the other cities also became increasingly unendurable. The end was a crisis which first broke the predatory system and finally eliminated the kingdom.

When the crisis of the payments by Byzantion came in 221 or 220, Tylis was ruled by a king called Kavaros. He was perhaps king from the 230s, though the exact date of his accession is not accurately known. We may assume he had ruled for some time before 220; his eventual intervention in the dispute suggests a canny politician and a king fully familiar with Greek diplomatic methods. The institution of kingship may well have been part of the original Galatian settlement of Tylis, which would make Kommontorios the first of the kings. Kingship, as opposed to chieftainship, did not go well with a community living by predatory raids, in which individual chieftains used their power to distribute wealth to their clients; these were a more suitable means of authority. And if Tylis was a state in which the ruling group, the Galatians, remained aloof from their Thracian subjects, it would be more likely that a king existed, if only to centralize the menacing and taxation powers which would maintain Galatian control; the demands of the king's clients and the other chiefs would not remain steady, but would necessarily increase – hence the steadily greater demands on Byzantion, and probably on the other cities.

We can therefore infer something of the kingdom's origin, of its social structure, of its political organization, and of its territorial extent. We know the king regularly levied tribute-blackmail on at least one rich Greek city, and no doubt enforced tribute payments, collected equally regularly and greedily, on the Thracians within his reach, and on the neighbouring Greek cities on the coast. On the other hand, it was not expansionist, unlike the Scordiscian state for example. It also appears that Kavaros' tribute will have been one of the major factors which led to the collapse of the state. It was, therefore, from the start a predator state. This would make it vulnerable to internal disputes over the division of the tax-take, and to any stronger power whom it alienated; it was, in short, inherently unstable.

The payment demanded by Kavaros from Byzantion in about 220 was for eighty talents. It is not altogether clear how long this level of payment had been so high, but for a time Byzantion clearly paid at something like this level. In 220/221, however, the city finally baulked at the demand. The eighty talents has been calculated to be the equivalent of 24,000 gold staters (eight times the original first payment)[38] and the city decided this could not be met out of Byzantion's own treasury. The alternatives were to refuse, thereby incurring a war in which the city's territory, much of which will have been owned by the city's oligarchs, was seriously damaged, or to shift the burden elsewhere; the city chose the second. The city government resolved to impose a transit tax, or toll, on ships passing through the Bosporos, thereby attempting to shift the weight of the tribute onto the Greek mercantile world as a whole. Complaints ensued. There is no real suggestion that the tax was exorbitant or unaffordable, but it would certainly increase shipping costs, and raise the prices in the cities to which the ships were taking the goods. In effect, as has been pointed out, Kavaros was compelling Byzantion to become his tax collector, and the merchants and shippers were expected to pay Kavaros' tribute, and therefore their customers; Kavaros was laying the whole Greek world under tribute.[39]

The complaints no doubt began with the merchants and ships' captains, but they were quickly taken up by their home cities. The cities appealed to Rhodes, currently the greatest naval and mercantile city in the Aegean region, to intervene – no doubt Rhodes will have been one of the original complainers as well. The Byzantines refused the demand from Rhodes to cancel the tax, and war followed, in which King Prusias of Bithynia joined, aiming to take advantage of Byzantion's plight to filch some of the city's territory on the Asian side of the Bosporos. The Rhodian tactics were, however, less violent, though perhaps more effective; they instituted a blockade of Byzantion, which no doubt meant that the passing ships would be protected from the Byzantine exactions, but also that they were prevented from calling at Byzantion. So Byzantion was both unable to collect the tax, and was deprived of the trade (and the customs duties) which was brought by the ships under normal conditions; further, the city was losing control of some of its territory. It could find no sympathizers. It was helped by Herakleia Pontike with cash, but by no one else – Herakleia was constantly at odds with the Bithynian kings; Byzantion's allies, King Attalos of Pergamon and the Achaian League, gave it no real support.

Byzantion was quickly forced to ask for terms. Ironically, or perhaps deliberately, it was King Kavaros who arranged the terms. He was probably feeling the pinch as much as Byzantion, since Byzantion was clearly not paying up, and would not be able to pay while the blockade continued. By the treaty Kavaros arranged that the city would give up collecting the tax, and would become the ally of both Prusias and Rhodes; Prusias returned the territory he had taken.[40] Nothing appears to have been said about Kavaros' original demand for the tribute, and it may have been abandoned, or more likely reduced. Alternatively, Kavaros may have simply agreed to collect it over a longer period, which in fact will have put Byzantion in a similar tributary position to the other Greek cities already overseen by Tylis. In any case it was clearly impossible to extract the full sum from Byzantion at once, and the result of the dispute was a modified victory for the city.

These characteristics made Tylis an insufferable neighbour and ruler, and its methods will have built up considerable resentment both in the Thracians who were in effect it serfs (and probably subject to enslavement and sale) and among the Greek cities. If Byzantion's experience is typical, the taxation regime applied to the other cities also became increasingly unendurable. The end was a crisis which first broke the predatory system and finally eliminated the kingdom.

Kavaros was, therefore, one way or another, deprived of a handsome sum of money. He was clearly greedy for it, for whatever reason. Possibly he had aimed to use it in wars in the Thracian interior, possibly he simply wanted to accumulate a large sum of money; the very large sums he had already collected had perhaps been distributed among the several chiefs of his kingdom, or used to pay mercenaries. If Tylis kept a fairly rigid separation between the elite and their Thracian subjects, its armed forces would necessarily be the followers of the elite plus any hired mercenaries Kavaros could recruit; the Thracians were no doubt not trusted and were kept disarmed. (One thinks of Spartan helots as an example, or serfs in many other parts of the Greek world, including Bithynia.) This would also mean that power within the kingdom was distributed among the Galatian chiefs, and Kavaros as king would be only *primus inter pares*, though no doubt richer than the others. Attempting to increase the tribute might have been a way for Kavaros to increase his internal power. The alternative means of getting money would be for him to impose greater demands on his own subjects, that is, the Thracians. The Galatians of Tylis, if they really were an oligarchic community whose contribution to the state was their military abilities and their armed followers, would not be taxed, but would expect to receive shares of the king's exactions; in other words, they were living on the tribute of the Thracians, and Kavaros' demands on Byzantion were probably fuelled by the expectations of handouts to his Galatians.

A new demand may have been the blow which finally brought the Thracians to rise against Galatian domination. The failure of Kavaros' scheme to mulct Byzantion will perhaps have made him impose these new demands. The details of the overthrow, as ever, escape us, but it does appear that it was a Thracian attack or revolt which brought about the kingdom's destruction.[41] Exactly which Thracians were involved, however, is not known. They could have been the Galatians' subjects, driven to desperation, but it could also be that Thracians from outside the kingdom felt increasingly threatened by the wealth being gathered by Kavaros; the move against Kabyle might have suggested that the kingdom was looking to expand. There was also a Thracian kingdom, ruled by a scion of the old Odrysian royal family, which may have inspired the Galatians' subjects to rebel, either passively, by merely existing, or actively, by intrigues. There was certainly a powerful Thracian kingdom in Thrace in the years before about 200, which was able to capture and sack at least one Greek city, Lysimacheia.[42] One might also suggest the possibility that the Byzantines, frightened by their experience of the demands of Kavaros and the war they provoked, might well have instituted intrigues themselves to secure his overthrow, though it would be surprising if they had not resorted to such tactics earlier.

The result was not only the removal of Kavaros, but the complete destruction of the Tylis kingdom, apparently sometime after 220. This speedy end was assisted by the intrigues of a man called Sostratos of Kalchedon, who became a favourite of the king. No doubt his influence was resented, and contributed to Kavalos' end.[43] The failure of his extortion campaign against Byzantion was also presumably an element in the kingdom's collapse.

The kingdom vanished without leaving a trace of its existence. The site of Tylis is unknown, the names of most of its kings are unknown, and the extent of the kingdom's territory can only be estimated. The fate of the individual Galatians was probably to be killed – it is likely that there were not many of them; otherwise, they might escape to refuge with the Scordisci or into the Galatian communities in Asia. That is another thing we do not know.

Settlers Eastwards

There is one further region into which Galatians moved in this period of confusion, migration, raids, and conquest. North of the Black Sea, in the steppe lands of the Ukraine, east of the Carpathian Mountains, there is some archaeological evidence of a scattered Galatian population. This is spread fairly widely, from Moldova to the lands north of the Sea of

Azov. Little information of this is recorded in any of the written sources, though one inscription is helpful and telling, so it is from archaeology that most of the information derives.[44] This has been noted already, but here more detail is appropriate.

The migrants came from the Pannonian settlers, and perhaps from Dacia, Bohemia, and Moravia. The route to the east led them to the great rivers flowing through the Ukraine south to the Black Sea, the Dniestr, the Bug, the Dniepr, and the lands along the north of the sea; at the estuaries of these cities there were a series of old Greek cities, founded 200 or 300 years before; Tyras at the mouth of the Dniestr, Olbia at the joint estuary of the Bug and the Dniepr, Pantikapaion at the Strait of Kerch between the Crimea and the mainland, and others. The Galatian migrants arrived at a time when the steppe was relatively quiet, with no great nomad conquerors rampaging. Not that there were no great movements at the time – their arrival is an indication of some restlessness, however. The evidence of their presence is scattered but extensive, though dating is difficult – since it was only by about 400 BC that a large Galatian population was firmly located in Pannonia, it must have been some years, or decades, after that date that the Ukraine Galatians arrived.

The archaeological evidence consists in part of constructed earthworks which are thought or presumed to be of Keltic construction, of burials identified as specifically Keltic, and of isolated finds of La Tène-type metalwork, which might imply the presence of Keltic workers, who may have been itinerant.[45] There is a concentration of Keltic materials in the upper Dniepr region, and a string of forts-cum-earthworks spread at approximately even distances from the upper Dniestr to the Dniepr. There is another concentration, this time mainly of burials and La Tène objects, in the middle of the Dniepr valley, in the area where Kyiv was later founded. The earthworks are largely in the open steppe, arguing a defensive purpose, but also close to or on the rivers;[46] the heavier concentrations of apparent occupation are in the zone of mixed steppe and forest north of the steppelands.[47]

There are also scattered Keltic place names and tribal names in this region, at least in the western part. The Costobogi (a similar name to the Tolistobogii in Asia) are recorded in the central area of modern Moldova, and the Britolagi have been located just north of the Danube estuary; on opposite sides of that river, above the estuary, are the Keltic place names Allobrix and Noviodunum. Such place names and the fortifications do suggest a permanent Keltic presence, whereas finds of jewellery, or even single burials, might be no more than the evidence of occasional visits or passing groups.

Exactly what all this amounts to is therefore less than clear. Many of the metalwork finds are in graves which are clearly not of Keltic people, but were probably Skythians – but the Skythians had been displaced by the Sarmatians during this time, though neither of these was more than an elite of warriors ruling over the same indigenous population. An earthwork, whether amounting to a fort or not, is not necessarily a permanent or long-lasting structure indicating the presence of inhabitants, but could be just a temporary camp. The concentration of a mixture of items at the upper Dniestr and in the area of Kyiv, however, are sufficient to imply the arrival of settlers in those places, living among the native populations, where their skills – in warfare, in metalworking – were welcome. Tribal names imply a ruling group, place names imply permanent settlers, and these imply the existence of organized Keltic states on the usual 'tribal' pattern. It is also possible that these groups arrived not from Pannonia, though this was the area of the heaviest nearby Galatian population, but derived from the Gauls who had moved into Poland; the place names by the Danube estuary could signal Kelts coming along the river.

The one worthwhile written source in this first period is an inscription from Olbia, at the mouth of the Bug.[48] The city had come under attack by an allied force of Kelts and Scirians. This looks very like the same sort of attacks made in Greece and Thrace and Asia Minor, if perhaps with a considerably smaller group of Kelts, if they were allied with others. The attackers encouraged the serfs working in the fields for the citizens to abscond into some sort of freedom, or kidnapped them. The attackers could have been based in some of the earthworks in the interior north of Olbia, or from one or more of the Keltic states in the east. On the whole, however, neither the settlements nor the raids seem to have had much effect on the local political or social situation in the lands north of the Black Sea. The presence of any Kelts was no doubt swallowed up by the indigenous inhabitants.

The eastward move of the Kelts produced a curious variety of results. The Scordisci state was an important local power in the Balkans for three centuries; the Tylis kingdom, a predatory state, went down to ruin after only sixty years; those Kelts who penetrated into the Ukraine were, like most steppe invaders or migrants, absorbed into the local population with scarcely any record. But the three were all different. The Scordisci was an expanding state typical of the Hellenistic period, only the Keltic origin of its rulers distinguishing it from other states all around the Mediterranean. The Tylis kingdom emphasized a different element in the heritage of the Kelts, the practice of raiding, which became institutionalized as predation on its neighbours; it was ended by those neighbours when the predations became too greedy or violent or both. In the Ukraine the migration was almost stateless, possibly predacious, possibly peaceful, perhaps both, but was far too weak in numbers to make much of a mark.

Chapter 5

Galatians into Asia

The Galatians who moved into Thrace in 278/277 were divided into several groups. Those survivors of the Greek and Macedonian campaigns who were commanded by Leonnorios and Loutarios were accompanied by their women and children. Of the suggested '20,000' people who comprised this band, probably half of these were dependents, which meant that the whole group moved fairly slowly.[1] It also suggests that they had all moved as a distinct group through Macedon and into Greece, alongside, or within, Brennos' and Akichorios' larger group, though obviously the warriors participated in the raiding and the battles.

There is no indication in the sources for this part of the history of the expedition that the women and children were present in the fighting at Thermopylai and Delphi, so it is likely that they had been left somewhere under guard and protection, perhaps north of the Spercheios River, while the fighting was going on. On the retreat through Greece they were evidently still a distinct group, or perhaps two groups under the two leaders, possibly annexing some men from other groups to replace any casualties – some of the women will have become widows during the fighting, and new husbands will have been valued. Their decision to separate from the main force and head into Thrace was no doubt a collective one, made after discussion, and possibly based on disgust at the failed leadership of the Greek expedition.

The decision to retreat, after their defeats at Delphi and Thermopylai, probably promoted or encouraged, the separation of the Leonnorios/Loutarios group from the main body; the main group aimed to return to the Banat area, the two dissident groups were looking for a new homeland. By moving as a unit, families and all, it is evident that the Leonnorios/Loutarios warbands had set out on the march into Macedon and Greece from the start with the intention of seizing that new homeland for themselves. They had failed in Greece, but their move into Thrace does imply an intention to continue that search.

It is not clear whether the warband under Kommontorios which formed the new kingdom of Tylis was composed of families or just of warriors, though some deductions can be made. The fact that they came directly from the Banat area into Thrace, and straight away established themselves there as the kingdom of Tylis would suggest that they were a migratory rather than simply a military group. In Thrace, therefore, when these movements had taken place, the Galatians were a set of separate forces which were quite distinct from the main body, which had returned to the Banat. Their intentions to find new homelands, particularly in Thrace, meant that they were therefore not so easy to shift, once they had chosen that new home. The main body, once it had been defeated at Delphi and Thermopylai, had immediately turned back and returned home, carrying whatever loot the men had collected, determinedly harassed by Thessalians, Macedonians, and Dardanians; the groups which split off had already cut their links with their original homeland, and were intent on conquest.

By moving into Thrace, both the Leonnorios/Loutarios and the Kommontorios groups found themselves in a cul-de-sac. They were not the only Galatian groups in the area. There was also the group which in 277 Antigonos defeated and massacred in the Chersonese; and there was the Tektosages, which had not yet linked up with the Leonnorios/Loutarios group; also there was the probably fairly small groups which Antigonos mopped up by recruiting them into his new mercenary army. Once he had done that he quickly gained control of Macedon, and this therefore blocked any retreat by the groups in Thrace back into Macedon. Kommontorios' group swiftly became established in its corner of Thrace, thereby excluding others. Behind them was Macedon, damaged but angry, and by no means finished – Sosthenes was in command until 277, then Antigonos soon after. Before them were the Straits – the Bosporos, the Propontis, the Hellespont – which were too wide to be crossed without the use of at least some ships or boats, and perhaps seamen as well. There were walled cities along the Thracian coast which they had passed on their migration, and were now part of Antigonos' kingdom, and which in most cases they could not capture, and there were fully alert governments on the Asian side, who were likely to block any crossing.

The Galatians in Thrace menaced the cities on the coast, ravaged Byzantion's territory, and managed to capture and loot Lysimacheia, which may have been recently damaged by an earthquake, and may also have been partly evacuated for this reason. The several small cities in the Chersonese are not mentioned in the only source on this episode – Livy writing nearly three centuries later – but one would suppose that most of those cities suffered, either seeing their lands ravaged, or finding that they were captured, or both; possibly they were among those whom Livy says 'sought peace' from the invaders, and paid tribute.

The Galatians occupied the Chersonese, once Antigonos had massacred his victims and moved on. Perhaps they could have settled there, but it was a narrow land, and the wealthy and extensive territory of Asia Minor was visible across the straits, and this attracted them even more. They sent envoys to negotiate for a crossing, contacting Antipatros, the Seleukid governor of the region, whom Livy called 'the prefect of the coast' – he was probably the governor of Hellespontine Phrygia. He refused them leave to cross, not surprisingly.

Livy now claims that the two Galatian leaders disagreed as to their next move – he calls it a 'revolt' – or maybe they decided to separate to try two different ways of crossing the water; since later they joined up again, whatever had been the supposed disagreement, it was not permanent; more likely it was a later interpretation from their brief separation. It looks more like a deliberate attempt to try several ways of crossing, so that if one group got across the other could follow. The separation may also be due to logistical reasons. If they had been in the Chersonese for some time, they will have largely eaten up the local supplies; when Leonnorios' group went off, their first priority was to 'ravage' – that is, gather or steal supplies of food – in the land they now occupied. Leonnorios took his force back towards Byzantion, a narrow crossing, while Loutarios attempted again to negotiate a passage with Antipatros, who was based at that moment in the Troad. This may in fact have been a ploy to keep Antipatros pinned down and allow Leonnorios' force to try crossing by another route.

The presence of the Galatian bands was a major burden for the people in Thrace. The settlement of Kommontorios' people in Thrace as the Tylis kingdom menaced the cities of the Pontic coast, at least until they came to an agreement with their new neighbour. Kommontorios eventually, but probably not until Leonnorios' force had moved on, instituted the more or less regular blackmail of Byzantion, beginning with a demand for 3000 pieces of gold – possibly an annual payment. Leonnorios' force sat in the city's territory, consuming supplies, and looting anything of value the men could find; the presence of Loutarios' band in the Chersonese was even more damaging to the cities there. The satrap Antipatros apparently continued resolutely firm in his refusal of passage across the Hellespont – clearly understanding how the Galatians would behave if allowed across – but at the Bosporos matters were different.

The political condition of Asia Minor, the land the Galatians were hoping to enter, was almost as confused and divided as the Thrace they were already inhabiting – temporarily, they hoped. The overall authority was the Seleukid king, Antiochos I, the son of the conqueror Seleukos I. Antiochos was an experienced ruler and commander, having been posted to the eastern provinces by his father to rule Baktria well over ten years before his father's murder. It had taken him some time to arrive in the west after his father's death, and once arrived he had had to cope with a series of problems. It had been his intention, as it has been that of his father, to cross into Europe and claim the kingship of Macedon, but the problems of Asia had delayed him. These had involved him in a brief war with Ptolemy Keraunos, and in another brief war with Antigonos Gonatas, both of whom were kings of Macedon in occupation, or claiming that position – Antiochos' own claim was based on his father's defeat of Lysimachos, king of Macedon and of Asia Minor. None of these three men claiming the post had been in occupation when they made their claims, and the one who succeeded in taking up the kingship, Ptolemy Keraunos, lasted only a year and a half.

Antiochos had tackled the main problem he faced – control of Asia Minor – with care, clearly anxious not to provoke local opposition. The country had been under Lysimachos' rule for twenty years, however, and, though Lysimachos had not been liked towards the end, that was not necessarily a reason to welcome yet another king. Antiochos' centre of government for the whole region was Sardis, the old Lydian and Persian capital. From there he faced a string of old Greek cities along the Aegean coast, many of them rich, famous, and vulnerable, but all of them autonomous to varying degrees. In the town of Pergamon, a little to the north and inland, Lysimachos' local treasurer, Philetairos, guarded his charge in a well-fortified castle. He had apparently accompanied Seleukos into Europe; after the king's murder he had secured Seleukos' body, performed the expected funeral rites, and then had handed the ashes on to Antiochos. This was sufficient to guarantee Philetairos his own, and Pergamon's, autonomy, but he also continued to hold and guard his treasure.[2]

The north coast of Asia Minor was also lined by a number of autonomous polities, a mixture of Greek cities and native kingships and lordships. These had all been menaced by the clear determination of Seleukos while he lived to impose his authority on them, and in response they had organized themselves into an alliance, which modern historians call the Northern League: Byzantion and Kalchedon, facing each other on opposite sides of the Bosporos, the king of Bithynia, the city of Herakleia Pontike, which had recently established its control over several nearby smaller cities, and whose navy was one of the main strengths of the alliance. The king of Pontos was loosely attached to the league, as was for a time Antigonos Gonatas.[3] The league had successfully maintained the independence of its members against Seleukos and then against Antiochos, who was just as determined in his pursuit of them as his father, but it had begun to break up by the time the Galatians arrived in Thrace. Byzantion evidently received no help against Kommontorios or Leonnorios from its allies, and meanwhile the Bithynian state was rent by a dynastic dispute, with two brothers claiming the kingship, and dividing the country between them. This had provided Antiochos with the opportunity to intervene and, he hoped, to establish his control, or at least his supremacy, on one of the Bithynian contenders, by allying with him and pushing out the other. But this was an idea which could occur to others.

The Northern War had been Antiochos' immediate concern,[4] but now that the Galatian bands had arrived at the Straits they provided an additional complication to an already complex matter. The Straits both separated and linked the two crises, and inevitably the two coalesced. When he arrived, Leonnorios quickly became fully acquainted with the political situation in the area, if he was not already: across the Straits was

Bithynia, a fractured kingdom under threat. It was either a perfect prey, or a Trojan Horse for entry into Asia.

Leonnorios and his band were hired by the Bithynian in occupation, Nikomedes, to squash his enemy brother, Zipoetas. This was agreed in a treaty which Leonnorios made with the whole Northern League. Possibly the league thought it was hiring a huge mercenary band, but Nikomedes was probably more alert to what the Galatians intended. At any rate, he not only used them to remove his brother, but to pursue his war with Antiochos. Moving them to Asia would therefore relieve Byzantion of the burden of the Galatian presence, and Bithynia of the threat of both Zipoetas and Antiochos I, at least for the moment. At the Hellespont, Loutarios' negotiations with Antipatros (Antiochos' governor) continued to meet with no success. Antipatros then dispatched men across to investigate the Galatians. They were sent 'to spy, under cover of being an embassy', Livy explains. They arrived in two triremes and three smaller vessels, which Loutarios' men seized, presumably having dealt with the agents first. For the Galatians, this procedure was even better than crossing by treaty, for they were not restricted by any conditions. Loutarios got his whole force across in 'a few days'.[5]

The two groups constituted themselves into two traditional Keltic tribes. When this occurred is not clear, though the beginning of the march against Macedon and Greece would seem to be the most likely time, for they operated from the time of the defeat at Delphi as distinct units. The Leonnorios group had the name Tolistobogii, and the Loutarios group were the Trokmoi. The origin of the names is unknown, but they may have been the names of the senior constituent elements of each of the tribes. It is clear from later details that each tribe consisted of several sections, each with their own names, and these remained in existence and in use within the larger grouping. The dangers involved in their travels, their fighting, and their search for a homeland are quite sufficient to account for their welding into clear political units, which existed for the next six centuries at least. The names, however, are only first recorded with regard to their campaigns in Asia after the elimination of Zipoetas.

Byzantion had suffered a severe ravaging of its territory, though more precision is not available. The city had asked for help from its allies, and had loyally opposed the Galatians' attempts to cross into Asia, which its allies did not want, at first. But when Nikomedes of Bithynia intervened, he and Byzantion saw an opportunity both to gain an ally against the brother and a neat way to get rid of the city's unwanted visitors, and a useful force to be used against Antiochos. It is quite possible that the Byzantines were the intermediaries in the negotiations, possibly even the instigators. The result was a treaty between Nikomedes and his allies (Byzantion, Kalchedon, Tios, Herakleia, and Kieros, and 'a few other tribal lands') on the one hand, and 'the barbarians' on the other. They were allies, not subjects or hirelings, whatever the Greeks might think to themselves.[6]

This treaty raises a wider point about the general situation. The Galatians are regularly described as barbarians in the Greek (and Roman) sources, and their behaviour in fighting is usually described as savage and cruel, though it was perhaps only a little worse than that of the Greeks themselves – who regularly destroyed cities, massacred defeated enemies, and enslaved survivors. In their diplomacy the Galatians generally conformed carefully to the accepted norms of the time and place.[7] In particular, a treaty between monarchies was made to last for the lifetimes of the contracting parties, by which it continued in existence until one of the parties died; alternatively a time limit, usually a number of years, could be included, and this latter was the preferred system for Republican states, whose magistrates usually served for only one year;[8] another alternative would be to contract for a particular occasion or task – such as delivering Nikomedes from the threat of his brother. To this system the Galatians clearly conformed: they had made an alliance with Nikomedes, and they respected it until the king died in c.255. It appears that he specified that the treaty must include a clause that the Galatians would be 'well-disposed to Nikomedes and his descendants'. This was not anything more, perhaps, than a hope, but the Galatians did assist one side in another Bithynian dynastic conflict after Nikomedes died, and otherwise kept the peace with the Bithynian kings until 230.

Nikomedes had been in a very difficult situation. He had been allied to both the Northern league and Antigonos Gonatas against the attempt by Antiochos I to re-establish Seleukid control over all the countries along the northern Asia Minor coast, but when Antigonos and Antiochos made peace (in 279 or 278) he was faced by the civil war with his brother, and so became extremely vulnerable, for that peace signalled the imminent dissolution of the league. Antiochos clearly now had the new capability to ally with Zipoetas and therefore drive out Nikomedes, or drive out both of them. Leonnorios and his warband were already enemies of Antiochos, who was denying them passage; so Nikomedes' alliance with the Galatians was a normal matter of the alliance of two powers facing the same enemy. By bringing them over the Bosporos, Nikomedes' ally Byzantion was relieved of their attentions, and by carefully listing the allies of Bithynia in the treaty, they also were being protected from Galatian attack, and Nikomedes was ensuring the continued existence of the Northern League. This was all within the normal methods of Hellenistic diplomacy and political behaviour.

The two Galatian forces, who actually got across into Asia at more or less the same time, joined together again to conduct the war for Nikomedes' kingdom, by eliminating Zipoetas, and were then encouraged by Nikomedes to continue the wider war by fighting his (and their) other enemy Antiochos – which would also remove the potentially dangerous Galatians from the Bithynian kingdom in the same way that the original agreement moved them away from Byzantion. True to their alliance with the Northern League, the whole joint warband, which at about this time had been joined by a third Galatian tribe, the Tektosages, which had been transported across the Strait in their wake, turned south to begin the looting of the rest of Asia Minor, Antiochos' territory. Nikomedes was at war with Antiochos; sending the Galatians south into the king's country was obviously a sensible military measure, and the worthwhile use of a willing ally. Moreover, it worked, and Bithynia's independence was assured from then on.[9]

No continuous account can be written of the subsequent events, though stories were later told which indicate that many of the cities of the western coast were threatened at one time or another; and yet there is a clear pattern involved. The three tribes operated to a clear plan in their campaign. In war they specialized in surprise attacks and fast movement, and they stayed nowhere for very long. They must have had centres from which they operated, probably fortified camps (perhaps like those known in the Ukraine), but none are specifically recorded. Their accumulated loot was no doubt substantial; we do not know what they did with it beyond holding on to it, and still held it a century later.[10] Some of it was no doubt sold, or exchanged for provisions, and it is known that they were accompanied, or followed, by numbers of merchants who would be happy to overcharge them. They could be defied from behind strong walls, if the will of the defenders was firm enough. Few, if any, Asian walled cities seem to have been physically captured, but any city they approached had its lands ravaged, at the least, and blackmail was paid by some. Rural inhabitants clearly suffered the most, and being outside the city when the Galatians arrived was to risk death, kidnapping, and enslavement. No doubt slave traders were part of the merchant group following them around.

It is reported in Livy that once the Galatians moved away from Bithynia they were divided, or divided themselves, into three 'tribes', the Trokmoi, the Tolistobogii, and the Tektosages, though this division had probably existed from much earlier.[11] In addition, they are said at one point to have had seventeen chiefs, who may or may not have included the original commanders Leonnorios and Loutarios and whoever was the leader of the third group.[12] The large number of chiefs implies that each of these three main tribes was composed of several sub-sections, each under its own chief. The numbers of Galatians is put by Livy at 20,000, of whom only half were 'armed' – that is, were warriors; he is referring at this point to the two groups which crossed first under Leonnorios and Loutarios, probably the Tolistobogii and the Trokmoi; the third group is perhaps also counted as '10,000', a vague figure which really just means 'a lot'. This is usually seen as too small for their intended task, and some would increase the total to up to 50,000 people, to include dependents, assuming that the '20,000' were fighters, though Livy is quite specific that only half were warriors.[13] None of these numbers, ancient or modern, can be taken as anywhere near accurate, all are mere estimates. Each of the three divisions, therefore, comprised in the region of a few thousand warriors, though we do not know how precisely they were divided or constituted. Whatever the precise numbers, this was a relatively small force, and once divided, as it evidently was almost as soon as they began to campaign, the campaigning units were even smaller; this needs to be kept in mind when we examine their campaigns.

Each of the three tribes was a distinct political unit and each of them was allotted, literally by lot, a part of the Asian territory as the area which it was to attack – the Trokmoi had the Hellespontine lands, that is, probably the Seleukid province of Hellespontine Phrygia, from the Bithynian border to the Troad; the Tolistobogii took 'Aiolis and Ionia' as their region, which was probably the satrapy of Lydia; the Tektosages are said to have had the Asian interior as their prey, but this is an extremely vague phrase in the circumstances, and probably results from a later circumstance; the earliest allocation was probably the southern area of Karia. This would imply that each of these tribes had a base somewhere in their raiding territory, though no such base has ever been located. If the allocated areas reflected the relative strengths of the three tribes, the Tektosages were the smallest, while the other two were roughly equal in size.

These political divisions might have allowed us to attribute to each tribe the raiding activities in the next year or so, but in fact the records of their activities tend to favour the territory of the Tolistobogii in 'Aiolis and Ionia'. The rich cities of the Aegean coast were their prey, though not one is recorded as having been captured.[14]

Kyzikos was the first Asian victim, and had its lands ravaged, presumably by the Trokmoi, who held the northern franchise. It was the first city they came to after leaving Bithynia, though those in the Troad may have been attacked by the Trokmoi after they crossed the Hellespont; at that point, however, it was rather more urgent that they join their fellows in the north. The evidence from Kyzikos is in a carved relief from the city showing Herakles, to whom the relief is dedicated, fighting a Galatian warrior, in which Herakles is using his club to good effect. It was a dedication by the officials of the city to the helpful Herakles, and evidently commemorated an episode in which the city was victorious over the Galatian attackers.

Kyzikos had its own diplomatic connections, independent of the Northern League, of which it was not a member – which is why, no doubt, it was attacked. Its closest connection was with Philetairos of Pergamon, and through him with King Antiochos. Both Philetairos and Kyzikos were therefore allies, or clients, of Antiochos, and Philetairos used the wealth under his control to establish political connections – for himself, particularly. Every year from 280 to 275 he gave something to

Kyzikos, and 'during the war against the Galatians' he supplied the city with barley and wheat. No doubt the lands of the city had been damaged in the war, and the food will have supplied the resulting deficiency; the city itself was not captured, though its soldiers fought the attackers, and the Herakles inscription was therefore a self-celebration by the city.[15]

The reference to 'the war' in the description of Philetairos' gift appears to date from 276/275, by which time the Galatians had begun their march into Asia, having dealt with Zipoetas, which appears to have taken over a year to accomplish. In the Troad, the city of Ilion was briefly occupied, though by whom is unclear. It could have been by Loutarios' warband who were in this area soon after crossing the Hellespont, when they were evidently looking for a place in which to defend themselves, perhaps while all of them were ferried across the Hellespont, and that city would be the closest to where they had landed. The place was regarded as untenable because it was unwalled, and was quickly abandoned. The alternative is that it was seized by the Trokmoi after they had dealt with Kyzikos.

This brief seizure of Ilion is a detail which rather suggests that this particular Galatian group, whichever it was, might have been looking for a new home as soon as they had crossed the Hellespont, or as soon as they had finished with the work in Bithynia. The difficulty is that this episode may instead refer to a later immigrant Galatian group, the Aigosages, who crossed in the same way decades later. The city had recently, under Lysimachos, been subjected to a forced synoecism, uniting it with a set of small and damaged cities nearby into the new city of Alexandria Troas. Not all of these victims, as they evidently saw themselves, were willing to accept this change in their status, though this might explain the 'unwalled' nature of the site. The place was reoccupied at some point, and later the Romans found it to be a 'village-city', implying a certain lack of fortification still in the 190s. Its unwalled state obviously made it vulnerable to the Galatians – any Galatians – when the band occupied it briefly and no doubt looted and damaged it; equally its unfortified state rendered if fairly useless for them as well.[16]

The information about the Galatians' attacks on individual cities in Asia Minor is only available in sources connected with the cities themselves, as with Kyzikos and Ilion, already discussed. There is no overall account of the campaigns such as is available for the campaigns in the European lands. The sources are, indeed, largely in the form of inscriptions, and are often personal, relaying individuals' experiences or activities, usually in the form of gratitude to a god. The events therefore have to be reconstructed from individual anecdotes, with the obvious attendant gaps and omissions and distortions. There were undoubtedly other places which were attacked of which we have no record, and any interpretation based on the facts we have now is tentative.

The division of the Asia Minor coastal area into raiding areas, one for each tribe, presupposes a considerable degree of advance knowledge of Asia and its geography amongst the Galatians from the start. This follows on from the similar information about Greek conditions shown by the expedition under Brennos. But while Greece may have been familiar to some of the participants from personal visits, or from mercenary sources – there had been Gauls in Sparta in the 370s[17] and in Syracuse earlier, and there had been a century of campaigning up and down the length of Italy – there is no obvious situation in which Galatians can have acquired personal knowledge of conditions in Asia. Visits by individuals are quite possible, of course, even likely, and during their stay in Bithynia no doubt plenty of information about the location of the cities and the wealthy temples was available, above all for Nikomedes and his court, who were no doubt quite happy to see the Seleukid kingdom suffer. The busier the Seleukid King Antiochos was kept by the raiders, the safer King Nikomedes in Bithynia would be. It must also be possible that second-hand information about Asia had reached the Gauls in Gaul itself, filtered through Massalia.

Massalia was a Greek colonial city in Gaul, founded from Phokaia in Asia three centuries earlier.[18] We have two clear cases where Asian Greeks automatically saw Massalia as the place to go in order to contact particular Gauls.[19] One of the three Galatian 'tribes', the Tektosages, had a 'branch' in south-western Gaul, and it was to their shrine at Tolosa that some offerings from the Delphian loot were sent.[20] A man whose wife had been carried off by a Gaul, went to Massalia in a quest to recover her. The Gauls of southern Gaul clearly could find out information about Asian Greeks without difficulty, just as Asian Greeks clearly knew plenty about southern Gaul.

It will not do to consider the Galatians to be mere ignorant 'barbarians'. Even in Asia they had contact with Gaul itself, overland by way of their Balkan homeland and through the lands of the Danubian Gauls, and they were evidently fully conscious of their western origins, both recent and more distant.

And, once across the Straits and in Asia, it would hardly be difficult to locate the most promising targets. The Bithynians, no doubt as concerned to be rid of their uncomfortable guests as the Byzantines had been, could probably suggest some targets – it is significant that Kyzikos, not part of the Northern league, was an early victim – as could the merchants who followed them to cash in on their loot.[21] It is therefore no surprise that one of the first targets of the Tektosages, who held the southern franchise, was the temple of Apollo at Didyma.[22] This had been for the previous thirty years one of the primary targets of dedications and presents by the Seleukid kings, even, or especially while it was under their enemy Lysimachos. Out of his loot from his Indian expedition, Seleukos I, for example, had given great quantities of spices and incense, and gold and silver vessels to the temples, and he had been financing the reconstruction of the temples as well.[23] (He had, of course, done this with the intention of establishing a position of political influence within Lysimachos' lands, just as Philetairos was doing in Antiochos I's lands, at Kyzikos, for example.)

The temple at Didyma was thus extremely wealthy. It was also, since 281 and Seleukos I's victory over Lysimachos, within Seleukid territory, and to the Bithynians and their Galatian allies this was enemy territory. A barbarian raid on one of the primary sanctuaries of the Seleukid enemy would inevitably attract the king's attention, and would significantly damage his reputation, especially as the temple was by no means so easy to defend as Delphi – and so he could be blamed for neglecting it. For Galatians who had been defeated in the Delphi raid, the chance to get revenge on the god who was credited with the victory there – Apollo in both places – would be sweet. The raid on Didyma seems to have been just about the first one mounted in this Karian region, and one may suspect the Bithynians' hand was involved in directing the Galatians towards it.

Like Ilion, Didyma was unprotected by walls or by soldiers. All but a few items – two in the treasury of Apollo's temple, half a dozen in Artemis' temple – were taken. The priests were bureaucratic to a degree, carefully recording lists of the gifts they had received, and then making new lists of the fragments and broken items that were left after the raid, no doubt determined to impress on donors their new poverty and misfortune. The items removed clearly included those presented by Seleukos in 288, which amounted to 3200 drachmae of gold, and over 9300 drachmae of silver, unless it had been spent or given away – and this was only one king's offering on one single occasion.[24]

In the same region was Miletos. The Milesians spent a good deal of their reserves during the next two centuries aiming to complete the building of the Didyma temple (though it never was completed).[25] The city itself suffered much less from the Galatians' attentions, since it was both walled and defended. But a group of women celebrating the Thesmophoria festival outside the walls were captured; three girls were so shocked by their treatment that they committed suicide; most of the women were ransomed.[26] One of the women so captivated her captor that he carried her off to Gaul, perhaps not unwillingly on her part. Her (Greek) husband followed by sea through Italy to Massalia to recover her; the end of the story is not clear, but if Kavaros (the captor) got to his own homeland in Gaul – presumably the country of the Tektosages – it is unlikely the husband will have succeeded in recovering his wife. The central point of the story from the point of view of Miletos was that it was necessary to keep the guard alert and the city walls in full repair. No doubt later Thesmophoria celebrations either took place inside the city, or, if outside, under guard. From our point of view one of the main lessons is that it is evidence of continuing connections between the invaders of Asia and the Tektosages in far-off Gaul, and that the Galatians' warlike powers were limited to open cities.

Miletos and Didyma, south of 'Aiolis and Ionia', were presumably also the targets of the Tektosages, an assumption partly encouraged by the story of Kavaros and his captive in southern Gaul. Also within their Asian franchise was Priene, which was close to Miletos. There the raiders met more resistance, more active than that at Miletos and more effective, but also somewhat costly. The evidence is a long inscription honouring a man called Sotas son of Lykos who organized the defence. The city was perhaps already on the alert. The raiders arrived in March (276) and made contact – at whose initiative is not known – with the Pedieis, a disaffected group who lived as serfs in the city's territory. They joined the invaders in attacking the city. If the Pedieis contacted the Galatians, this may have been the reason for the attack (and for the apparent foreknowledge of the attack within the city), with the serfs guiding the Galatians to what was thought to be a soft target; if the contact was at the Galatians' initiative, this would argue a most active intelligence gathering system by the raiders.

Priene, under Sotas' persuasions, resisted. It was not just a matter of facing a looting rampage by the Galatians, but also of fighting a rebellion by the Pedieis, who, as a subject peasantry, were clearly all too willing to turn the tables on their masters; the invasion therefore would become a social revolution, which in the ancient world normally meant a massacre of the losers. It cannot have taken much to persuade the Prienians to fight back under such circumstances. It was also a combination of a resentful rebellious peasantry with the greedy invaders which may explain the unusual savagery of the fighting: prisoners captured in the countryside suffered 'outrages', Greeks caught out in the country were killed, the country temples were looted and defiled, and as they withdrew, the farms and buildings were burnt. (It may therefore be assumed that the Pedieis who joined the raiders withdrew with them.) The details may seem particularly savage, but they were no worse than the Greeks inflicted on each other.

The citizen militia, horse and foot, were mobilized, apparently at Sotas' initiative, and marched out to confront the raiders. This appears to have been sufficient to drive them away, but they were not pursued too closely – they clearly had plenty of time for their killings and destructions as they withdrew. The fighting went on for some time with the militia attempting to secure the country buildings and to rescue captives. Sotas arranged that strong points in the countryside were occupied, where forces would be available to interrupt any raiders, thus implying that the raiding went on even after the main force withdrew, presumably mainly by the unreconciled Pedieis; the inhabitants of the countryside were brought into the city for their safety (or to stop more Pedieis getting away).

The Prienian resistance was only partly effective. It would seem that considerable numbers of captives were removed – or in the case of the Pedieis, escaped – and perhaps many more were killed; singling out Greeks for killing was presumably the work of the Pedieis – the Galatians were more prone to hold captives for ransom, or sell them into slavery (a Greek custom also, of course). Property damage was evidently extensive. The country temples and shrines were particular targets, partly because they held treasures, or were assumed to, but probably also because to the Pedieis they were the symbols of their subjection. If, as is theorized, the Pedieis were the descendants of the original inhabitants of the land, conquered and subdued by the Prienian citizens, the Greek gods would not be their gods.[27]

These three places, Didyma, Miletos, Priene, are geographically close together: Priene is only fifteen kilometres from Miletos, which in turn is only twenty kilometres from Didyma. It is thus highly probable that all three were subjected to raids by the same group of attackers, and that seems to mean the Tektosages. Going north from Priene, the first place known to have been attacked is Ephesos, though the only indication is that a woman taken captive there later committed suicide; the story is probably fictionalized, but it certainly fits the pattern of the time; the city was not even attacked, it seems.[28] A more firm and detailed account of a Galatian event is from Erythrai, which is on the end of a long peninsula, where the advance of the attackers would seem to have been signalled well in advance. The city had prepared by placing a prominent and wealthy citizen, Polykritos, in charge of the defence, supported by the elected generals of the year. Their preparations included getting arms, no doubt embodying the citizen army, and collecting money, perhaps by a special tax. Polykritos himself went out to meet the approaching Galatians, who were commanded by Leonnorios (which is our best evidence that his command was of the Tolistobogii). Negotiations ensued. Polykritos promised to pay tribute, and the Galatians took some hostages to guarantee payment. Polykritos collected the money, delivered it, and recovered the hostages.[29]

This sequence of events at Erythrai demonstrates once again that the Galatians did not necessarily indulge in wanton destruction and barbarity. This they resorted to with the aim of inducing their victim to negotiate and pay either blackmail or ransom, a normal recognized method of warfare. They could be bought off and were fully capable of entering into peaceable negotiations, and of making agreements which they would then keep. It is customary to decry these procedures as the payment of 'Danegeld', which in English history is a pejorative term which implies the likelihood that the raiders would soon return and make more demands. This was certainly the case at Byzantion, where the kingdom of Tylis imposed regular and increasing payments on the city, and it is evidently what Ptolemy Keraunos thought would happen if he succumbed to Bolgios' demands. But the Galatians in Asia were in search of two things: wealth and a new homeland, and while collecting wealth was an immediate interest, the search for a new homeland was perhaps their real priority. There was, they must have soon realized, very little possibility of acquiring the latter in the western parts of Asia Minor, packed solid as it already was with cities, most of whom were walled and bristling with weapons – none of the cities so far mentioned was captured, except unwalled Ilion. The Erythraians may have paid the Galatians to go away, but they did so on the basis of a well-armed and alert city, and on a cold-blooded calculation that it would be cheaper to pay than to endure the ravaging of their countryside and a war. So the raiders campaigning among the cities of western Asia Minor were for the moment in search of wealth rather than land, hence their particular attention to the temples, which they knew were liable to hold considerable hoards of wealth, and hence also their willingness to be bought off. To the Erythraians, the bargain was probably worthwhile, so long as the Galatians did not return.

There is evidence also, though much less detailed, of fighting near Pergamon, commemorated by a statue group set up at Delos later to honour the whole Attalid family. It included verses which state that Philetairos fought the Galatians successfully, which fits well enough with his friendship towards the Greek cities, such as Kyzikos, which had also fought them.[30] The claim, however, is somewhat vague, and may not imply much in the way of fighting; self-glorification after a minor success was not unknown at the time. Also inland, at the city of Thyateira, a man saw his son captured and then rescued, and put up a tablet in remembrance, and gave thanks to Apollo. This is precisely dated to 275 BC.[31] Neither of these cities, note, was captured, and perhaps not even seriously attacked.

These Galatian raids, stretching from Kyzikos to Didyma, all took place in the lands ruled by King Antiochos I, and it was his responsibility to combat the invaders. Individual cities such as Kyzikos, Pergamon, Priene, and Miletos could defend themselves against such minor attacks, and did so with some success, if at the cost of some danger to the city's territory outside the walls. Others might bribe the invaders to leave, as at Erythrai. Open sites such as Ilion and Didyma were indefensible except by a royal army. In the case of Ilion in fact, measures were soon taken by Antiochos I to provide a refuge at nearby place called Petra, probably on a stony hill ('Petra') in an area of high land.[32] This place was to be politically attached to either Ilion or its neighbour Skepsis, one of the cities which had re-established itself rather than continue as part of the synoecism of Alexandria Troas. Petra was to be available to the peasants living on royal land nearby as a refuge. The date of the documents in which this is recorded is about 275, and so it fits into the history of the time; probably the measures were taken as a result of the brief occupation of Ilion by the Galatians a year or so earlier and their continuing ravages.

It has to be said that, if the expressions of horror are laid to one side, the Galatians' campaign was rather less than successful. Only unfortified places were captured; loot came from unprotected temples and from ravaging the countryside, or from bribes to leave. This was not a campaign of widespread terror and devastation. A calculation of their strength suggests that the three tribes were in fact not particularly powerful. If, as is suggested, two groups commanded by Leonnorios and Loutarios numbered about 20,000 people, half of whom were families, each man commanded only about 5000 warriors, which is about the force a reasonably large city could field; the Tektosages, coming along later, seem to have been perhaps even fewer. 5000 warriors was a force which would certainly threaten a powerful city, though casualties were clearly to be avoided if possible; when a royal army came up they would necessarily need to retire quickly, or consolidate all three into a larger central force.

The defensible cities could therefore look after themselves, with a man in charge to stiffen civic spines, and the Galatians could be effectively denied them; areas without defences could be provided with places of security into which their populations could move if necessary, as at Petra in the Troad, or in the fortified posts in the countryside of Priene organized by Sotas. But this did not solve the major problem, which was the presence in Antiochos' territory of a hostile army liable to damage any cultivated land, any villages they could find, any undefended towns, and any open temple. The only security would be to drive them out, to gather an army, as had Sotas at Priene, and defeat the invaders in battle, though it is not likely that many cities could field an army capable of meeting any of the tribes in battle. The alternative might be to pay them to refrain, as did Polykritos at Erythrai – though this would only work if both sides could be trusted, though there is no evidence that the Galatians broke any of their agreements.

In the absence of the complete annihilation of the invaders, therefore, as by Antigonos, it would be necessary to pin down the Galatian armies to a particular region or regions by means of a negotiated treaty. Treaties were something they evidently respected, judging by the agreements made with Erythrai and with Bithynia. If Antiochos could bring them to accept a treaty, then western Asia Minor would be secure for the rest of the king's life, at least. It would also provide the Galatians with what they were aiming for, a new homeland, and no doubt this aim had quickly been understood by their victims and by the king.

There were probably arguments in the royal court and in the cities about the morality of this procedure, since it was evidently a sort of blackmail on an international scale, whereby the Galatian threats would seem to be successful. And yet the settlement of groups of Greeks or Macedonians on someone else's land was hardly an unusual business, and there were many such colonial cities in Syria, and some in Asia Minor. The only difference would be that the lords of the land would be Galatians, not Greeks, though to be sure the resulting society would certainly be different. This may well be the background to the distinctly poor territory they were eventually provided to settle on; it was also territory scarcely under detailed Seleukid government, and so a cynic would say it might as well go to the Galatians if it would keep them quiet. It was also no doubt in the king's mind that by settling them they would be a source of mercenaries, just as his brother-in-law Antigonos had calmed his kingdom in part by recruiting them.

To understand what took place it is necessary to recall the political situation in Asia Minor which present from the Galatian invasion. The

Galatians were allies of the Bithynian king and so also of his allies in the Northern League. They had divided themselves into three armies, each of which was raiding its own part of western Asia Minor, which in fact meant the cities and temples and farmland from the Bithynian border to the edge of Karia.

Karia in fact appears to have been left alone, possibly by agreement with its satrap, possibly because it was a mountainous and intricate land with many cities, all fortified, which made it very difficult to attack. As a region it tended towards independence, but exactly who ruled there in the 270s is not known. It had been under Pleistarchos, a brother of King Kassandros of Macedon, until about 280; it is generally assumed to have slid under Seleukid control when Pleistarchos died, and to have been governed by a Seleukid satrap, but nothing is certain; the failure of the Galatians to attack it in the 270s is suggestive that it was protected in some way, possibly by its fortifications, perhaps by a local treaty between whoever exercised government there and the Galatian force which had the southern franchise, the Tektosages.[33]

The three tribes were clearly operating independently of each other, and this was obviously the purpose of their separation. The treaty which Polykritos of Erythrai made to fend off the Galatian attack was with Leonnorios, the commander or leader of the Tolistobogii, operating in the central region, but the other two tribes were not involved. This division of the enemy forces provided Antiochos with the opportunity of tackling them singly.

The most dangerous of these, and the one operating closest to Antiochos' own headquarters at Sardis, was the Tolistobogii, under Leonnorios. The first necessity would be to collect a sufficiently large army to face the Galatians in battle and then to compel them to stand and fight. If each had about 5000 warriors, they could be tackled by the royal army. They had a tendency to move fast, though, and they were furious in fighting, and they had a competent cavalry contingent as part of their force. Leonnorios was clearly a capable commander, both militarily and diplomatically. There is no indication in fact that the three tribes were together in the fight, and it was probably with the Tolistobogii alone. Antiochos would need an army of double the Galatians' size at least, and probably larger, to ensure victory; a Hellenistic army was composed of a phalanx of sarissa-armed infantry to which was attached light infantry and cavalry; it was a formidable army, but it could be vulnerable in open country when faced by an unorthodox enemy – like the Galatians. A secret weapon would also help.

The preliminary manoeuvring is nowhere detailed, but the one place which the Galatians would have to defend was their camp, which will have held both their families and their stored treasure. Antiochos, once he had located the camp, would need only to advance and threaten to attack it, at which point the Galatians would have to come out in its defence. The site of the camp is not known, but from the range of the Tolistobogian army's actions – Ephesos to Pergamon and inland to Thyateira – the base was somewhere in the region of Magnesia on the Hermos. Sardis, Antiochos' headquarters, was further up the Hermos River Valley, and Thyateira was on its Lykos tributary of the Maiandros. It may be presumed that the battle was fought in this area.

Antiochos fought and won his battle. It became famous because he used elephants, which apparently the Galatians had not encountered before, at least not in battle. They scared either the Galatians or, more likely, their horses; and they were also capable of breaking down, or climbing over, the necessarily flimsy defences which is all that the Galatians can have had time to construct at their camp.[34] The victory will have been followed by a negotiated peace – there is no indication that the Tolistobogii were destroyed, only that they were defeated. It is said that Antiochos allocated them territory in the interior, a matter which will be discussed later.

The overall record of the Galatians in warfare in Greece and Asia Minor was therefore very mixed. They had twice defeated the Macedonians, but had been defeated twice in Greece, at Delphi and Thermopylai, and their retreat had been very costly. They were very good at ravaging enemy territory by surprise attacks, which reduced the number of opponents they might have to fight, but were defeated in the only battle they fought. Their reputation was as destructive savages, and yet Antiochos deliberately refrained from annihilating them when he could probably have done so, and then permitted them to settle within his kingdom. Despite losing so many battles, therefore, this band of Galatians had succeeded in their aim. This suggests that their leader Leonnorios was not simply their military commander but a clever diplomat.

This was a victory over only one part of the Galatians. The other two armies were not involved, though it is possible that they sent some of their warriors to assist the Tolistobogii. We have little or no information about the Trokmoi, whose raiding territory was in the north, and who were probably the group who attacked Kyzikos and possibly Ilion. The Tektosages, however, can be traced still raiding for some time after Antiochos' victory, yet in their southern area. After their success at Didyma, and partial failures at Miletos and Priene, they evidently moved away. They are said to have been originally allocated the interior,[35] though it seems that at first they operated against those southern Aegean coastal cities, which were clearly a richer prey than the inland cities. They do not seem to have attacked Karia, but there are signs of raids into Lykia, and on cities along the great Royal Road heading east towards Syria. That they later went raiding in the interior does not mean they were not originally allocated the southern Aegean coast as well, only that they eventually concentrated on communities in interior Asia Minor, and so this was assumed to have been their allotted territory from the first in later accounts.

It is necessary at this point to discuss the dating of that Elephant Victory. Several dates from 278 to 267 BC have been argued for; 278 is, of course, far too early, for the Galatians were still occupied at Byzantion and in Bithynia at that time and 267 is also outside the likely range. The evidence for this late date (usually actually reckoned to be 269 or 268) is an inscription from a pair of villages, Neoteichos and Kiddioukome, near Laodikeia-ad-Lykon, which reveals that captives taken from these villages had been ransomed by two local officials.[36] This is the only indication that raiding continued as late as this – except possibly raiding into Lykia; this is also the Tectosages' raiding region.

It is clear that Galatian raids were still happening in the area a little before the stone with the inscription was set up, which is calculated to be in 267. It is also clear that this was a very local affair, in which the captives were ransomed by a local official. From this it is too much to suggest that the Elephant Victory, generally regarded as the decisive battle which stopped the Galatian raids, was fought just before the events mentioned on the stone. No reference to such a victory appears on that stone, only a reference to the ongoing war.

To understand what was happening it is necessary to realize that the three warbands were operating separately, and had been since they left Bithynia, and that the Elephant Victory was fought against just one of the bands, the Tolistobogii. The area where the villages were is in the south and interior, and therefore this was the area allocated to the Tektosages, who were not forced to settle down by the treaty which followed the Elephant Victory (which was, obviously, with the Tolistobogii), and who could therefore continue their raids where the Tolistobogii could not.

The date 274 for the Victory was long assumed, or calculated before the village-ransom story intervened. That was also the date of the outbreak of the First Syrian War, between Ptolemy II and Antiochos I.[37] This was superficially a quite independent development, in which Antiochos had intrigued with Magas, the Ptolemaic governor of Cyrene, who wanted to obtain his political independence. Antiochos' daughter Apama was given to Magas in marriage, which signified an alliance, for the moment, and this was an obvious affront to Ptolemy. Ptolemy was therefore faced by possible war on two fronts; he succeeded in stopping Magas' attack in Libya, and then turned to attack Antiochos in Syria. The timing of the outbreak of this war is certainly in 274, and it is perhaps best to see that the Elephant Victory by Antiochos, was, for Ptolemy, a dangerous moment, since it seemed to mean that Antiochos would be free to engage fully in the Syrian War, while Ptolemy was preoccupied with Magas.

The calculation evidently went wrong. Magas' attack on Egypt failed, either to preoccupy Ptolemy or to reach Egypt. The Elephant Victory did not end the Galatian war, since only one of the tribes was involved, and the others could continue raiding; it did, however reduce the problem in Asia Minor. Antiochos must leave some of his forces in Asia Minor rather than send them against Ptolemy, and this may have been an element in Ptolemy's decision to fight. No doubt Leonnorios was conscious that he had an opportunity to reach terms with Antiochos because of the Egyptian war. So Antiochos was faced by what he had planned for his enemy, a war on two fronts, against Ptolemy in Syria, and against some of the Galatians in Asia. The ransoming of the village prisoners therefore was part of the continuing war, and bears no relation to the Elephant Victory.

Raids continued, in the south of Asia Minor, for up to twenty years after the battle, wherever it took place. These raids therefore were the actions of a part of the Galatians who had not been involved in the battle – and the obvious group who were at war still at that time was the Tektosages; their allocation of the interior as their raiding territory is in fact what they did, not necessarily what was their original assignment. Their original region for raiding was the south, Karia, as is suggested by their activities in the Miletos area. Denied any attempt to attack Karia outside the Miletos/Priene region, either by treaty or by the prospect of fighting in a particularly difficult country, and perhaps driven away from the southern coast by local or royal resistance and counter-attacks (as at Priene) they raided instead along the handy route of the Royal Road, along the fertile lands of their Maiandros valley and further east.

A few places can show their work. At Themisonion the citizens hid in a cave, supposed to have been divinely revealed to them, at the moment of danger.[38] The city of Themisonion was in fact only founded in 251, so either the raid there had come very late in the raiding period, or more likely, it came earlier than that date if the people of the area were only formed into a city afterwards, and the citizens recalled the raid as a traumatic moment in their pre-urban history. Fifty kilometres to the north, and directly on the Royal Road, was Laodikeia-ad-Lykon, in whose territory was found the villagers' inscription referring to local people being captured and released, the war still continuing; this raid, according to the dating of the inscription, probably happened in 269 or 268. Seventy kilometres further east along the Road, at Apameia-Kelainai, a city which had been the local capital for King Antigonos I for a couple of decades and so might be expected to have reasonable defences, there was another divine intervention, whereby the local river god Marsyas raised a flood, so deterring a Galatian attack.[39] The date of this event is not known, but perhaps between the ransoming of the villagers and the attack on Themisonion would be appropriate.

Two cases of Galatians penetrating into Lykia are recorded. One is from Tlos in the south-west part of that country, recorded, or referred to, in an epigram of Stephanos of Byzantion. He mentions that Pisidians, Paionians, and Thracians were involved in the raid along with the Galatians; how many is not stated and one wonders if the poet were simply including other notorious frontier raiders because they had that reputation, though it might be that deserters and malcontents from all three had banded with

Galatians to exploit the disturbed situation.[40] This, however, might better be dated to the disturbed period of the war of the brothers in the 230s. The other Lycian record is from Limyra, close to the south coast, recorded on a stone inscription which seems to have been added to the balustrade of a circular temple after the temple had been built. The temple was built in the 270s, but the stone, and certainly the inscription, is probably later; this is not good evidence really for any raid.[41] These southern raids, in so far as they are definitely by the Galatians, may be attributed to the Tektosages, though it is probable that they took place in the few years following the Elephant Victory – that involving the two villages was in 269 or 268, and this may well be the last; it might be, however, that these had nothing to do with the settlement of the Tektosages.

The question arises why Antiochos did not finish the job he had evidently begun with the Elephant Victory. The Tolistobogii, pinned down by their treaty until at least 261, when Antiochos died, presumably settled down in their new homeland; the Trokmoi may have continued raiding, but no evidence exists either way, though it might have been fairly easy to provoke them to battle. The Tektosages clearly did continue raiding for a few years. The answer is that the king was distracted from this task by the outbreak of war with Ptolemy II, the 'First Syrian War', which was a much more serious matter than the raids of relatively small Galatian forces in inland Asia Minor, especially since one, and possibly two, of those forces had already been neutralized by being given land to settle on. So from 274 onwards Antiochos was fully occupied in Syria for several years, defending his inherited territories there.[42] By about 270, if it is possible to generalize from the single case of the village near Laodikeia, the raids were on a small scale, and any captives could be easily rescued by paying a ransom.

Antiochos' major reaction in Asia Minor to these raids was to fortify his defences. So far as can be seen no city with good defences was ever taken by the Galatians, in Greece or Macedon or in Asia Minor. The Royal Road, however, was clearly vulnerable if such raids returned. The standard Seleukid response to long-standing dangers such as this was to fortify, in particular to found cities which were populated by Seleukid colonists/citizens, who governed the cities, owned estates in the neighbourhood, and lived within the fortifications.

This was the basis of the kingdom's defence in Syria against the current Ptolemaic attack, and seems to have been the response in Baktria, under Antiochos' rule while his father was still alive, against nomad attacks. Now it was applied systematically in Asia Minor. A string of such cities were founded along the Road, Laodikeia-ad-Lykon and Apameia-Kelainai were two of them, and both had been subjected to attack, and not taken. Both were in fact existing urban centres, taken up, re-founded by the imposition of Greek and Macedonian settlers (who became the instant ruling group when settled in the cities), and given new names adopted from the Seleukid royal family. More such cities were founded further along the Road, especially in the vulnerable stretch north of Pisidia between the lakes and the mountains in the centre of the peninsula – Apollonia, Metropolis, Antiocheia, Seleukeia, and others. These also formed a guard against raids made by Pisidians out of the mountains to the south.[43]

These cities anchored Seleukid power firmly in this south-central region, and the royal foundations were supplemented by other cities planted, or organized, by important estate holders who were to a degree partly independent of the royal authority. Themisonion, for example, was apparently founded by one Themison; north of the dense concentration of cities south of the lakes was Dokimeion, founded by Dokimos, one of the most agile and slippery of the Macedonian officers in the confused period after Alexander's death; further east were two cities, Lysias and Philomelion, founded by a family of local lords, also Macedonian soldiers, who can be traced for four generations as commanders for a series of Seleukid kings, and even further, perhaps to the mid second century; and the man whose steward the villagers of Kiddioukome and Neoteichos thanked for rescuing the captives was Akhaios, probably a younger brother of Seleukos I and the founder of a notable family with much influence in Asia Minor for the next two centuries. One of the results of the Macedonian conquest was the imposition not only of these cities of Macedonian type, but the establishment of men such as these who possessed large estates and were established as the new ruling aristocracy. The raids of the Galatians had the effect of forcing further city-founding and driving existing cities to build or improve their fortifications. And this pattern of society had its effect eventually on the Galatians themselves.

The Galatians in Asia Minor had therefore upset the balance of power, first by protecting the Bithynians and the Northern League, in effect by guarding them, so that by the end of the First Syrian War, in 271, their independence was no longer in question. Second, they had forced some cities, such as Kyzikos and Priene and Pergamon, to develop and employ their own forces in their own defence, and had promoted a social revolution by the establishment of numerous new Seleukid colony cities in various parts of the land, simultaneously energizing urban autonomy and extending the territory allocated to the new cities. They had dealt a terminal blow to Seleukid hopes of controlling the whole of Asia Minor, and therefore using that as their base for recovering Macedon. They had established themselves, with or without Seleukid permission, in the centre of the country, the further division of which they had promoted.

Chapter 6

Mercenaries

Kelts in all regions were readily recruited as mercenary soldiers by every Hellenistic state in the eastern Mediterranean. Even in the preceding period, they are known to have been recruited by Dionysios I, the tyrant of Syracuse, and by his later imitator Agathokles. Dionysios sent some of his men to assist Sparta in its Theban War in the 370s and 360s.[1] As a result when the invasions of Greece and Asia came, the Galatians' fighting abilities were not unknown, and their ability to create civil disorder was also known. Plato referred to them as warlike as well as having a large capacity for alcohol.[2] In the Hellenistic period notices of their employment occur somewhat irregularly, but sufficiently frequently to imply that Galatians were employed as mercenary soldiers throughout the period, and in every state of any size, though there were some exceptions and variations.

In a sense King Nikomedes of Bithynia might be said to be the first employer of Galatians as soldiers in the Hellenistic period, but the agreement he and they made in 278/277, by which the army under Leonnorios was brought across the Bosporos, was a formal alliance, sealed by a written treaty, rather than the mere hiring of a band of warriors by the king.[3] When joined by the army under Loutarios there was another treaty, or alliance, directed against the Seleukid kingdom. The Galatian campaigns in Asia Minor which followed showed that they were operating as an independent political unit or units, but not under control of Nikomedes. In that very time, while the Asian campaigns were still continuing, other Galatians were also recruited by other kings. The earliest notice of their employment in the region is by Antigonos Gonatas, who recruited Galatians after having defeated, and he claimed, exterminated a major warband at the Battle of Lysimacheia in 277. It is generally assumed that these were survivors of that murderous battle, but this seems highly unlikely – such survivors would surely scatter distantly from their enemy.⁴ More probably there were other smaller bands roaming the Macedonian countryside who could easily be recruited once Antigonos had a victorious and cohesive Macedonian force at his disposal. In other words, the alternatives for the Galatians were recruitment or annihilation.

The employment of Galatians by the kings was therefore begun remarkably quickly, within two or three years of the first invasion of Macedon.⁵ The earlier employment in Sicily and their brief appearance with Sparta in the 370s were secondary effects from the activities of the Gauls in Italy. It is odd, however, that other Greek states than Sparta failed to use them, even while recognizing their usefulness in battle. Once Antigonos demonstrated that quality again, however, other kings quickly took note, at least of their fighting abilities. By 274 Pyrrhos in Epeiros and Ptolemy in Egypt had recruited substantial numbers, and then soon discovered that they were much more difficult to control than other soldiers.

It also quickly became clear that they were not familiar with normal Hellenistic military practices when defeated. They contributed to Pyrrhos' defeat of Antigonos in his invasion of Macedon, but then Pyrrhos stood by while his Galatians looted the Macedonian royal graves at Aigai.⁶ This was one of the factors – his own feckless political behaviour was the main one – which alienated the Macedonians who had welcomed Pyrrhos in the first place.

If Pyrrhos had a force of Galatians in his army in 274 in his invasion of Macedon, and he had only returned from Italy the year before, he must have recruited the Galatians during late 275 or early 274, virtually as soon as he arrived from Italy, unless his son Ptolemaios, whom he had left to watch affairs in Epeiros while he was away, had begun recruitment a little earlier. It was only in 275, with his defeat in Italy, that Pyrrhos was reduced to commanding a small army (said to be only 8500 strong),⁷ and it was only in 274 that he seems to have determined to attack Antigonos in Macedon. In the same way, the fact that Ptolemy II had a force of 4000 Galatians in his employ in Egypt, also in 274, implies that he had recruited them some time earlier, and so we arrive again at 275 as the likely time of their recruitment.⁸ This was only three years after the Galatians' retreat from Greece, but only in that year or 274 did Antiochos

I gain his Elephant Victory. These two Galatian defeats, in Europe and in Asia, made them employable; together with the killings at Lysimacheia, the defeats tamed the Galatians to some degree, and made their form of warfare less frightening, though probably also less effective.

The defeats greatly reduced their hopes of loot, because resistance to any of their raids would obviously now be effective – as it often was in the campaign in Asia – but they also opened up the promise of pay as mercenary soldiers for their young men. There was much less likelihood of their achieving wide conquests after these defeats, though, as Kommontorios showed at Tylis, and the Galatians in Asia also, smaller niche-kingdoms were possible, and even new states in less salubrious regions. The men were also, at least at this time, reported to be cheap to employ, which suggests a certain desperation in their homelands, or perhaps a lack of research into standards of pay by the chiefs.[9] This discrepancy in pay will not have lasted long once the Galatians and the Greeks began talking to each other; it may have been one of the root causes of a Galatian mutiny which took place at Megara (against Antigonos) in 265. Nevertheless, the speed with which advantage was taken of the recruitment possibilities by the kings is remarkable.

No doubt also the display of self-sacrificing resistance in the battle between Antigonos' and Pyrrhos' armies was impressive. Antigonos' Macedonians and his elephant corps surrendered quickly once their defeat became clear, but the Galatians fought on until massacred.[10] (Admiration has been expressed for their constancy, but their conduct, after it was clear that their side had been defeated, must be regarding as a pointless waste.[11]) The surrenders by the Macedonians were in fact, fully in accordance with normal military Hellenistic practice, and both they and the elephant corps were instantly recruited by Pyrrhos into his own army – indeed he used the elephants with their Indian mahouts at once, turning them around in the middle of the battle to attack their former fellow soldiers in Antigonos' army. The Galatians clearly did not understand this practice and went on fighting until destroyed. No doubt some of them will have survived, but the myth of their military effectiveness was destroyed. Their earlier defeats had sent the same message. A parallel myth of loyalty to their paymaster was started. Both myths were, of course, equally untrue.

Then it was Pyrrhos' turn to discover the difficulties of commanding Galatians. Antigonos, defeated, fled the battlefield and took refuge in Thessaloniki. Pyrrhos quickly occupied western Macedon and Thessaly. In the process his Galatian soldiers arrived at Aigai, the old Macedonian capital, where the former kings were buried. Tombs like these, under the heaps of soil and very conspicuous, were familiar sights to Galatians, who buried their leaders in the same way. They also buried them, as did the Macedonians, with treasures. As they will have done elsewhere on discovering such a site, the Galatians set to work to dig up any treasures they could find in the Macedonian royal tombs.[12] This naturally incensed the Macedonians, and quite probably many of those Macedonian soldiers who had recently surrendered to Pyrrhos will have deserted back to Antigonos when they heard the news – they were, after all, Macedonians, whoever was king. Pyrrhos himself paid no attention to the vandalism and desecration – he could scarcely afford to dismiss or punish the perpetrators, since his army was still relatively small, so he ignored their conduct; he surely knew the problem this was going to cause him. This was therefore yet another reason for his new unpopularity in his conquered kingdom. His subsequent decision to leave Macedon and move into Greece, taking his Galatians with him, was presumably in part a result of the change in Macedonian attitude towards him, as well as an effect of his own constantly restless spirit. Antigonos swiftly recovered the lost parts of Macedon when Pyrrhos had left.

In the same year as this battle in Macedon, Ptolemy II experienced his own Galatian problem. In 275 his viceroy in Cyrene, his half-brother Magas, married the daughter of Antiochos I. This apparent alliance was an obvious threat to Ptolemy in Egypt, who now had open enemies on both of his international borders, north in Syria and west in Cyrenaica. Magas soon proclaimed himself king, and so became a clear and active threat to Ptolemy, for one reason for his self-promotion was to lay a claim to the Egyptian kingdom, and in 274 he launched an invasion of Egypt from Cyrene. Antiochos I, a little later, also indicated an intention to fight on Magas' side, though for the moment he was preoccupied in Asia Minor (see the previous chapter).[13] Exactly when the fighting began in Syria is not clear, but Antiochos was busy in Asia Minor all through 275 and into 274 winning the Elephant Victory. Ptolemy therefore had a year's warning of the developing trouble, and one of his preparations was to actively recruit more soldiers, including those Galatians.

Recruiting Galatians was clearly a process which, conducted from Egypt, will have taken some time. The potential recruits had to be contacted, presumably by a soldier, an officer, in Ptolemy's service, persuaded to join, probably paid an advance, then transported to Egypt. Where the contract was made is not known, but it must have been in the Balkans or, less likely, Asia – though maybe Antiochos would have been pleased to see Galatians leaving to serve elsewhere, but also annoyed that they would be reinforcing Ptolemy. The number of men recruited is put at 4000, which will have required at least fifty, and perhaps more, ship-journeys to move them to Egypt. Yet they were embodied and organized by the time Magas' invasion began late in 274, so the recruitment had probably begun, like Pyrrhos', in 275.

Magas' rebellion against Ptolemy was halted by a rising against him by his Libyan subjects, taking advantage of his absence from his new kingdom in his attempt to claim the kingship in Egypt. As a result he had to turn back to secure his Cyrenaican base; there has to be a strong suspicion that intrigue by Ptolemy lay behind the Libyan rebellion.[14]

The most curious aspect of the crisis is that Ptolemy's Galatians themselves then rebelled and are said to have intended to 'take over Egypt', in Pausanias' words.[15] What this might really mean is difficult to discern, but it can hardly be that they intended to overthrow the Ptolemaic government and seize power. 4000 soldiers were hardly enough for such a task, given that Ptolemy could dispose of an army ten times that size, while the Galatians had been in Egypt only a short time, perhaps only a few months. Then most of them probably could not speak Greek, and they would hardly be familiar with the political situation in Egypt except in the most superficial way. They would clearly need guidance in their exploit. To seize Egypt was actually Magas' aim, which suggests that it was being attributed to the Galatians because both they and Magas were rebelling against the same man at the same time. So we may take Pausanias' words as being an inaccurate summary of their intentions – or perhaps simply a later assumption that that is what they intended to do.

Yet it must always be remembered that, in these early days of the Galatian presence in the eastern Mediterranean, the aim of most of the

Galatians who had not returned to the north to found the Scordiscian state was to find new homes for themselves. This was the case at Tylis and in Asia – both of which, it may be noted, succeeded in this aim – and it is from groups in these areas and familiar with the aims of those larger groups that the recruits probably came. So when they saw the Ptolemaic government in difficulties, and that most of its army had been sent to face Magas to the west, or to face Antiochos in Syria, they may well have thought the opportunity was right for them to strike for a new homeland. This need not mean 'Egypt' as a whole, but just an area carved out of the Ptolemaic state. Their Balkan fellows had carved out two new states in that way, and their Asian fellows were being allotted land by Antiochos at his own expense, even as the Ptolemaic Kelts were in rebellion; by putting Ptolemy under threat, they may have felt that Ptolemy II might do the same, perhaps in Syria somewhere, perhaps as military settlers (cleruchs) in Egypt; there was, after all, a generation-long tradition of planting settlers in new cities throughout Syria, especially in the north, and of allotting estates to Greek cleruchs in Egypt.

Ptolemy, faced by threats on both of his borders, could not afford to succumb to yet another threat, and one in the very centre of his power, not even by buying off the rebels – mutineers, he might call them – for fear of stimulating imitations. Not surprisingly, he reacted with the sort of savagery which was normally attributed to the Galatians themselves. How it was achieved is not known, but he induced the rebels to move to a desert island in the Nile, and there he let them starve and fight each other to death.[16]

There is so much here which requires explanation that it is difficult to know where to start. The very idea of a group of recently recruited mercenaries, who were obviously ignorant of the country they had been taken to, mounting an attempted *coup d'état* within only months of their arrival is both astonishing and ludicrous. It surely implies that something else was going on beneath the surface of events. One would expect that, at least, the idea had been put into their heads – or rather in the hands of the Galatians' leading officers – by someone much more familiar with Egypt and its government than they were. If that interpretation is reasonable, the obvious instigators would be either Magas or Antiochos, who had already conspired together to form their political and military alliance and launch the First Syrian War. Magas' attack clearly came before Antiochos was ready, and the rebellion in Libya which forced him to turn back in his attempted invasion is a mirror image of the Galatian 'rebellion' in Egypt. Mutual intrigues by those allies to destabilize Ptolemy, and by Ptolemy to force Magas to retreat, would seem the best explanation for the prevention of Magas' invasion and the prevention of Ptolemy's military reply, both rulers operating to undermine the enemy by instigating rebellions behind the front line. But one must also, in that case, if the Galatians were to be included in the plot, assume that an agent in Egypt persuaded the Galatians, or at least their officers, to mount the *coup*, and it must have been someone of influence in the Egyptian regime if he was to be persuasive. Given the Galatians' recent history, Antiochos, being more familiar with them than Magas, might be the most likely instigator, especially if at least some of them had been recruited in Asia.

The matter of persuading the Galatians to move to a desert island is equally unexplained and mysterious. Ptolemy could only do this if he had already brought the rebellion to an end before getting them to move, perhaps by agreeing mendaciously to some of their demands. The move was, therefore, their punishment, and was also Ptolemy's way of warning others who might rebel or mount a *coup*. Whether he expected them all to die is not known, but he was certainly ruthless and unscrupulous enough to intend that from the start and angry enough to see that it was carried out. Since they were isolated it would seem he had 'sealed off' the island, no doubt using his fleet, to prevent any escapes – but equally there is also no doubt that he will have been unsuccessful in this, at least in part. (One may recall the ease with which Brennos passed the Spercheios by calling up large numbers of swimmers.) It is highly unlikely that all 4000 men killed each other, or starved to death, and some would be able to swim to the shore. It suited the story put about afterwards to end with the rebels' deaths. Starvation would thus be the original intention. Mutual killing amongst the rebels was a bonus. And that mutual killing was presumably the result of political developments amongst the survivors, some of whom were no doubt enraged at the situation to which the plotters had brought them.

The story was not finished with the extermination of the island prisoners, either by death or escape, or by the capture of the last few to survive. The court poet Kallimachos included in his *Hymn to Delos* a reference to the Keltic attacks on Delphi, and added to that account an explanation that Ptolemy himself had participated in the suppression of Keltic outrages on the Nile island – he even claimed that it was survivors of the attack on Delphi who took part in the Egyptian affair, and suffered the just punishment – which was, of course, quite possible.

The whole interpretation of events in this way was propaganda, with Ptolemy appropriating to himself the defence of civilization against the barbarians in imitation of Antigonos' rescue of Macedon, or Antiochos' defence of the cities of Asia. This was a matter which could, more convincingly be attributed to both Antigonos and Antiochos, whose victories were rather more impressive than Ptolemy's, and yet Ptolemy's interpretation was not wholly outrageous – a Galatian force of 4000 men rampaging through Egypt would be a formidable threat, and could cause enormous damage. That his means of suppression did not entirely succeed in preventing later rebellions and mutinies only shows that savagery of itself is generally counter-productive. The magnitude of the crisis was perhaps responsible for Ptolemy's brutality, though it may not have been uncongenial to him to inflict all those deaths. But to allow the Galatians to survive, hostile and within Egypt, would seriously undermine his regime, and might even cause its collapse; there was a lot at stake, and the interpretation of Pausanias that they meant to 'take over Egypt', may not be too wide of the mark. Ptolemy's proclaiming that his victory over them was equal to those of his contemporary kings may really be a sign of his relief.

So the Galatians once more had a major effect on international affairs, for one result of the war with Magas, and Ptolemy's inability to follow up Magas' retreat, was to leave Cyrenaica as an independent kingdom for the next thirty years. By the time the Galatian rebellion in Egypt was over, Antiochos had been able to reach Syria with his forces, so that Ptolemy's intended attack on the Seleukid territories failed to have any effect, and Antiochos was able to threaten Ptolemy's territory. Antiochos was himself distracted from finishing his work in Asia Minor by the outbreak of the war, so that Galatian raids (by the Tektosages) continued for some time after his initial victory over the Tolistobogii.

Employing Galatians as mercenaries was therefore a difficult art. Pyrrhos took some of them with him into Greece in his final fatal campaign, and they were inherited by his sons, until the leaderless army surrendered in its entirety to Antigonos. The result was that Antigonos ended by employing Pyrrhos' mercenaries, including the Galatians. Antigonos continued to employ them, and others, but faced a mutiny of one of his Galatian units at Megara in 265, which he resolved by attacking them and killing most or all of them – the Ptolemy solution, and one he had resorted to in the Chersonese fourteen years before. (Of course, it would only be cosmic justice if this group included those who had rifled the royal tombs, but that seems unlikely.)[17] Massacre seems to have been the automatic default position in face of Galatian hostility, by whatever king or regime faced the problem.

From then on, there are only occasional notices of Galatian mercenaries until the late 220s, a fact which may be put down to the general lack of source material for that period rather than their absence. It is to be noted that at least four Galatian groups – at the Thracian Chersonese, in the war between Antigonos and Pyrrhos, in Egypt, and at Megara – were subject to suppression by massacre. This is surely an indication of the fear they engendered in their employers; it was obviously dangerous to recruit them.

The early instances in the 270s of kings recruiting Galatians meant that other kings did the same, but in all cases this obviously had to be done with some care, especially after these early awkward experiences. Antiochos II had a unit of Galatians in Antioch before 246, acting as a guard for his second wife Berenike, a daughter of Ptolemy II. When he died in 246 some of the men of this bodyguard murdered Berenike and her son in the palace. This was either part of a conspiracy with some of the local citizens, two of whom are mentioned as partaking, or on instructions from the new King Seleukos II. The instigator of the killings is, however, usually said to have been Antiochos' first wife Laodike, with whom he had been reconciled in the recent past.[18] One reason for it was that a Ptolemaic invasion of north Syria was approaching the city, and it would be very likely that, if Berenike and her child fell into Ptolemy's hands the boy would be proclaimed as the new Seleukid king, a rival to the two sons of Antiochos II; one Ptolemaic governor, in fact, did assume that the boy had succeeded.[19] (It is also quite possible that Antiochos left instructions for their killing in the event of his death.) This was the start of a new Syrian War, the third. A second result was a dispute between Antiochos II's and Laodike's two sons, which developed into a dynastic war lasting twenty years, the 'War of the Brothers'. Naturally, since there were three armies involved, all of which always needed more men, Galatians were recruited by all sides, above all by the younger and politically weak of the two brothers, Antiochos Hierax, but the Galatian relationship with Hierax appears more as an alliance than as a recruitment of mercenaries. (See next chapter).

One Galatian and one Seleukid officer, the first a mercenary, the second a royal officer, joined together to murder Seleukos III during his invasion of Galatia in 223.[20] This in fact is a good indication that, despite the earlier troubles, by the middle of the third century the Galatian mercenaries had become integrated into the Seleukid military system, whereas at the start of the 270s they had been still following their own traditions. It is rather chilling to find that the assassins of choice, both to kill Seleukid rulers and to kill those conspiring against them, were Galatians.

Another Syrian War broke out in 221 and shortly afterwards a new great war began in Greece. Once again there was widespread recruitment of Galatians. The Galatians involved in the great armies that were formed grew from a few thousands in the early years – the 4000 Ptolemy killed is the highest number recorded until the 220s – to a much greater overall total. Those mentioned for that time in the sources are never counted, though the mutinous group at Megara was big enough to require the full Macedonian army to put their mutiny down, and it is likely that Antigonos' early recruits numbered in the several thousands. From 223, however, the sources improve, notably thanks to Polybios, whose continuous account begins at that point, together with Livy, who was working from a different perspective, but often based himself on Polybios for eastern matters. For the time in which great battles took place the sources are almost adequate.

In 221 the Seleukid king Antiochos III, who inherited the throne when his brother was murdered, was young and inexperienced, was threatened by rebellions both in Asia Minor, where his cousin Akhaios was moving into independence, and in Iran, where the viceroy of the eastern territories (or the 'Upper Satrapies'), Molon, came out in active rebellion. Exactly what Akhaios' aim was at that time was not clear, but Molon, along with his two brothers, one of whom was the governor of another eastern province, clearly aimed to displace Antiochos and make himself king of the whole kingdom. To add to the difficulties Antiochos was persuaded to attack Egypt, partly as a means, it was hoped, of uniting the rebels against a common enemy. That ploy was a failure.

Two expeditions commanded by generals appointed by Antiochos failed to stop Molon. Sending such commanders had been the policy of Antiochos' advisers, but the failure of both the generals and the advisers meant that Antiochos had to lead an expedition himself. Akhaios was for the moment loyal, and in Egypt there was a dynastic crisis and the succession of a young king amid a series of murders of members of his family. This political and dynastic paralysis, and the failure of a Seleukid invasion of Ptolemaic Syria, produced no Ptolemaic reaction, so despite the existence of a Ptolemaic war, it was apparently safe for the king to go on a campaign to the east. Antiochos seized control of his government and then of his army and marched east, meeting and defeating Molon in Babylonia.[21]

The two contending armies each included a contingent of Galatian soldiers. In Antiochos' army they are called the Rigosages,[22] and were, it may be assumed, a particular tribe or nation of Galatians hired through their rulers, and so fighting as an auxiliary force under their own leader. On Molon's side the Galatian contingent are simply designated as 'Galatians'.[23] In neither case are the numbers of the soldiers mentioned, but both units were large enough to stand in the line under a separate command. Their individual actions in the battle are not recorded.

The hiring of a complete community, such as the Rigosages, was highly unusual. Normally, as seems to have been the case in the armies of the 270s, the Galatians were enlisted as individuals, or perhaps as relatively small warbands, or units; no doubt separating the men from their Galatian leaders was seen to be a safety measure. Nikomedes of Bithynia had, of course, hired a whole community, and had used them successfully, but he had also swiftly redirected their warlike energies into Asia Minor as soon as possible. Later Attalos I hired a similar group, the Aigosages, but abandoned them almost at once as uncontrollable. The group who mutinied against Antigonos Gonatas at Megara may have been a communal hiring, possibly originally by Pyrrhos, though this can only be an assumption. The large group in Egypt who rebelled were evidently not cohesive, at least not at the end. Hiring a specific communal unit, probably under its own king or chief, such as were apparently the Rigosages, was clearly dangerous, since the force was under less than total command – Nikomedes lost control of his allies as soon as they moved south. Like the Megaran mutineers, such a force might rebel if it felt that it was in a strong enough position to win its point; its leader might possibly accept a bribe to change sides at a crucial moment. The war against Molon was an internal dynastic dispute where loyalties were indefinite and confused, though it seems that the Rigosages did apparently stay loyal; their subsequent history, however, is quite unknown.

The hiring of a whole national group was not repeated in the Seleukid army, nor were any Galatians recorded as being enlisted in any other of Antiochos III's wars until the last battle at Magnesia in 190. It would therefore seem that he did not want Galatians in his force except in the most serious of emergencies, of which revolt and rebellion in the Roman war were the only occasions in the course of his reign. The preparations for Magnesia was such an emergency, and his army was substantially smaller in that engagement than in his earlier battles, hence perhaps the resort to hiring Galatians.[24] In the war with Molon, Antiochos was reduced to the forces he could mobilize in Syria and Mesopotamia alone, and not even all these; for Akhaios had taken a force into Asia Minor to campaign against Attalos of Pergamon, and another unit of several thousands, the 'Kyrrhestai', was in obdurate rebellion. That is, Antiochos only resorted to hiring Galatians as a matter of dire necessity. The hiring of a full independent Galatian nation in 221 was evidently such a case, as was the hiring of Galatians in 190.

What is even more surprising is that the opposing army, under Molon, also had a substantial Galatian contingent. Molon had governed the Iranian provinces for some years, and it seems unlikely that he had contact with the usual sources of mercenaries. Numbers again are unknown, but he had an army only a little smaller than that of Antiochos, so it would seem that he was as desperate to find extra troops as was the king. Molon's army was mainly comprised of Seleukid forces which had been already stationed in Iran and the Upper Satrapies, which had been his viceroyalty until he rebelled, and so where Molon got his Galatians from is a puzzle. It is possible they were recruited from prisoners captured from the earlier armies sent against him, but most of these men seem to have escaped rather than were captured (and there is no record of any Galatians in those armies). It is also possible he had recruited them from Galatia in preparation for his rebellion. Otherwise the only supposition is that they had been posted to the eastern provinces as garrisons some time before, and were gathered up at the start of the rising (which would have course contradict my conclusion reached in the previous paragraph). It seems equally unlikely, since it was not necessary in the Seleukid military system to recruit mercenaries for garrison duty; there was a constant flow of recruits thanks to the conscription of young men for short service. The only possible origin of the men is in the war in which Seleukos III was killed. He was fighting at the time in Galatia, and the men might have been recruited then. We do not know.

It is also a puzzle where Antiochos found his Galatian unit. The best guess is that he had hired them in Galatia itself, and it was a constituent part of one of the Galatian states. Possibly they were inherited from his brother's army, perhaps more likely they were hired by Akhaios while he was still loyal and passed on to Antiochos in the emergency of Molon's rebellion. Again we do not know.[25]

It is, however, clear from the description of Antiochos III's army in the several campaigns during the next thirty years that Antiochos' armies were normally fielded with no Galatian contingent. In the great force he brought to attack Egypt in 217, which was defeated at the Battle of Raphia, only one Galatian, 'Lysimachos the Galatian' is mentioned, clearly an officer; there were no Galatian private soldiers so Lysimachos was an officer in one of the Greek or Macedonian contingents in Antiochos' army; he must have been thoroughly Hellenized to take on such a role successfully. There are no Galatians in the escalation of Seleukeia-in-Pieria in 219, none are referred to in the conquest of Palestine in 218, none in the Elburz campaign in 211, none in the Battle of Panion in 200, none in the Thracian campaigns in 196–194. The absence of Galatians is consistent all through, from the recruited group in the war against Molon in 220 to the Battle of Magnesia in 190. Most of these campaigns are described by Polybios and he details the various units of the army with great care; Cretans, Thracians, and Arabs are all, for instance, listed and numbered, as were any mercenaries. But there were no Galatians. It is clear that Antiochos did not recruit Galatians for these campaigns, and since he clearly had no prejudice against employing mercenaries as such, he may well have had a dislike of Galatians in particular; more likely he did not need them, having naturally sufficient resources from internal recruitment for his needs.

One might explain their absence in the early campaigns (except that against Molon) as due to the lack of contact with Galatia, because Asia Minor as a whole was under the domination of Akhaios or Attalos I (or before that, Antiochos Hierax) until 216. But from then on Antiochos had secured control of much of Asia Minor and could have recruited in Galatia if he wished, but he clearly did not choose to do so until he needed extra forces to face the Roman invasion in 190. At the Battle of Magnesia he had 2500 Galatian cavalry and 3000 Galatian infantry, which fought on either side of the phalanx in two groups of 1500. It was clearly possible for him in 190 to recruit a large Galatian force – 5500 men is the largest Galatian force recorded in any Hellenistic army – so their absence in other armies of the king can only be due to his refusal to recruit.

An explanation for this curious abnegation may be in the events of 223–220. In 223 his elder brother Seleukos III was murdered in an officers' plot while on campaign in Galatia, and one of the murderers was a Galatian called Apatourios. Then in Molon's rebellion the rebel army included a strong Galatian contingent, whose pressure may well have compelled him to enlist the Rigosages. However well the Rigosages marched for Antiochos in that war – no decisive battle took place, for much of Molon's army deserted to the king before the fighting began – Antiochos had little reason to trust Galatians as a whole, and the employment of the Rigosages may have been an uncomfortable experience. Only when he suffered from a lack of numbers in his regular forces in 190 did he recruit them again.

This abstention from Galatian recruiting is in strong contrast with their presence in other armies. At Raphia Ptolemy IV had several thousands in his force, brigaded with Thracians (which may be a clue as to where both groups were recruited, though they may also have been Cleruchic forces;

that is, Galatians domiciled in Egypt); some of this brigade are said to have been only recently recruited – it was 6000 strong, so we may assume the Galatians numbered about 3000.[26] There were Ptolemaic posts on the north Aegean coast, with an appointed governor, who could have acted as their recruiter. This was not, however, an important element in an army of 70,000 men.

Of all the Great Powers of the time, Macedon should perhaps have been the most reluctant to employ Galatians, given its disastrous experience at their hands. Despite Antigonos Gonatas' success at the start of his reign, when he had recruited Galatians to rid his kingdom of other Galatians, he had experienced troubles later when Pyrrhos' Galatians had rifled the royal tombs at Aigai, and when the large contingent in his own employ at Megara mutinied and had to be massacred. In addition, the Macedonian kingdom was hardly wealthy in comparison to the Seleukid and the Ptolemaic states, and mercenaries were expensive. On the other hand, the Macedonian population and manpower had been seriously reduced in the preceding century due to the wars and expeditions and invasions, so employing mercenaries was a way of conserving the essential manpower base of Macedonians, and it was they who gave Antigonos his authority.

From the 220s and the new kings who took office in that time – Antiochos III in 223, Ptolemy IV in 222, Philip V in 221, all in their teens when they took power – and once the manpower and stability of the kingdoms could be seen to have recovered, there is a clear indication that employment of Galatians by Ptolemy was increased, but, like the Seleukid kingdom under Antiochos, recruitment by Philip ceased. At the Battle of Sellassia in 222, King Antigonos III Doson, Philip's uncle and regent, had only 1000 Galatians on the strength.[27] Philip did not recruit any at first, but in 218 he did employ some Galatian cavalry (no numbers given) in his war against Sparta.[28] In his later wars, however, no Galatians are mentioned, even in 197 when he was desperate for extra numbers of troops to face the Roman attack. On the other hand, in that year he had contacted the Scordiscian state to form an alliance against the Dardani. He had defeated yet another Dardanian invasion, the sixth or seventh of his reign; the Scordiscian alliance would help to deter such attacks from then on, but it does not seem that the alliance allowed Philip to recruit Scordiscian Galatians. This was a version, if one still categorizes all Galatians as chaotic barbarians, of the hiring of tribes; in fact, it was an international agreement of a typical sort, allying with the enemy of one's enemy.[29] Later Philip planned to activate the alliance to destroy the Dardanians completely, but this was prevented by his death.[30]

Philip's son and successor as king, Perseus, was similarly strapped for soldiers in his own Roman war, and at the start of the war he had added 13,000 mercenaries to his national army of 30,000 men; of these mercenaries 2000 were Galatians.[31] At the end of the war, as defeat loomed, Perseus projected a scheme to hire an army of 20,000 Bastarnai, half cavalry, half infantry, under their own king, Klondikos – a hiring of, or an alliance with, a whole community, like Antiochos' hiring of the Rigosages. The Bastarnai were in all likelihood a Keltic group (some claim them as German) who had been migrating into the Balkans and the Ukraine at the time. In the end Perseus decided he could not afford the cost. He attempted to change the deal to hiring just 5000 cavalry, but the Bastarnai King Klondikos pulled out of the agreement.[32] Had Perseus risked hiring the whole force, the Battle of Pydna might have had a different outcome; on the other hand, the Romans were as leery of the Galatians as the Macedonians, and being beaten in battle by a great Macedonian-Bastarnai army might just have so enraged them that they would have put forth an even greater effort to achieve victory. And the prospect of 20,000 Bastarnai – who appear to have been migrating in search of new homes – loose in Macedon was a good reason to pull out of the agreement. Perseus would hardly be popular at home if, having won the Roman war, he found the Bastarnai would not go home, or at least not go away.

The market for Galatian mercenaries changed gradually. From initial enthusiasm in the 270s, the kings became steadily more wary and kept their hirings to only a few thousands – Perseus is said to have been too stingy (or poor) to pay Klondikos, but hiring 20,000 Galatians and admitting them to the kingdom would clearly be both very expensive and dangerous. The subsequent extinction of the Macedonian kingdom in 167 therefore removed one of the major markets for Galatian soldiers. The Seleukids had already lost ready geographical access to Galatia once again in 188, but at his great victory parade at Daphne in 166, Antiochos IV included a division of 5000 Galatian mercenaries.[33] The collapse of the Seleukid state, which followed Antiochos' defeat in Parthia later, effectively closed that market also, since they were, as Perseus had found, too expensive (a major change from the first hirings, when they were thought to be a cheap alternative to hiring Greeks). The Ptolemies continued to employ them, and the wealth of the dynasty was clearly enough to afford them, but their appearance is so infrequent that one must assume that they were few in number.[34]

The Pergamene King Attalos I had as much reason as Antiochos III and Ptolemy II to be wary of Galatian mercenaries, but in an emergency he was just as willing to take the risk. In fighting Akhaios in 217 he turned to hiring a whole nation of Galatians, the Aigosages. They came over from Europe, families and all, on a promise of land on which to settle – more evidence of continuing Galatian migrations – but they proved to be both superstitious and unreliable, and were clearly aiming to settle first and fight later, if necessary. Attalos, however, was the one who repudiated the contract, though by the time he did so they were over the Hellespont and in the Troad. They inevitably became a public nuisance to everyone else in the area, until, ironically, it was the Bithynian King Prusias I who attacked and destroyed them – another massacre. One would suppose the survivors – there will have been some – who escaped, moved into Galatia for refuge.[35]

All the Great Powers were clearly in the market for Galatian recruits at various times, but increasingly only on their own terms. The strictly limited numbers of all those who were employed suggests that great care was being exercised in recruiting them once the habits and behaviour of the Galatians were understood. The single attested case of a whole Galatian nation being employed successfully, in Antiochos III's fight with Molon (and discounting Nikomedes' exploit), can be explained as a desperate measure in a time when the available Seleukid manpower was very limited; it was also ended very quickly, since Antiochos did not use them in the fighting against Ptolemy and Akhaios which followed. All other cases were hirings of smallish numbers, in the low thousands, and the men were, again, employed usually for brief periods in times of shortage of military manpower – at Raphia by Ptolemy, at Magnesia by Antiochos, at the start of the Roman war by Perseus. The Galatians were clearly valued as mercenary soldiers, but their presence was hardly welcome and they were kept for most of the time at a distance.

Chapter 7

Galatia and its Wars

The essential element to note for the history of the Galatians for the two centuries after their settlement in Asia Minor is that they remained as three distinct 'tribes', each of which, once it was occupying a specific territory, was actually an independent state. They had arrived as three separate mobile states, which divided the Seleukid enemy's territory into three areas from which each conducted separate military operations.

Just as it is necessary to avoid the term 'tribe' in referring to each Galatian political entity, it is also necessary to avoid the word 'raid' in referring to the Galatians' military exploits. Both are denigratory and imply a lack of organization and intelligent direction. Their 'raids' were, in fact, military campaigns with specific objects in view. They were conducted in a particular way, which their Greek opponents did not like – the mass charge, naked champions, and so on – but this does not make them any the less military. The one set of battles we are informed of in detail – against Vulso's army in 189 – show evidence of advance planning and firm command. They were in fact not very good at battles, and their victories were very few. Their original aim, as already remarked, was to secure a territory on which to settle; afterwards they aimed at retaining those territories.

It became clear very soon in their first Asian campaigns that the land from the Aegean coast to Armenia was already divided among existing states. It was going to be necessary therefore for each tribe to persuade at least one of the established states to agree to allot them land. At that point peace could be made, and presumably the tribe and the allotting state would become allies.

The land they gained was in the interior of the peninsula, high above sea level, dry in summer, cold in winter. The Tolistobogii were first, by a treaty with Antiochos I in 274 after the Elephant Victory.[1] They took over the upper valley of the Sangarios River, including the town of Gordion and the temple town of Pessinos. The Tektosages continued raiding for some years, but it seems probable that the Trokmoi were settled by treaty at the same time as the Tolistobogii. The Trokmoi took a large area east of the Halys River, with a centre at Tavion. The Tektosages were allotted land between the other two tribes by Mithradates I of Pontos in the early 260s, including Ankyra; this must have been organized before 266, when Mithradates died. By that date all three had taken over their new homelands.

This was all achieved, first by a suspension of fighting by a truce, then by a treaty agreed between tribal leaders and the king. Technically, this will have made the new Galatians in some way subjects of the king, since it was part of his kingdom they were receiving. This was perhaps of little account, for the Tektosages were settled by Mithradates but on Seleukid land, and the Trokmoi were settled on land which may not have been part of any kingdom. Certainly from the time the three tribes became settled they behaved as independent states.[2]

Much of the land which now became 'Galatia' had been Phrygia until then, and was inhabited by the descendants of the subjects of the ancient kingdom of Phrygia, destroyed by the Assyrians and Lydians centuries before. The Tolistobogii, the first settlers, took over the prime part of the region in the western part of Galatia, with the temple city of Pessinos within their territory. Neither of the two urban centres in their territory, Pessinos and Gordion, was damaged, and they did not, it seems, interfere with the rites or with the priests at Pessinos. It is another indication that the Galatians were not the ravenous raiders and destructive looters as they are so often depicted. There is, however, some evidence from Gordion that the Keltic practice of human sacrifice was practised, as well as the sacrifice of other animals. The evidence is not wholly conclusive, being archaeological, but it was a practice common with other Keltic groups, and it is hardly surprising that it was practised by the Tolistobogii.[3]

To the east of the Tolistobogii, on land higher, drier, and colder, and centred on the ancient town of Ankyra, were the Tektosages, whose territory was narrower than the others, but stretched well to the north to the northern mountains. The Trokmoi were even further east, in the poorest and most thinly populated part of Galatia, where part of the land was mere sand. In total, these three states occupied a land which was roughly oval in shape, perhaps 400 kilometres from east to west, and 200 from north to south. It was thus a relatively large area, but thinly populated even after their arrival. Antiochos and Mithradates were not giving away territory which was of much value.[4]

The geography is rather odd. The Trokmoi's western boundary was the Halys River, a clear geographical line, and this became the Tektosages' eastern border. Their western border is less clear, and was presumably negotiated with the Tolistobogii, already in occupation. In fact, the latter may have surrendered some territory to give the Tektosages a reasonable area, which would help explain the relatively small size and curious shape of the Tektosagian territory. The Trokmoi could hardly be expected to give up their clear western boundary, and because theirs was an extra dry country they obviously needed a larger area than the others. No doubt the continued raiding by the Tektosages was almost as unsettling to the other two tribes as it was to Antiochos and Mithradates, and all concerned would be relieved to see them settled.

These new settlements had separated Pontos on the north coast from the southern and western Seleukid lands in Asia Minor, and provided Pontos with a certain shelter from Seleukid annoyance. The Trokmoi, settled east of the Tektosages, were also clear of Seleukid annoyance by the relatively remote situation of their new land. The intervening territory was Kappadokia, under the authority of a local ruler; it became a recognized kingdom in 255 when the king married a Seleukid princess.

The settlement of the three Galatian tribes therefore began in 274, but the process continued for several years. The three tribes seemingly operated separately, according to the several agreements made by the original rulers – mainly probably with Antiochos I, no matter that Mithradates interfered. There was surely considerable disturbance within the new states. The local Phrygian ruling class will no doubt have objected, but probably fruitlessly: possibly the Phrygian peasantry did not, or did not care – one overlord was probably like any other. There is, however, no hint of civilian troubles, though, given the lack of sources, this is not surprising. Yet some indication might have been expected if disturbances had been wide or long continuing. The relative smallness of Galatian numbers perhaps helped here, since their capacity for oppression would have been limited.

The main geopolitical result of the three tribes' settlement in central Anatolia was to decisively limit the authority of the Seleukid king, not only in the areas in which the Galatians settled, but in the surrounding states as well. Pontos is an obvious benefactor: no matter the precise nature of the intervention by Mithradates, the fact of the Galatians being settled in lands between his kingdom and that of the Seleukids placed him in a much more independent situation. Seleukid kings had claimed suzerainty over Pontos since the time of Seleukos I; this was no longer a realistic notion. Ironically, this did not directly cover Bithynia, though that kingdom remained allies with the Galatians for the next forty-odd years.

Seleukid power had already been truncated by the success of the northern kingdoms and cities in asserting their independence, so that Bithynia, Herakleia Pontike, and Pontos were all by 270 or so formally independent states. Nikomedes' policy of turning the Galatians against Antiochos' lands had thus been highly successful. He secured control of his whole kingdom and his throne, and he prevented Antiochos from returning to the attack against him and his allies.

The treaties which permitted the three tribes to take over their sections of 'Galatia', as the land must now be called, had a further effect. For example, Antiochos' treaty with the Tolistobogii, agreed after the Elephant Victory, did two things: it allocated land in Phrygia on which the tribe could settle, and it established peace between the two parties during the lifetime of Antiochos I; we do not know the timing on the Galatian side which was equivalent to the king's lifetime, but there is no hint of any hostilities between them in the years following the treaty – so long as one accepts that for the moment the three states were acting independently, and that the later raids in the south were by the Tektosages alone, with whom Antiochos did not (yet) have a treaty. After all, the Tolistobogii had achieved their aim by their agreement, which was to acquire a new homeland. It seems reasonable to assume that something like a treaty also established the other tribes in their new homelands. Mithradates of Pontos is supposed to have settled the Tektosages around Ankyra, but since this was technically Seleukid territory and had been publicly recognized as such in 280 by Seleukos' defeat of Lysimachos, no doubt Antiochos I made an agreement to this as well; the Trokmoians' settlement was also presumably agreed.

These treaties were successful in solving the Galatian problem if that is seen as a matter of raids or terrorism. The Galatians clearly had certainly indulged in raids and theft, before being allocated their new homeland, but this had only been a secondary aspect of their aims. It bears repeating that their primary aim was always to settle in a new homeland, and that their mode of warfare in the 270s was aimed at persuading the reluctant local powers to accommodate them. Therefore, once settled in Galatia, they had no obvious motive to go raiding again. Politically, once settled they became a group of weak states, and were therefore vulnerable; staying quiet and peaceful was protection. By their treaties they had become part of the state system of Asia Minor.

The purpose of Mithradates I in settling the Tektosages south of Pontos was probably defensive, in that they formed a barrier protecting his kingdom from any aggression by the Seleukid king. In addition, by a treaty with the Tektosages he established peace with them, and could prevent any raids by them on his own territory while he was alive. The Bithynian kingdom had done the same by its alliance with the whole Galatian group when they crossed into Asia in the first place, an alliance, it may be noted, which remained in effect until 230. The treaties with Antiochos I had the same result.

By the 260s, therefore, the Galatians were settled in their new homelands and were also pinned down by a series of treaties made with all the kingdoms surrounding them. The cities they had been attacking in their campaign against the Seleukid kingdom were now out of their reach, in effect protected by the treaties of the Galatians with the kings, of which the cities were dependents. However, these treaties gradually expired, either after a number of years, or more likely on the deaths of the kings who concluded them; Mithradates I died in 266, Antiochos I in 261, and Nikomedes I in 255. From this point, therefore, the Galatian state or states were no longer either restrained or protected by those treaties, though the power of the successor kings was probably sufficient to prevent them from resorting to war at once, certainly in the case of Antiochos II. Nor is it clear that the Galatians still wished to indulge in wars; having achieved their main aim they were no longer internally compelled to go raiding; any young men who were so attracted could fulfil their aggressive impulses by enlisting as a mercenary somewhere. Instead the Galatians could operate as normal states and enter into treaties, or wars, as they chose.

This interpretation conflicts, of course, with the generally accepted assumption that the raids continued, and that they terrorized the Greek cities during the next century or so. Yet the evidence for raids after they were settled is thin to non-existent. There were certainly instances of warfare in which the Galatians were involved in Asia Minor, and these will be discussed in sequence in the rest of this chapter, but it will be worth considering the difference between state warfare, which I will maintain is what happened, and 'raids', for which I can find no evidence after the three tribes can be considered to have settled, that is, after, say, 268.[5]

Before considering the Galatians' wars, it is necessary to examine the states themselves, their society, and their governing system. In the geopolitical circumstances of their settlement in the new homeland it was obviously necessary that the Galatians organize themselves in such a way as to be able to act as a normal Hellenistic state. They were clearly not willing to be a kingdom – the three distinct 'tribes' continued to be their basic organization until Roman times, and rivalry between the three, to put it no stronger, may be assumed. It seems that Leonnorios remained as leader, or chief, of the Tolistobogii from the time they were in Europe until after 274, and he was evidently the pre-eminent war leader. He was able to conclude the treaty with Erythrai, and perhaps with other cities, and Antiochos I, but there is no sign of him ever being king, nor any other man being suggested as such in any of the three tribes at this early period.[6]

A loose political association was clearly preferred, in which the three tribes retained their identities as states. We have no direct information from the settlement period as to how they were internally organized, but Strabo has a passage in which he claims to be describing their organization 'long ago'. The account he gives is evidently based on information from before the emergence of the Galatian monarchy under Roman auspices in the early first century BC and therefore it refers to conditions at some point or period in the two centuries before then. The description he gives may be taken as a reasonable overview of the conditions in the early years, without the details necessarily being wholly accurate.[7]

There are two main theories of the development of the governing system of the states. One is that Strabo's description refers to the earliest period after the settlement, and that few changes took place until the upheaval of the Roman Republican period, in which Roman warlords trampled across the country, and several disasters happened. The other theory assumes that Strabo's description refers to the situation in the second century BC, after the Galatians had been in occupation of the new lands for a century. There were a series of military conflicts in the first half of that century, which would have triggered changes. This, of course, implies that we know little or nothing of their condition in the first century of their presence, and that they were not capable of organizing themselves, which is patronizing. Given that the three states made international treaties with the surrounding kingdom on several occasions in the third century, it is clear that they had a good understanding of the diplomatic system they had intruded upon; and given that individuals happily took service as mercenary soldiers, a good understanding of the political (and military) systems of those states is clear. But the main thing is that the governing system Strabo described is one which is very similar to that which operated in other Keltic tribes; and it is distinctively Galatian. I conclude that Strabo's description is a good indication of the Galatian governing system from the start. (Strabo came from Sinope, close to Galatia on the Black Sea coast, and he may be presumed to have had access to good local information; he was a careful investigator, and we may accept that his account bears a reasonable relationship to what existed.)

A central authority for the three states as a group existed in the form of the Council (*boule*) at which each of the subdivisions of the three tribes was represented. Each state was divided into four tetrarchies, each of which had a tetrarch, a judge, and a military leader, with two subordinate commanders. How these were chosen is not stated, though heredity or wealth or achievement could be the criteria, probably a combination of all three. In an early account, as the tribes left Bithynia, they are said to have had seventeen chiefs and two named leaders (Leonnorios and Loutarios), so the quadripartite system was a later adaptation, though based on Keltic tradition.

The Council of tetrarchs met at Drunemeton, whose name implies that this was a shrine or grove or *nemeton*, a vague word implying a tree-surrounded sacred space. The meeting took place either in a building or in a grove of (usually) oak trees. Its location is not known – though Pessinos has been suggested, but if so why not call the place by that name?[8] Strabo's description of the Council's functions is that it was the court for judging murder cases for the whole three tribes, but he then notes that its 'power' passed to the new kings who emerged in the first century BC. There is no indication that the Council had more than legal functions, though it was perhaps consultative.

The Council met once a year and all the political notables of the three states attended. It is not conceivable that they simply paid attention only to murder cases. Informal discussion of mutual problems is to be expected, and one of its obvious functions would be to smooth over disputes between the tribes, which, to be sure, are not recorded anywhere, but which surely existed.

The three states were self-governing, and conducted their own foreign affairs, a matter which implies internal consultations. Examples are when the Tolistobogii assisted Ziaelas to gain the Bithynian throne in 255 after Nikomedes' death; both the Tolistobogii and the Tektosages attacked Pergamon into the 230s, while next year it was the Tolistobogii alone doing the fighting. They were clearly acting as independent states.

The society which the Council and the tetrarchs headed may be seen as oligarchic in political terms. The invading Galatians no doubt became the rulers and the chiefs. The Phrygian natives will have composed the peasantry. In the few towns there was an exiguous middle class. The lords established themselves in castles and manor houses, collected some taxes – or perhaps tithes would be the appropriate term – , supervised local affairs, and probably interfered with the peasantry as little as possible. Much of the area which became Galatia was dry; pastoral farming, particularly of flocks of sheep, appears to have been the main livelihood of all classes. The river valleys, and areas of particularly fruitful soil, would support agriculture, but true wealth lay in the flocks of sheep. There were perhaps some Phrygian lords still surviving, who integrated themselves into the Keltic culture as they could.

The internal arrangements in each tribe was one of extreme decentralization. Below the level of the tetrarchs there was a large number of chiefs – 183 of them, a massive increase on the 17 in 278. Settlement in their new homeland would clearly permit a more expansive society, and a chief could build up a small province of his own by establishing a fortified manor house and lording it over the local peasantry. In addition, there were an unknown number of units each with their own names, of which we know the names of a few – Voturi, Okondiani, Ambitouti, Artigniakon – all of which, as it happens, were part of the Tolistobogii. (The Rigosages hired by Antiochos III in 221 may have been another of these.) Each tribe was therefore deeply subdivided, and identities were no doubt as multiple as in any Greek city. It would perhaps be difficult to motivate the whole tribe into a single action.

The evidence for Galatian rule and presence in the new lands is first of all the written material, such as Strabo and the Hellenistic historians, who give evidence for the settlement itself. In more detail there is place-name evidence, in which a number of Keltic names for particular locations in Galatia are known, though it has to be said there are not many of them. The preceding Phrygian and Greek names continued to be used, an indication that the Galatians were not numerous enough to impose many of their own names on this new land. Then there is a considerable amount of archaeological evidence from Galatia, burials and cemeteries, and finds of La Tène-type metalwork, which are likewise clear evidence of settlement, but only if they can be specifically identified as Galatian; finds of jewellery and metalwork are ambiguous, since they are valuable and movable objects. They could be evidence either of the presence of Galatian settlers, or of trade; there are finds of this material all over Asia Minor, often well outside the Galatians' homeland. A number of sites indicate that they were fortified by the Galatians. These are often called *oppida*, and the term implies the presence within an encircling wall or earthwork of a settled population; perhaps a dozen places show such evidence.[9]

While individual elements in this catalogue might be disputable, particularly when taking the presence of isolated items of La Tène jewellery as a mark of the Galatian presence, the sheer concentration of *oppida*, burials, cemeteries, and other finds in a clearly geographically restricted area is wholly convincing of the presence of Galatians. The indigenous population on which the Galatians imposed themselves was Phrygian, and the fusion of the two peoples appears to have been fairly rapid, although there is evidence of Phrygians still speaking their particular language well into the Roman period. A number of scattered notices show that, particularly in the rural areas, the Keltic language also continued in use throughout the Roman period. What the balance was between them, and between them and Greek, is impossible to judge, except that urban areas tended to use Greek, perhaps in combination with one of the other languages; it was above all in the rural areas that the older languages survived.[10] The penetration of Greek into the interior area only took place in the Galatian period, not before, and the Galatians are thus, somewhat ironically, identified as agents of Hellenization. At Gordion, for example, a series of graffiti record twenty Greek names out of thirty identifiable names, with just two others certainly Keltic – and this was before 189, when the town was abandoned. At Abydos in 197 an inscription lists four men with Greek names and identifies them as Galatian.[11]

Ancient historians remark on the increase in the number of Galatians,[12] and this may be accounted for by the continued immigration of reinforcements from Europe, though there is no actual evidence for this. The number of Galatians who originally settled in each area was probably no more than 10,000, perhaps less, but in a new land their numbers would certainly increase. The fusion of Galatians and Phrygians is likely to have been rapid, particularly in the acquisition of wives and concubines from the Phrygian population by unmarried Galatian warriors. The Galatian territory was untroubled by invasion or war for a full generation after 274, so there was plenty of time for intermarriages and procreation. It is highly probable that the Phrygian population, which undoubtedly had its own memories of independence and of its own kings, may well have welcomed the opportunity to participate in a new independence after several centuries of subjection to alien Lydian, Persian, and Macedonian rulers, even if they were being ruled by yet another alien group.

There is, however, an indication that other Galatian groups did arrive in Asia Minor after the original settlers. One specific instance is the arrival of the Aigosages in the Troad by arrangement with Attalos I in 217, though they became such a nuisance that Prusias I of Bithynia massacred them, supposedly to extinction. Antiochos III employed the Rigosages in 221, a Galatian nation which may have been part of one of the Galatian states. Within Asia Minor there were other possible Galatian groups, living fairly close to, but outside, the Galatian borders. These may be later migrants, or chieftain groups who had split off from the original conquest tribes – but the evidence is late, and they may not be Keltic at all.

The Galatians were always regarded by the Greeks, and later by the Romans, as 'barbarians'. This has had serious consequences for the study of the people and the states they formed. The various meanings of 'barbarian' have led to the assumption that they were politically unorganized and unsophisticated, wild in their warfare, and fit only to be Hellenized or Romanized. In the Greek time, of course, the term primarily meant that they did not speak Greek, which, at least for the upper layers of Galatian society, was probably not correct, but it also implied that their society was not organized into *poleis*, cities, which is probably correct. There were a few old urban settlements in their area, but none of these was set up as a *polis* until the Roman period, and Gordion at least was abandoned.

But there is, first, no reason why they need to be organized in a way recognized by Greeks and Romans as 'civilized', which would presumably mean as city states. A political organization obviously existed from the start in each part of Galatia, capable of command and of making treaties. The migrants were set down in the midst of a possibly hostile population, and they were surrounded by other political units – cities, kingdoms, empires – who may be, or may become, hostile. Setting up a governing system, no matter how exiguous, was a way of stamping their authority and presence on this new home, and inevitably it was the sort of organization with which they were already familiar which was used.

This would ensure their continuing control of the land to which they had been assigned, and provide a framework for assigning estates and lands to individuals. Strabo is quite definite this organization was set up 'long ago', which to be sure is vague, but no more than two centuries before his time. Above all, it is the international situation in which they found themselves which demands that they organized themselves into a recognizable and effective government quickly. They were new to the area, very much resented, and obviously vulnerable. This would require that they integrate or dominate the local population quickly, fortify their settlements at once, and erect a government which would be able to treat with other powers and command in war.

In considering the international position of the Galatian states it is also necessary to avoid characterizing them as composed of out-of-control barbarian raiders, likely to set off on a raid at any moment. Instead they must be seen as three of the many independent states in the Mediterranean world, which varied in size from single cities to intercontinental empires. 'Their governing interest was in their own profit and advantage, for which they would change any allegiance of break any pact.'[13] This is a description of the supposed conduct of the Galatians, and is to a degree denigratory, based on Greek and Roman perceptions of barbarian conduct, but it is also a description of the conduct of any and every Hellenistic state, with the exception of 'breaking any pact', of which no instances by the Galatians can be found, and none are listed; it is a reasonable characterization of the Galatian states, but not only of them.

From their arrival in Asia, the Galatians stood by any treaties they made. They were allies of Nikomedes, who was at war with Antiochos I, and the Galatian invasion of Seleukid Asia Minor was therefore a logical extension of Nikomedes' treaty with them, and of his war with Antiochos. The Galatians were no doubt unscrupulous, but then so were their contemporaries; Nikomedes' use of them is one case, and one may also instance in particular Ptolemy II, whose conduct was best described in the words above quoted, and as deceitful, murderous, and conscienceless.

Once established, therefore, and organized, the Galatian states must be seen to have operated internationally with the same priorities as every other contemporary state – with the aim of maintaining or increasing their own wealth and security, and ensuring above all their own political continuance. The initial problem was that one of the three tribes was constrained (and protected) by a treaty – that of the Tolistobogii with Antiochos I – though all three were parties to the alliance with Nikomedes. The situation of the Trokmoi is always unclear; it may be that they were the weakest of the three tribes, and it is certain that they were settled in the poorest part of Galatia: evidence of their presence in the form of archaeological finds and place-names is thin on the ground in that region.

King Mithradates of Pontos and the Tektosages formed an alliance against a Ptolemaic maritime intrusion into the Black Sea, and this is a good indication that their alliance dated from the time he allotted land to them. The date of this event is not known if it actually took place; doubts have been cast. Mithradates may have been moving from hostility to friendship with Antiochos, while Antiochos had been involved in the settlement of the Tolistobogii by their Seleukid treaty, so they were now counted as Seleukid friends, or perhaps clients. So the Ptolemaic raid on the Black Sea coast would be part of Ptolemy II's strategy to destabilize the recent settlement in Asia Minor. The force which landed was driven off by a joint Pontic-Galatian force, which captured some of the ships' anchors. Also named as an ally in this fight was Ariobarzanes, Mithradates' son, who was presumably joint king with his father (who was about eighty years old by 270). If Pontos had earlier been subjected to the Tektosages' raids, the alliance will have stopped them, and opposing Ptolemy's attempt to disrupt the new settlement would have been in accordance with both their interests.

By then, perhaps in the early 260s, the Galatian states were at peace with all their neighbours. They were still capable of mounting their own expeditions, as the Tektosages did in alliance with Mithradates, and they were still no doubt perceived as a restless threat by their neighbours, perhaps as a result of internal rivalries, but they also saw their neighbours as threats to themselves – which made them normal states of the time. Galatian restlessness would be taken as given for some time; it would take a period of peace and quiet on their part to convince former victims or nearby communities that they were no longer a threat.

The deaths of kings automatically extinguished the treaties they had made. When Nikomedes of Bithynia died, at some time in the late 250s, possibly in 255, his two sons disputed the throne – a repetition of the situation in 279, and the same solution was adopted. The elder of the two claimants, Ziaelas, had been driven into exile by his father, and was excluded from the succession in favour of a younger son by a different mother. He made an agreement with the Tolistobogii, or perhaps he activated the clause in his father's treaty which extended the alliance beyond Nikomedes' death. The succession struggle pitted the Galatians against a substantial coalition of guardians appointed by Nikomedes for his chosen successor in his will – Kings Ptolemy II and Antigonos Gonatas, the cities of Byzantion, Kieros, and Herakleia. This last was the most active, it seems, and it was the only one within reach of the Tolistobogii; it was therefore the enemy of both Ziaelas and the Tolistobogii, and it was quite reasonably attacked (though this has usually been interpreted as a Galatian 'raid').[14] In the end Ziaelas succeeded, as a result of mediation by Nymphis of Herakleia. The Tolistobogii might well have celebrated their success against such a coalition of enemies, though how active the kings were in the affair is not known. Politically, one result was a renewed alliance between Ziaelas and the Tolistobogii; another was enmity between Herakleia and the Tolistobogii.[15] This was all quite reasonable military and political conduct by them, but it was nevertheless depicted as an act of spite and is too often listed as a typical Galatian 'raid' on an unoffending city, though it was not a raid, and Herakleia was an open enemy.

One reason for seeing these Galatian wars as 'raids', apart from researchers' laziness in continuing to accept an old interpretation, is probably the Galatian method of war. This, as Greeks and Romans both knew, consisted mainly of a charge by the mass of warriors. This was certainly frightening. It had succeeded often enough that the Galatians in Asia saw no reason to change it, and they continued to employ it against the Roman army in 225 at Telamon, and in Asia in 189 against the army of Manlius Vulso. This, to well-drilled hoplites and legionaries, clearly looked barbarian; hence their attacks were 'raids', despite the obvious political and international involvement. But it is time such a false interpretation was abandoned.

The alliance of the Tektosages and Pontos expired on the death of Ariobarzanes in about 250; his participation with his father in the alliance had extended it beyond Mithradates' own death in 266. The 'Galatians' – presumably the Tektosages – freed from the treaty restrictions, immediately invaded Pontos. The new king, Mithradates II, was a child, which was perhaps an added incentive for the attack, and it is evident that the new government of the kingdom, presumably a regency, did not have the time to renew the old treaty, if they had even thought of it.

The exact reason for the war is not known, but it was more than a mere raid on the kingdom; there had presumably been a build-up of enmity between the two states, but the quarrel had been restrained from war while Ariobarzanes lived. The invaders laid siege to the city of Amisos on the Black Sea coast. Herakleia intervened by sending supplies into the city. Foiled in the siege, the Galatians attacked Herakleia – the friend of their enemy, and looted what they could seize. This is all perfectly normal international behaviour – Ptolemy III attacked the Seleukid kingdom in very much the same way and with the same excuse four years later – that the peace between the kingdoms had expired, and that he felt like gaining a cheap victory. We are not told why the war began between Pontos and the Tektosages, but it only became possible once the treaty expired. There was surely more to the issue than a new king's minority.

The point of this discussion of these minor political crises is to emphasize that the Galatian states, once established, operated in the same way, and with the same priorities, as all other contemporary states. In each case the cause of the fighting was different. In Bithynia the Galatians were invited in by Ziaelas; in Pontos the treaty with Mithradates and Ariobarzanes had expired and they were perfectly entitled to declare war, though something more than the child king's minority was surely involved.[16] Herakleia was clearly acting in a hostile manner by interfering against the Galatians, both over Ziaelas and at Amisos. All this is perfectly normal political behaviour, and is to be expected in a diplomatic system which was centred on treaties which lasted only during a royal lifetime.

The third royal death in this period was that of Antiochos I in 261. He was succeeded by his son Antiochos II, who had no conflict with the Galatian states. This immunity was perhaps enforced by the extensive fortifications of Antiochos' territory carried out by his father, and which he continued to extend, but it is more likely to have been because he made new treaties with the Galatian states, to replace that, or those, which had expired with his father.

Antiochos II was busy enough without the complication of a Galatian war. His first wife Laodike was from the family of Akhaios, and so they were cousins. (It was Akhaios' steward who was responsible for ransoming the villagers seized at Neoteichos and Kiddioukome about 269.[17]) Laodike lived in Ephesos later in Antiochos' reign when he was briefly married to

Berenike, the daughter of Ptolemy II. (He returned to Laodike in the last years of his life, leaving Berenike in Syria.) He was responsible for building or developing some of the new and/or reconditioned cities in Asia Minor which formed the defence line. He married his daughter Stratonike to the ruler of Kappadokia, Ariarathes, who dated his kingship to 255, the year of the marriage, though he had evidently been the effective ruler in Kappadokia for perhaps two decades already. This was the territory south and east of the new Galatia, even drier and winter-cold. The promotion of Ariarathes to the status of king was the direct result of the marriage; it also put Kappadokia into a subordinate alliance with Antiochos, who recognized it as an independent kingdom. This is one more state which geographically hemmed in the Galatians. We do not know what the relationship was between Ariarathes and his Galatian neighbours – the Trokmoi – but he had survived without difficulty for twenty years as their neighbour, so one might suppose they were in a treaty relationship analogous to that between the Tektosages and Mithradates I.

One of Antiochos' military exploits was to take his army into Thrace. This area was one of the regions to which the Seleukid kings had long laid claim, from Seleukos I's defeat of the earlier ruler, Lysimachos, though since Seleukos' murder no Seleukid king had approached it. The date and extent and context of this expedition are all unclear and disputed, as ever in this dark period for historical source material, but it took place in the 250s (he reigned 261–246), and Antiochos certainly conducted sieges of Byzantion and Kypsela, so his forces penetrated deep into Thrace.[18] One result was the repossession of the city of Lysimacheia by the Seleukid king, where Antiochos' coins were issued. The absence of the Tylis kingdom in every discussion of the event is notable, and implies that it was resolutely impartial, though the siege of Byzantion cannot have pleased the Tylis king. The tributary relationship with Byzantion implied by the payment of frequent sums of gold pieces to the king of Tylis clearly did not require the Tylis king to come to the city's defence or assistance. Antiochos' expedition implies strongly, along with his alliance with Kappadokia, that he had no fear of any hostile Galatian activity in Asia. From this one would conclude that he probably had binding treaties with the Galatian states from very early in his own reign.

This comfortable international situation ended with Antiochos' death and the crisis which followed. In 246, in January, Ptolemy II died, and was succeeded by Ptolemy III, who married Berenike of Cyrene; she brought Cyrenaica with her as her dowry and so joined that country with Egypt again; as a result an independent Cyrenaica was no longer available to the Seleukids as a distraction when a war began with Ptolemy. In June or July of the same year, Antiochos II died, leaving one wife, Laodike, in Ephesos with her two sons, Seleukos and Antiochos, and the second wife, Berenike (Ptolemy III's sister) in Antioch in Syria with an infant son, another Antiochos. All earlier treaties between the two monarchies ceased to have effect, and Ptolemy III soon began a campaign to disrupt the Seleukid kingdom. Some Seleukid governors and cities recognized the child Antiochos as the new king, but most recognized Seleukos.[19]

The child was quickly eliminated. A plot, probably instigated by Laodike, procured the murder of Berenike and her son. Ptolemy discovered this when he landed at Seleukeia-in-Pieria and marched into Antioch. From there, using reinforcements from Egypt, he occupied north Syria and Kilikia as far as the Euphrates River and the Taurus Mountains, the political heart of the Seleukid state. In Asia Minor the elder son of Antiochos II and Laodike assumed the kingship as Seleukos II, and set out to recover his lost territories. He commissioned his younger brother as joint king at some point and put him in command in Asia Minor. The date of this commission is not clear, but Antiochos remained in Asia Minor while Seleukos campaigned in Syria, so Antiochos will have become much more familiar with Asia and its politics than his brother.

Seleukos slowly recovered Syria and Kilikia, but not all of his lost lands: Ptolemy kept control of the imperial capital of Seleukeia-in-Pieria and of a string of small Kilikian cities; but Seleukos regained Antioch, and this became the replacement capital. In Asia Minor, Antiochos, having gained the nickname Hierax ('the Hawk'), acted independently, apparently encouraged by his mother, who perhaps favoured him from the first. The dynastic war, however, only began when Seleukos had recovered Syria, made his peace with Ptolemy in 241, and then tried to reassert control in Asia Minor. The succeeding 'War of the Brothers' which followed lasted until a truce in 237, but soon recommenced and lasted for almost another decade. Seleukos' peace with Ptolemy III came at considerable cost, for Ptolemy secured control of many cities along the southern and Aegean coasts of Asia Minor, and in the Thracian Chersonese. Lysimacheia had therefore remained in Seleukid control for little more than a decade.

The legacy of that war, the Third Syrian, was to weaken decisively the Seleukid Empire: apart from the losses in the west to Ptolemy, the far eastern province of Baktria broke away into independence, and its neighbour Parthia was soon conquered by nomad invaders. The effect in Asia Minor was even more serious. The various kingdoms failed to renew their Seleukid allegiance, at least to Seleukos, who was in Syria. A long series of ports and cities on the coast from Seleukeia-in-Pieria to Lysimacheia and the Hellespont were taken from Seleukid control.[20] The independent kingdoms of the interior and the north could now dabble in the Seleukid divisions. Parts of the Seleukid territory broke away into effective independence, notably Karia in the south-west, where the satrap Olympichos became effectively an independent ruler, going so far as to make arrangements with the Antigonid kings of Macedon for his protection.[21] The dynasty of Philetairos in Pergamon moved in the same direction of independence.[22] The longer the crisis of the dynasty lasted, of course, the more entrenched the new conditions became.

Details as ever are sparse, but the main event of the Brothers' War was an offensive against Antiochos by Seleukos out of Syria, probably in 239. Two years before, Seleukos, freed from the Ptolemaic war by his peace treaty, had indicated that he would be resuming full control throughout the empire, to which intention Antiochos demurred and recruited his forces. Antiochos had also secured alliances with Kappadokia and Pontos, where two of his sisters were married to the kings (but these women were also sisters of Seleukos). He was also allied with some or all of the Galatians, whose forces reinforced the local levy of troops from the Seleukid cities. Seleukos' invasion penetrated west all the way into Lydia, the local centre of Seleukid power, but then he turned north-east into the territory of the Tektosages, where a decisive battle was fought near Ankyra. Seleukos' opponent was an army composed of the forces of Mithradates II of Pontos, Antiochos Hierax, and the Galatians – this must be seen, therefore, as a triple alliance, the Galatians being the Tektosages, since Ankyra was in their territory. Probably outmatched in numbers, at the end of a long line of communications, and well inside hostile territory, Seleukos was defeated.[23]

The Galatians (Tektosages) evidently took the view that the victory was due to them, even though Antiochos was apparently in overall command, and it is certain that it was their territory which had been invaded. They insisted on changing the terms of the agreement they had with Antiochos.[24] It seems that he did not agree to this new arrangement, and 'paid a ransom'. This break therefore marks the end of the alliance of Antiochos and the Tektosages. With Seleukos defeated and for a time believed to be dead, the alliance was no longer needed; probably the agreement had been that the alliance should last for the duration of the war against Seleukos. It seems also, though on minimal evidence, that Mithradates in Pontos removed himself from the triple alliance at once, perhaps as a consequence of the break between Hierax and his Galatian allies;[25] he certainly never appears with his former allies in the later fighting. The new king of Pergamon, Attalos I, proved to be hostile to Antiochos at once, but Olympichos in Karia was neutral, so it seems.

The general assumption about this is that the Galatians were disappointed at their share of the loot acquired in the fighting.[26] This is hardly a sufficient reason for such a decisive alteration in the political relations, and notices are clearly based on the assumption that the Galatians were still a wild undisciplined force with no political sense – Justin likens them to bandits; it may also be a result of Attalid propaganda.

Antiochos may already have been thinking of carrying the war into Syria to displace his brother entirely. Seleukos had gone east with an expedition to attempt the recovery of the eastern provinces, protected by the truce with his brother. He failed in this, but by leaving he removed any pressure on the kings of Asia Minor. One result may have been the separation of Antiochos and his former allies, no longer under pressure from Seleukos.

The one enemy left for Antiochos in Asia Minor was the Pergamene ruler, Attalos I. He was a grandnephew of Philetairos, and had inherited the position from his cousin Eumenes I in 241. Eumenes had only a small territory, which he had concentrated on expanding during his reign, and both Eumenes and Philetairos had devoted much attention, energy, and resources to establishing good relationships with a series of cities in western Asia Minor, which gave them potential allies in a crisis, and helpful friendships at the least. The wealth which Philetairos controlled was available for hiring mercenaries, as well as subsidizing the local cities. The kingdom was small but had considerable potential.[27]

Attalos inherited the family propensity for expansion; he was one of the predators aiming at exploiting the dynastic Seleukid division to his own profit. The withdrawal of Seleukos II back to Syria after his defeat at Ankyra was followed by a peace, or a truce, between the brothers in 237.[28] It was this which permitted Seleukos to march off to the east, but it also meant that Asia Minor became a cockpit of continuing hostilities.

The role of the Galatian states in all these events is difficult to discern, since what few sources there are were concerned above all with the Seleukids or with Pergamon. Antiochos in Asia Minor had a series of allies with whom he was in treaty relationships of some sort. He had alliances with the Tektosages and Mithradates of Pontos, both of whom had fought beside him against Seleukos, but who broke off the alliance at some point after the Battle of Ankyra. Ariarathes of Kappadokia was his brother-in-law; Antiochos himself married the daughter of Ziaelas of Bithynia, who was, of course, in a treaty relationship with the Tolistobogii. (These marriages did not necessarily signify close political relationships – Mithradates was married to another of Antiochos' sisters – but at least they indicated a scheme of friendships, and perhaps an unlikelihood of hostility.) The one potentate in the region who was outside Antiochos' system was Attalos of Pergamon.

Antiochos' ambition was to overthrow his brother, and to do this it would be necessary to secure control over Attalos, who, equally ambitious, would inevitably seek to profit if Antiochos moved against Syria. No doubt Seleukos' move east was done in part with the assumption that Antiochos would soon find himself in trouble in Asia Minor; if Antiochos moved against Seleukos, the latter would inevitably seek Attalos' alliance. When Seleukos' eastern expedition ended in defeat in 235,[29] he returned to the west, with his army, and this was probably the signal for Antiochos to seek to remove the threat of Attalos in his rear.

The main evidence for the wars which soon followed is a broken and fragmentary statue base from the sanctuary of Athena at Pergamon, which commemorated a series of victories achieved by Attalos I. The reassembled fragments can be arranged in various ways so as to provide different but arguable histories, so that various solutions are possible. There are seven separate fragments, six of them recording a different victory by Attalos and his forces – no defeats are mentioned; and all the sections have to have some words restored. It is a precarious base for any historical discussion.[30]

The reconstruction of events must begin with the new alliance of Antiochos Hierax with two of the Galatian states, which was agreed sometime after the Battle of Ankyra; this gave Antiochos renewed strength. Two battles are recorded between the allies and Attalos' forces; the first, against 'the Tolistoagii the Tektosages and Antiochos', was fought close to Pergamon, near the temple of Aphrodite, which indicates that the allies had invaded Attalid territory. The second battle was against the Tolistobogii alone, and was fought near the sources of the Kaikos River, not far from the city of Pergamon, probably also within territory ruled by Attalos. It seems best to link these two fights and place them within the period of the alliance of Antiochos with the two Galatian states. This does not seem to have lasted very long after Ankyra, and so the fighting probably took place in the mid-230s. Three other battles of the war were recorded, one 'against Antiochos' alone in Hellespontine Phrygia, one 'near Koloe' (possibly in Lydia), and one near Harpassos in Karia. In these fights the Galatians were not involved, so they may be placed later in the 230s, after the alliance with Antiochos ended.

If this arrangement is plausible, it means that the two Galatian states, having twice suffered defeats at the hands of Attalos, pulled out of the war. Antiochos, however, could not, and continued fighting for some years. The result was that he was repeatedly defeated (at least according to this Attalid record). No matter how edited the record is, it is certain that Attalos was eventually victorious in the war, and extended his power throughout the Seleukid territory in Asia Minor which Antiochos had been ruling, as far as the Taurus Mountains. (This is not to say that this is the total of the fighting in the war; it is, after all, an Attalid victory monument in which no defeats are admitted and in which victories could be manufactured out of minor fights; the complete record of the fighting is out of our reach.)

Attalos had achieved the conquest of Seleukid Asia Minor by 228, so the fighting against Hierax had taken place before that date – and the war had probably lasted six or seven years, or there had been two wars, one between Attalos and the allies, the second between Attalos and Antiochos. Attalos used his victories to enhance his reputation, and chose to emphasize that he had been fighting the Galatians. He posed as a champion of Hellenism against the barbarians, though most of the fighting was actually against Antiochos.

It must be assumed that the defeats inflicted on the Tolistobogii and the Tektosages knocked them out of the war altogether. The second battle, against the Tolistobogii alone, might imply that Antiochos failed to turn up to the campaign. The Galatian states no doubt then made peace with Attalos, leaving Antiochos to fight on alone, with or without a contingent of Galatian mercenaries in his employ. Antiochos eventually attempted an invasion of Mesopotamia, but was driven away, and took refuge in Thrace with the Ptolemaic governor there. But there he was killed by a band of Galatians led by a chieftain called Kantarates – unless this was an assassination by Ptolemaic mercenaries.[31]

Antiochos died in 227, which puts all but one of the battles listed by Attalos I before that date, beginning probably in the early part of the period of the war/s. During that time the Galatians and Ziaelas of Bithynia also fought a war, in which Ziaelas was killed.[32] The reason for this war is unclear, though it is probable that it was connected in some way with the war between Antiochos and Attalos. Ziaelas had married his daughter to Hierax, and was allied with the Tolistobogii after they had assisted him to gain the throne. The killing is explicitly dated after Attalos' victory over the Tolistobogii. Perhaps Ziaelas allied himself at one point with Attalos, and so found himself attacked by Attalos' enemies; clearly his alliance with the Tolistobogii was broken at some point. Ziaelas' death is generally dated about 230, which puts the war between Attalos and the Tolistobogii before that date. So the Tolistobogii–Bithynian war took place between 235 and 230.

Given that the Galatians are regarded by historians as 'barbarians', and so treated as liable to break treaties and be generally treacherous, it would be normal to suppose that they had betrayed Antiochos, and had left him to fight on alone. We cannot, however, conclude from the record that this was the case. The terms of the alliance between Antiochos and the two Galatian states are not known, and to know if a betrayal took place we need that information. Antiochos Hierax has a bad reputation as a wild boy in the sources and the literature, so his own behaviour may have caused the rift. The involvement of Ziaelas is also curious, and essentially unexplained, unless his delivery of a daughter to Antiochos was the trigger for a political alliance.

The previous record of the Galatians in international affairs would in fact suggest that they were as scrupulous as any other state in adhering to the letter, and perhaps even the spirit, of any treaty to which they were party. They faithfully carried out their obligations to Nikomedes; the Seleukid kings had no complaint about the settlement treaties, once they had been agreed; Ziaelas made an alliance with the Tolistobogii to gain the Bithynian throne, and this was carried out; the Tektosages fought beside Antiochos at the Battle of Ankyra, and these two tribes joined him in the invasion of Attalid territory, after which the alliance was severed. We do not know why, though we have no reason to assume it was a Galatian betrayal; it could just as likely have been a betrayal by Antiochos, (who did not join with the Tolistobogii in the second battle against Attalos) or a result of a clause in their alliance.

Attalos busily exploited his victories. He gained control over the former Seleukid territory as far as the Taurus, which put the Galatian states and Kappadokia on his northern flank; this expansion was no doubt gratifying, but his real strength lay in western Asia Minor, and there he dominated, by one means or another, the well-urbanized Aegean coastlands, or at least those not under Ptolemy's control. He must have understood from the beginning that the victory over Antiochos Hierax was never going to be enough to secure permanent possession of his winnings, and a glance at the geography will have shown him clearly that it would be very easy for a Seleukid army to come over the Taurus and sweep up all his new conquests as far as the Aegean. His control of Asia Minor, which the new extent of his kingdom seemed to give him, was purely temporary.

Attalos set about convincing public opinion that he had performed a great service for the civilized world. This involved labelling the Galatians as barbarians, exaggerating the threat they had posed both to him and the Greek cities, and possibly fashioning a link between the Galatians, the Seleukids (his obvious next enemy), and barbarism. His propaganda included written accounts of his victories, suitably slanted (which later became one of the main sources of the events for historians), dedications such as that which is the main source for the information we now have about the war, and commissioning the Great Altar at Pergamon, displaying dead and dying Galatians of heroic size, musculature, and beauty – of a barbarian sort, of course. There were no doubt other elements to the distorted story, including offerings at the major Greek shrines at Delos and Delphi and on the acropolis at Athens. It seems to have worked, for, even to this day, the Attalids are still seen as strong defenders of Hellenism and civilization against barbarism.

Chapter 8

Galatia Facing Pergamon and Rome

The last battle recorded in Attalos' list of victories was against 'Lysias and the generals of Seleukos'.[1] Lysias was probably a member of one of the notable families which, like that of Akhaios, had come into the possession of large estates in Asia Minor – there was a city with his name, probably founded by a member of the family, the members of which can be followed through four generations at least.[2] Lysias may have lost these lands by taking the side of Seleukos II against Antiochos Hierax, or by taking the side of Seleukos II or III against Attalos; the notice of his fighting Attalos' forces suggests the latter.

The wording of Attalos' notice suggests that Lysias was leading his own force alongside that of 'the generals of Seleukos' and therefore that he had independently stood in opposition to Attalos' occupation of Seleukid Asia Minor, and had succeeded in raising a substantial force to do so. No doubt there were other men displaced and angered at Attalos' presumption – Lysias' contemporary Akhaios, the grandson of the earlier man of that name, who possessed extensive estates in Asia Minor and had posed for a time as loyal to Seleukos III's brother Antiochos III, before striking out for a kingship of his own, is probably another. This attack by Lysias and a Seleukid army against Attalos may have come during Attalos' initial conquest of Seleukid territory in the early 220s, or it may have been as part of an expedition which is known to have been sent by Seleukos III; whenever it happened it was defeated.

Seleukos II died in an accident in 226, and Seleukos III was assassinated in 223 (one of the assassins was a Galatian, Apatourios, who was presumably a soldier in his army). Neither king therefore succeeded in the dynastic aim of recovering control of Asia Minor, even after Antiochos Hierax had fled and been killed. But the next phase of the contest came in 222 when Akhaios (the younger) was sent in the name of the next king,

Antiochos III, to reverse Attalos' conquests, and succeeded in driving Attalos back to his small ancestral kingdom around Pergamon. Akhaios was, of course, a member of a cadet branch of the royal family which was settled in large estates in Asia Minor, a grandson of the Akhaios who ransomed the villagers of Neonteichos and Kiddioukome, and he was a cousin of Antiochos III.[3]

Akhaios operated for a year as Antiochos III's viceroy and avenger in Asia Minor, but then, having defeated Attalos, he allowed himself to be proclaimed king. The basis of his decision to make himself king was evidently his victory and his familiarity with the region as a native, and the evident loyalty to him of his army.[4] Having claimed the royal title he had intended to challenge Antiochos in Syria with his locally-recruited army, but that army refused to march out of Asia Minor,[5] so he had to be content with being king in Asia Minor alone. (In this he was a successor of Antiochos Hierax – and of Attalos). Ostensibly the reason for the army's refusal was that the men refused to fight against the king – meaning Antiochos – but the more likely reason is that the men were now thoroughly domiciled in Asia Minor and had no wish to be taken to fight in Syria; it is likely they were commanded by their local lords, who similarly may not have been inclined to distant expeditions. Asia Minor had been separated from direct Seleukid rule by this time for a full generation, under Antiochos Hierax, and then Attalos; the army's decision was clearly a gesture towards regional independence. Akhaios succeeded in taking over the former Seleukid territory, but not in suppressing any of the local potentates –Attalos of Pergamon retained his inherited base. Indeed Akhaios probably relied a good deal on the local lords to assist him in governing. From his position as king he was removed (that is, defeated, captured, and executed) by Antiochos III by 212.[6]

In all this the Galatians were completely uninvolved. There is no reference to any Galatians, other than the assassin Apatourios (whose actual origin is not known), in any of these events – with one exception. The final, approximately dated, notice of Galatian political and military activity was in the war against Attalos in about 236 or 235, when he defeated the Tolistobogii (assuming that date is correctly calculated).[7] The Galatian retreat from that war, and the breaking of the alliance with

Antiochos Hierax, which is implied by that and by the story of a Galatian attempt on his life (though that was in Thrace, and the 'Galatians' may not have been from Asia Minor),[8] also obviously involved a Galatian peace agreement with Attalos. This peace would last until Attalos died (in 197). It may also be that a treaty was negotiated between the Galatians and one or more of the surviving Seleukids. There is no record of this, but the failure of any Seleukid king to display any concern about any official Galatian involvement in their wars in Asia Minor or in Europe tells its own story – the Galatians were thus in all likelihood in treaty relationships with Seleukos II, Akhaios, and Antiochos III, as well as Attalos I – a perfect neutral position, which entirely suited a minor power. It has already been noted that Antiochos III was evidently reluctant to employ Galatian mercenaries: it seems he was determined to have nothing to do with the Galatian states either, though it will be argued later that he perhaps made an alliance with them, which would explain their silence in the sources during the king's reign.

Antiochos III made it a regular practice in his wars to contact an enemy of his enemy first, preferably in that enemy's rear. In 216 he made contact with Attalos when preparing for his war with Akhaios;[9] a similar contact with the Galatians would also make sense, since their position would be on his right flank as his forces advanced westwards from Syria towards Akhaios' power base in Lydia. This would isolate Akhaios, surrounding him with neutrals or enemies, and it might suggest that Antiochos had learned a lesson from the wars of his father Seleukos II, who ended his life during fighting his own Asia Minor coalition of enemies, and was defeated. The fact that Antiochos' brother was assassinated by a Galatian during a war against Attalos will also have bothered the Galatians, and they were no doubt anxious to ensure that they as a state were not involved; a neutrality agreement will have suited both. These are speculative notions, of course, but they arise from the general geopolitical situation within Asia Minor.

The one exception to the statement that Galatians were not involved in the wars and campaigns in Asia Minor after 235 was when Attalos, under pressure from Akhaios in 218, brought over a new Galatian nation, the Aigosages, from Europe. In return for a promise that they would be settled somewhere, they were to serve as mercenaries in Attalos' army, an adaptation of the old agreement between Nikomedes and the first Galatians to come into Asia. This, of course, was well before Attalos' self-promotion as the champion of Hellenism against barbarism, which is signalled in his later celebrations.[10] The Aigosages arrived, it seems, from Europe, though their more distant origin is not known, but they could have come all the way from the northern Balkans, or possibly from Thrace, where the Tylis kingdom still existed, though it was to collapse about the same time – they may have been refugees from that collapse. They could also have been domiciled for some time independently in Thrace, but Macedon, under its new King Philip V, was once more looking to expand, and the area might have been less than comfortable for a Galatian warband; we must suppose that they arrived in Asia by Attalos' invitation, not spontaneously.

The Aigosages were used in Attalos' campaign through Aiolis and Ionia during 218; the local cities were surely reminded all too clearly of the Tolistobogii's campaign sixty years before. In a passage showing blatant signs of Attalid propaganda, Polybios claims that a string of cities were 'visited', and 'joined him willingly and gladly'. Force was, it is admitted, required at times, but in fact force, or at least the threat of force, is constantly implied throughout the campaign. Then Attalos turned his horde north into Mysia and drove out the governor appointed by Akhaios. The campaign ended with the Galatians facing (and presumably threatening) another group of cities along the Hellespont; with these cities Attalos then 'entered into friendly relations', presumably after calling off his Galatians.[11] That is, in sum, Attalos brought a horde of Galatians into Asia, a horde which was admittedly largely out of his control at times, and sent them through western Asia Minor to overtly threaten any city they could reach. Many of these cities had bad memories of the Galatian raids half a century before, and in the end, when the Galatians took advantage of an eclipse of the sun to stage a panic, Attalos in effect decided that they were too much trouble. When Attalos claimed that the Galatians were barbarians, he will have had the Aigosages in mind.

Attalos then had the gall to claim that the horde had 'rendered no service of vital importance' – other than establishing his authority over a large section of northwest Asia Minor, that is. He then, having conducted them to the Hellespont area, allowed them to settle there.

That is, having used them, he abandoned them. It was a prime example of the unscrupulousness and faithlessness of which Hellenistic kings were capable – the sort of behaviour the Galatians are repeatedly claimed to have displayed, but rarely, if ever, did. To claim later that he was the champion of Hellenism against barbarism must have left a sour taste in the mouths of the cities he had subdued, and even more for those he had abandoned to the mercy of the Aigosages.

The settlement of this group of Galatians is at times claimed to be a 'military colony',[12] as a sort of Galatian version of a Hellenistic city foundation. Yet there is no evidence for this. Attalos had certainly agreed to provide land for them, which he did, but then he had no more to do with them. He promised to attend to any of their 'reasonable requests', but this was never fulfilled; further, he made no attempt to defend the local cities – with which he had just established friendly relations – against them when they broke out of their camp.

The Aigosages, now unrestrained, it seems, by any treaty or contract, began to expand the territory they had been allotted, first by attacking Ilion, laying siege to the town (which therefore must have been fortified since the place was seized by the first Galatians in the area). If they had any agreement with Attalos about their conduct, Attalos did not record it. The citizen levy of Alexandria Troas came out, relieved the siege, and then drove the Aigosages away. They camped again, this time at Arisbe, a little further along the coast of the Hellespont, in the territory of Abydos. The threat they posed was clearly hardly serious. Alexandria had fielded an army of 4000 men, and had succeeded without difficulty, and apparently without fighting, in moving the Aigosages on. But they were a potential source of mercenary manpower for Attalos, or for Akhaios, or for anybody who might choose to hire them, and so to the other kings they would be an obvious threat, quite apart from their propensity to attack the local cities, at least the small ones. Prusias I of Bithynia brought his army to Arisbe and destroyed them in their camp, supposedly killing all the men and many of the women and children (and survivors were no doubt enslaved). As a reward the Bithynian soldiers were allowed to loot the Aigosages' baggage.[13]

Attalos' behaviour in this affair was thoroughly inconsistent with his Hellenic pretensions. He claimed in his propaganda that he was a saviour of Hellenism against the barbarians of Galatia, adopting the surname 'Soter', producing the great altar in Pergamon to celebrate his achievement and other grandiose sculptures, and probably texts also, which became the basis for the pro-Attalid interpretation of the events visible in later histories, including that relating to the Aigosages. But in his relations with those Galatians he displayed all the elements of the carelessness of others, bad faith, and self-centredness which are attributed to the 'barbarians'.

This is the only notice of any Galatian activity in Asia Minor between Attalos I's victories and the arrival of Antiochos III in his campaigns, first to suppress Akhaios, and then to curb the ambitions of Attalos. By 212 Akhaios and his independent Asia Minor were no more and Attalos had been successfully confined to Pergamon and its vicinity once more – though he had gained some territory, including access to the sea at Elaia, in the most recent conflicts. Having achieved the pacification of Asia Minor and the restoration of Seleukid authority in the west, Antiochos turned to the east to aim for the same success. In his absence Asia Minor had a modicum of peace.

Not so Greece, where warfare broke out repeatedly from 217 onwards. Attalos briefly intervened in the fighting there in 208, but this left his kingdom open to attack by Prusias I. It is not clear how this brief war connected with the defeat of the Aigosages by Prusias nine or ten years before, if it did, but the conflicts were waged in the same territory, and were probably latterly about control of that territory; this was, of course, the region through which Attalos had campaigned with the Aigosages in 217. Attalos had intervened in Greece on the Roman side in their Macedonian War, and against Philip V of Macedon; since Philip was Prusias' brother-in-law, suspicions must exist that Philip had instigated Prusias to the attack, but they are not supported by any firm evidence.[14]

The Galatians of Asia Minor came into contact, indirectly, with the Romans for the first time shortly afterwards, in 205, when a Roman delegation came to Pessinos on a religious mission in aid of their war against Carthage. Pessinos was the city of the temple of Kybele, but it was also part of, or attached to, the territory of the Tolistobogii.

The Romans had called in at Pergamon first, where Attalos was regarded as a friend and ally. They acquired assistance from him, who sent them onward to Pessinos with a favourable message for the priests there. At Pessinos the message and the request were powerful enough for the priest there (or priests) to permit the delegation to remove the holy basalt stone of Magna Mater (the Roman name for the goddess Kybele) – or what was said to be that stone – and carry it back to Rome to be installed in her temple there.[15] Attalos was no doubt pleased to imply to the Romans that he had authority in Pessinos, but this was many miles outside his borders. This, of course, was the traditional method for any king to extend his influence, though Attalos was probably moving on Pessinos for the first time. It seems likely that the Tolistobogii were displeased at his intrusion into their area. This is, again, the first time one of the Galatians had contact with the Pergamene king – so far as we know, at least.

The Romans went home with their prize. The priests were no doubt taking the long view, fully appreciating that their gesture gained them friends at both Pergamon and Rome – and this had been Attalos' motive also, and it was no doubt yet more of the active propagandizing which lies behind the story in Livy. A branch of Kybele's temple in the great city of the west was a valuable addition to the priests' own influence. All, except the Tolistobogii, could be pleased with their work, and the Roman delegation will have gained some information about conditions in Asia Minor, while those in Asia Minor began to understand the sheer power being wielded by the republic.

The Tolistobogii had included Pessinos in their territory when they settled in their new homeland, and it counted as the main urban centre for the Tolistobogii in their early years, but they do not appear in the story of the black stone; later, however, there is strong evidence of Galatian influence in the temple administration. The temple was thus in all likelihood not a completely independent entity; it was geographically within the region called Galatia, and Galatians were actively involved in it. The absence of any reference to these Galatian in Livy's account was thus presumably the result of their absence from his source; it would be most likely that this source, given the manifestly pro-Attalid cast of the story, was Attalos and his propaganda. The Romans had sent the delegation as a result of an interpretation of one of the Sibylline Books which claimed that moving the stone of the Magna Mater to Rome would bring victory over Hannibal. It was more a tribute to Roman anxiety and superstition than anything else – though Hannibal did evacuate his forces from Italy in the next year.

Antiochos returned to work in Asia Minor in the 190s, after his victory in Syria in the latest Ptolemaic war (the 'Fifth Syrian War'), to enforce his control in the neglected areas. The war had allowed him to mop up the Ptolemaic coastal cities in Asia Minor taken by Ptolemy III fifty years before, in a leisurely but careful double naval and military campaign during 197. A naval expedition from Syria sailed round to the Aegean to Ephesos, collecting the surrenders of cities, and an army marched from Syria to Sardis. And still the Galatian states remained neutral, though now heavily overshadowed by the enclosing power of Antiochos. On the other hand, Antiochos went on to repeat his grandfather's expedition into Thrace in a series of campaigns beginning in 196 which confirmed his authority there; he clearly had no fear of being attacked while away, in the 190s any more than earlier.[16]

Antiochos' success was resented in some of the cities he claimed. At Lampsakos on the Hellespont, for instance, a complaint went to Rome over Antiochos' threat to its independence. (This is in the very area where Attalos, Prusias, and the Aigosages had contested for power earlier; before then it had been under Ptolemaic influence, now Seleukid.) The city took advantage of contacts with the Asian Galatians and through them with the Gauls in Gaul, by sending their envoy, Hegesias, to Massalia. There he contacted the local Gallic tribe, which gave him a letter to be delivered to the Tolistobogii; the exact relationship of the two groups of Kelts and how this will have helped this city is not known, but Hegesias and the city seem to have felt it was helpful. Perhaps the Kelts in Gaul were one of the parent tribes of the Asians, but the episode argues for continuing contacts between the Kelts in East and West. The connection between Lampsakos and Massalia was similarly indirect: both cities were colonies of Phokaia several centuries earlier. From Massalia Hegesias contacted that city's ally Rome, voicing his complaints.[17] He could point to support at home from one Galatian state, and perhaps Attalos.

It was an opportune moment, for Rome was beginning to become seriously worried by the growth of Antiochos' power. The Thracian expedition had shifted Antiochos' power decisively westwards into Europe; his territory probably now bordered on that of Macedon, with whom Rome had just fought a difficult war and which was hardly a Roman friend. Antiochos claimed to be the heir of the conquests and claims of his ancestor Seleukos I and his grandfather Antiochos II, and when these claims were examined they included Macedon. In addition, the Antigonid and Seleukid kings had frequently intermarried and had stood together more than once against Ptolemaic power. It may be also that Antiochos had contacted the Scordiscian state in the Balkans, which was in turn in contact with the Italian Gauls in northern Italy, another recent Roman enemy and in a restless subject area. Antiochos generally, having defeated Ptolemaic Egypt and greatly increased his territories and his naval power, appeared to some Romans to be becoming too menacingly powerful. Complaints of oppression by Antiochos of supposedly free cities, such as Lampsakos, were very much grist to the mill of the Roman anti-Antiochene policy as it was developing.

Also it may be noted that the Keltic diaspora which stretched from Gaul to Asia were apparently in contact with each other and with the original Keltic homeland, just as had been the case back in the days of the first invasions of Asia, and just as the Greek cities and their colonial offshoots were.

In Thrace Antiochos came into contact with a Galatian people, from whom he recruited some troops.[18] He also contacted the cities along the coast of the Sea of Marmara and the Black Sea from Lysimacheia in the Chersonese to Odessos and Kallatis on the Black Sea, establishing his suzerainty over them, and supplying political and economic support. These included the cities recently freed from the Tylis kingdom's oppressions. It would seem that, as suspected in the case of Attalos I's Aigosages, and those hired by Antiochos, there were still Galatian warbands based in Thrace two decades after the end of the Tylis kingdom – or perhaps they were survivors of that kingdom's destruction. Alternatively the Galatians he recruited came from the Scordisci state, and action which will certainly have alerted Rome to his political range of action, and which will have certainly been interpreted as a menace.[19]

The result of the mission of Hegesias to Gaul was a letter of recommendation to the Tolistobogii in Asia. This is the first indication for forty years that the Asian Galatians were being drawn into wider affairs. For that proved they had been the most peaceable of Asian states.

More important in the wider scheme of things, this was a straw in the wind which would within a few years bring Antiochos into a disastrous war with Rome, and the Galatians in Asia likewise, but separately. This was Antiochos' doing; there is no real indication that Rome wanted a war, though it was certainly becoming apprehensive about his power, but Antiochos intervened in Greece in 192 to overthrow the political settlement which Rome had imposed at the end of its latest Macedonian War (in 196). In retaliation Rome took the part of the three cities on the Asian coast, including Lampsakos, which had objected vocally to being under Antiochos' authority.

For the decisive campaign Antiochos brought up an army which was much smaller than he was able to produce for his wars against Ptolemy; why he so limited his force is difficult to understand; it may have been that he underestimated Rome's military, or that the conflict was taking place on the very far western border of his empire, or that he feared a renewed war with Ptolemy behind his back, though it may actually have been simple over-confidence. But he did reinforce his own army with 5500 Galatian mercenaries,[20] recruited presumably from the Asian Galatians, though there is no evidence for their origin and some may have been those he had recruited while in Thrace or from the Scordisci. The cavalry Livy describes as 'Gallo-Greek', which means Asian Galatians; the infantry therefore may have been recruited in Thrace. (Gauls from Italy, who were being conquered by Rome at the time, would no doubt have been willing to serve.) In the crisis of the Roman invasion of Asia, the Galatian states took Antiochos' side, as did Galatia's eastern neighbour King Ariarathes IV of Kappadokia. No doubt the Asian Galatians knew perfectly well Roman attitudes to Gauls, and that this would surely transfer into a similar dislike of Galatians. There was one Galatian exception, a chief called Eposognatos, who was probably of the Tolistobogii tribe.[21] His motive seems to have been to secure some sort of authority for himself over the tribe, using Roman help; in the event the ploy failed.

The assumption of Roman enmity was a self-fulfilling prophecy. The participation of the Galatians, either as mercenaries, or more likely officially as a state ally of Antiochos, certainly earned them the enmity of the Roman commander, the consul Cn. Manlius Vulso, who took over the legions in Asia after the defeat of Antiochos' army at Magnesia. It seems probable, though Livy does not specifically state it, that the Gallo-Greek cavalry were an official force sent out by the Galatian states. There is some doubt because Livy does state clearly that the Kappadokian contingent had been sent by the king, and he seems to make that a contrast. Maybe the Gallo-Greeks were partly mercenary.

This was, in a sense, a personal expedition by Vulso, for he does not seem to have had any official authorization for it from Rome; on the other hand, a Galatian force had taken part in the war on Antiochos' side, so they were Roman enemies. Vulso had arrived in Asia after the main fighting was over, and was therefore faced by a long wait in idleness while the peace agreement was discussed and ratified by the Roman Senate. Inactivity was anathema where glory and riches were possible. He persuaded the soldiers to accept the new campaign, no doubt after a preliminary campaign of persuasion amongst the officers. He held out the prospect of loot, and the traditional enmity of Rome for the wild Kelts was emphasized. Whatever doubts there may have been as to the official nature of the Galatians was ignored. The soldiers cheered him.[22]

The approach to Galatia was not easy, since the truce with Antiochos prohibited the Roman army from operating in some areas, and the king's son Seleukos was watching carefully to detect any breach of the truce terms. They did, however, allow the army to march through other regions which had been neutral, or were Seleukid enemies. On the road Vulso extracted sums of money from a variety of cities, money clearly needed to purchase supplies for his forces; these contributions are classified as 'bribes' in the historians' accounts, and the Roman army's march must have seemed rather more like a campaign of extortion to the victims, the sort of predatory march traditionally attributed to Galatians, though the alternative might have been to sack the city.[23]

The Galatians themselves became Vulso's victims in part because they had not been included in the truce between Rome and Antiochos, which was negotiated after the Battle of Magnesia. Why they (and the Kappadokians) were excluded we do not know. It may have been forgetfulness by Antiochos, though this is hardly likely; Vulso in his speech to the soldiers had pointed out that they had supplied 'auxiliaries' to Antiochos, and he claimed that the Galatians had been the king's ally.

Vulso appears therefore to have interpreted the Galatians in Antiochos' force as troops supplied by the Galatian states, and so the Galatians were king's allies, which was surely correct. (Kappadokia was also omitted from the truce; it seems unlikely that Antiochos should have deliberately ignored their participation on his side; it was thus presumably at Roman insistence that these were omitted, as allies of the king, no doubt this was done with a view to later extortion – Ariarathes was judged to owe 600 talents, though this was reduced later to 300.)

The campaign of Vulso sheds some light on the Galatian political system. It seems clear that the chief Eposognatos spoke for nobody but himself and his immediate entourage, which will make him the chief of only a section of the Tolistobogii. He contacted Vulso with a plan, but could not carry it out. He is said to have been in contact earlier with Eumenes II, the new king of Pergamon (a Roman ally). Eposognatos was seeking to profit in the peace, and had refused to help Antiochos, but he was the only chieftain to take that attitude.[24] This makes it clear that the rest of the Galatians were unwilling to join with Eumenes or with Rome, and that they maintained the alliance with Antiochos. When the alliance had been agreed is not known, but there had been numerous occasions when negotiations could have happened during the previous thirty years, and being Antiochos' ally can explain the long peace of Galatia over that time.

Whatever agreement existed between the Galatian states and the Attalid kingdom had expired when Attalos I died in 197, so what Livy was reporting was a refusal by the Galatian state to agree to a new treaty when Eumenes II became king. This may have been in part due to a Galatian pursuit of neutrality during the previous decades, but more likely it was because they had concluded a treaty with Antiochos earlier, perhaps in 216, when he moved directly against Attalos. In the circumstances this would preclude them agreeing one with Eumenes, since the two kings were at enmity. The Roman attack was resented by all three Galatian states, so probably all three had been allies of Antiochos.

Eposognatos claimed to be able to keep the Tolistobogii out of the war with Vulso, though he was wholly unsuccessful; he presumably approached that particular tribe because he was a member of it, but the result also means that the Galatian states as a whole were anti-Roman. He reported to Vulso that they were preparing to resist the Roman invasion of their lands. The fact that Eposognatos could contemplate such a scheme suggests again the looseness of the independent Galatian states, in which it was possible for a single chieftain to act on his own, and with some plausibility to claim that it was possible to detach one of the three tribes from the communal resolve. This of course implies that the states could act independently – though, of course, he actually failed to persuade the Tolistobogii to do so – which in turn implies an earlier discussion and decision that the three states would act together. The annual Council meeting would have been the place for such discussions.

On the other hand, there seems to have been something of a disagreement between the chiefs of the three tribes over the defensive strategy. The Tektosages, under the command of a chief called Komboiomaros, occupied Mount Magaba, ten miles to the east of Ankyra; the Tolistobogii (commander Ortiagon) and the Trokmoi (commander Gaulotos) occupied a mountain to the west of Ankyra, which Livy calls Mount Olympos. To both places they had removed their families and their goods for refuge. It is notable that the Tektosages stood out from the rest, as they had done at the time of settlement, and as they had been late in joining the crossing to Asia. Note that the Tolistobogii removed themselves from their own lands in order to join with the Trokmoi, and that both strongholds were in the Tektosages territory. Note also the failure of all the Galatian states to defend any of their towns. Whatever differences the three tribes had in earlier cases of foreign policy, they were cooperating on this occasion.

Their disagreements on strategy were thus not that serious, for the Trokmoi entrusted their families to the Tektosages, while some of their warriors joined the Tolistobogii.[25] The three were obviously allied. This, in fact, might have been a disagreement, but it could also have been a generally agreed plan of defence. The idea was that the Roman forces would find it difficult to assault the mountainous positions, which were well prepared with fortifications and supplies. The Galatian force occupied the higher parts, and in a siege the Romans might run out of supplies before the Galatians did.

It may be noted that, despite the Galatians' supposed reputation for raiding and informal warfare, they were acting in a rational and disciplined manner, with a clear military plan in mind, and their forces remained under the commanders' control all the time. Consultations beforehand had clearly taken place. The one omission, as Livy noted, was that they relied almost entirely on a passive defence, and had not equipped themselves with missile weapons, which Vulso had in large quantities – consisting, Livy explains, of javelins, skirmishers' spears, arrows, and balls and sling stones.[26]

On the other hand, the Galatians fielded a powerful cavalry force – no doubt survivors in many cases of the Battle of Magnesia – whose role should have been to harass the Roman besiegers. It made a first contact at the Roman camp called Caballum, where Vulso occupied an existing 'Galatian stronghold' – presumably an *oppidum*. He was not expecting an attack, and the 'advanced guards', outside the Roman camp, were driven back by the Galatian charge. From inside the camp the Roman cavalry came out and drove the Galatians away, supposedly in disorder. This would seem to have been a Galatian reconnaissance, partly to locate the Roman force, and partly to see if they were alert. The Roman cavalry was fairly small in numbers, as usual – there had been 3000 at Magnesia – and if it was able to drive the Galatians away easily, so therefore the Galatian force involved was also small. Livy's account is very obviously doctored to imply a Roman victory, and disguises Vulso's discomfiture and lack of ability.

The Roman forces were encouraged by the prayers of a squad of *galli*, from the Kybele temple at Pessinos, who were reprising their generosity over the holy black stone several years before. And yet the Roman soldiers were perhaps surprised by the complete absence of the inhabitants at Gordion as the army moved steadily forward. They had evacuated the town; the Roman soldiers sacked it nevertheless; the town, which had developed peacefully as a normal Hellenistic town over the last century and a half (since Alexander's visit), was not reoccupied for the next century. The Roman forces were joined by Attalos, the younger brother of King Eumenes, who brought with him 400 Pergamene cavalry to reinforce the defeated Roman horse, and the whole force camped in front of Mount Olympos. Vulso's first reconnaissance of the enemy's position, protected only by his cavalry force, was interrupted by a sortie of the Galatian cavalry, who were twice the number of his guard; the Galatians trounced the Roman/Attalid force, and drove them and Vulso helter-skelter back to the camp. Three days later a new reconnaissance was undertaken, this time with the whole Roman force as Vulso's guard. A feasible approach route towards the Galatian camp on the mountain was located, and preparations were made for the assault; the Galatians replied at once by posting an advanced force of their own to block the route of approach.

The Roman army had been fighting virtually continuously for the previous thirty years, and this army had recently won a major battle. It was a mixed force of legionaries, light-armed auxiliaries, and cavalry, so capturing a mountain stronghold constituted no real difficulty and was well within its collective capabilities, requiring little or no command decisions. By contrast, the Galatians' experience of fighting in that time constituted no more than small groups employed as mercenaries by other armies and a force of cavalry at Magnesia; the Galatian states had not been involved in any full-scale fighting between the war with Attalos in the 230s and that in alliance with Antiochos – and had been on the losing side on both occasions; it was not a contest between equally skilled forces.

Vulso picked out his light-armed troops, mainly non-Italian auxiliaries – Thracians and Trallians are named – and with their missile weapons they drove the men of the Galatian advanced force, minus their casualties, back into the main camp. The legionaries, the heavy infantry, came along behind the lights, climbing the mountain side more slowly after them, and they all took a rest in front of the Galatian camp. The Galatians came out from their camp for the fight, forming up before the rampart and the gates, but were driven back into the camp once again by the Roman light forces and their missiles, and these then bombarded the camp interior. The legionaries at last came forward to the assault, but the Galatians broke before the threat could be really launched, and fled out of the camp. Many died by falling over cliffs in getting down the mountain, or were picked off by the Roman and Attalid cavalry which had been left in the lower land.[27] Large numbers were taken prisoner, to be sold as slaves later.

Casualties on the Roman side were not recorded, but were certainly few, since the troops had mainly fought at a distance from the enemy – perhaps there were more among the cavalry than the infantry; it is noticeable that Vulso used allied forces rather than Roman citizens in the front line. The Galatians are said to have suffered 40,000 dead or captured, but even Livy, normally credulous over numbers, is sceptical of such a figure. The loot was very satisfying; Vulso restrained the men under his direct command and directed them to pursue the fleeing enemy, but a detachment arrived later and collected much of the booty from the Galatians' camp.

Vulso moved the army forward to Ankyra. Negotiations began with the Tektosages on Mount Magaba, but failed to bring a peace agreement, and in the process of making contact Vulso nearly fell into an ambush; his cavalry escort was again scattered and driven back.[28] The Galatians – Tektosages and Trokmoi, so Livy says, though he had earlier claimed that the Trokmoi warriors had gone to join the Tolistobogii – left their camp on Mount Magaba, since it was now clear that a mountain defence meant defeat, and formed a battle line (50,000 strong, so Livy says, presumably getting his figures from Vulso's report). Contingents of Kappadokians under King Ariarathes and Paphlagonians under King Morzius were present; the Galatian cavalry was placed on the flank, but was being used as infantry.[29] Vulso used the same tactics as before. The Galatian line was bombarded by missiles from the lights, and this so disordered the line that the whole broke up. It was not necessary to launch the legions into the attack, as before.[30]

It is evident that Galatian warfare was not of the type which required close hand-to-hand fighting, but was perhaps more of the gesturing and informal type, perhaps with champions fighting in front of the main line; probably the infantry was effectively untrained, conscripted peasants, and the cavalry was no doubt formed from the aristocracy. Many of those fleeing the field discarded their weapons, or perhaps never had any. Galatian military tactics were thus in effect non-existent, as they did not get an opportunity to make a great charge. Their excellent cavalry was dismounted and placed as infantry on one flank, a waste of a most useful force, which could well have broken into the legionary squares if it had taken them in flank – it had happened to a legion at the Battle of Magnesia.

The overall, long-term strategy of the Galatians, on the other hand, had nearly worked. After the second battle – at Mount Magaba – when the Galatian envoys asked for peace, Vulso demanded they meet him in Ephesos to receive his terms, since winter on the high plateau was approaching. Had the fighting, or the stand-off, lasted much longer, the Roman forces might have been trapped by the winter snows, so prefiguring what actually happened to Corbulo's forces two and a half centuries later.

Vulso had been careful at the first battle to make a serious attempt to secure the booty from the Galatian camp, but failed; he was more successful in the second battle, since no fighting took place at the Galatians' base. They had apparently gathered much of their treasure together into the camp, and Vulso greedily examined it. Livy claims, perhaps eventually from the words of the boastful Vulso, that it amounted to all the loot gathered by the Galatians in their raids, but Livy does not know a great deal about the Galatians, nor it seems did his main source, Polybios. His description of the booty simply claims it had been gathered over 'many years'.[31]

The Galatians had displayed staggeringly inept military tactics in the fighting against Vulso's army. Any group which had experience at raiding, which was necessarily a process demanding forethought, care, and a grasp of tactics, would never have allowed themselves to be locked up, separately, on a couple of mountains, when they had an effective cavalry arm, some of which were dismounted for the last battle – or to fail to supply themselves with the most obvious weapons; if they fought from behind ramparts, missile weapons, such as the Romans used, were the most obvious weapons of defence.[32] It all is further evidence that the Galatian states had been peaceable and had renounced raiding.

In the event the peace treaty was delayed and was finally made at a meeting at Lampsakos, while Vulso, having discussed the matter with King Eumenes, was on his way back to Rome. This took place, therefore, after the wider peace settlement imposed at the meeting at Apameia which dealt with all Asia Minor except the Galatians, and was a separate agreement from it. The terms were actually a treaty between Eumenes and the chiefs of the 'Gauls', and consisted simply of an agreement to keep the peace.[33] They included a curious clause that the Galatians should cease 'wandering about with arms', which is usually taken to mean that they should stop raiding, though it is hardly a good description of such mercenaries, but since they had not indulged in raiding for decades, it may actually have been an attempt to prevent them enlisting as mercenaries – a misunderstanding of recent history in Asia by the Romans seems also likely. It would seem to have been the practice, therefore, of the men seeking employment, to move from one potential employer to the next. Such a prohibition is unlikely to have succeeded, and the Romans will have made no attempt to enforce such terms.

The Roman involvement in the treaty was perfunctory at best; one has the impression that Vulso was primarily interested in the booty he could acquire. As a peace treaty it was careless and without effect. By the treaty Eumenes' relations with Galatia were restored to the position which had obtained under Attalos I until 197. Eumenes, having acquired the former Seleukid lands in Asia Minor, succeeded to the position of Antiochos Hierax, Akhaios, and Antiochos III – and his predecessor's (Attalos I) brief conquest in the 220s. After all this repeated change of rule it is not surprising to find that the Roman *diktat* at the peace treaty was disputed with vigour by all those except the Attalid king. It was a recipe for repeated warfare.

Chapter 9

Collapse and Recovery

The Roman Senate may have dictated the terms of the Treaty of Apameia, and Cn. Manlius Vulso may have arranged the peace treaty between King Eumenes and the Galatian states, but the Roman enforcers had then gone back to Italy and their triumphs. The Asia Minor states were left to themselves to settle down in the new conditions and exploit them. Most states were unhappy about the situation and within a few years they were busy going to war or intriguing to rearrange matters. It was the same reaction as in Greece a little earlier: the Romans having left the local states and removed themselves took it for granted that the others would stay away – as Antiochos had failed to do, to his later regret. In Greece the Romans quickly returned; in Asia, further away and without any power of any real consequence, it was local states who set about rearranging matters; the Roman reply was merely the occasional visit of a senatorial delegation, often ineffectively attempting to exercise some control.

The separate agreement between Eumenes and the Galatians did not involve the Galatian state in more than observing peace with the king. No territory was taken from the Galatians, though Eumenes received the reversion of Antiochos' lost Asia Minor lands, defined as Hellespontine Phrygia (the area through which Attalos I and the Aigosages had campaigned thirty years before), Greater Phrygia and Phrygia Epiktetos, which were Galatia's neighbours to the west, various territories to the south of Phrygia, and Lykaonia, south of Galatia.[1] This took the Pergamene boundary once again to the Taurus Mountains and along the southern border of Kappadokia, and it made Eumenes' kingdom the western and southern neighbour of the Galatian states, a reversion to the extended kingdom briefly gained by Attalos I in the 220s. To the east and south of Galatia there was Kappadokia, whose King Ariarathes had paid talents to the Romans in the peace treaty, but by marrying his sister to

King Eumenes he had possibly transformed their enmity into friendship, though a marriage 'alliance' was a poor basis for political decisions. To the north of Galatia there was Paphlagonia, whose King Morzeos of Gangra was a Galatian friend, and Pontos, along the Black Sea coast, an energetic power for the moment.

The peace agreed between Eumenes and the Galatian states at the behest of Manlius Vulso is nowhere detailed, other than in a very brief summary.[2] It must be assumed that an agreement was reached, but Vulso did not wait to enforce its terms or oversee it, being in a hurry to reach Italy, and it is unclear if Rome was a party to the treaty. Since the Asian states went to war with each other only two years later, it seems reasonable to suppose that the terms as agreed formed little more than a truce, neither being at all satisfied with them. The terms imposed on other states in Asia in the Apameia treaty were also a source of annoyance to them and their neighbours, and Bithynia, the Galatians, and Pontos were all uneasy at the growth of Pergamene power, as were its weaker neighbours, and Rhodes. No doubt this was, in part, the Roman intention.

The repercussions of military defeat in the Galatian states were severe, over and beyond the casualties suffered and the prisoners taken away. The practice of the tribal authorities of carrying their treasure with them on the campaign had resulted in much of it being seized by the Romans, either looted by the Romans or confiscated by Vulso. In addition, it may be assumed that looting and destruction had taken place everywhere within reach of the Roman army during its advance, certainly in Gordion. Vulso had succeeded in keeping control of most of his troops on the early part of the approach march, largely because he was able to extract fines and tribute and subsidies ('bribes') from a succession of cities, out of which he could buy supplies and pay the soldiers' wages, but in Galatian territory he could loose his soldiers to go off to fend and forage for themselves. The army camped at Gordion, whence the inhabitants had fled before their arrival. The town had been the major market centre, and it had been left stocked with goods:[3] no doubt these had all been stolen, consumed, or destroyed by the time the Roman army moved out. Archaeological investigation suggests that the town suffered destruction as well as a sack.

The confiscation and seizure of the public treasures drastically reduced the resources of the Galatian states, but also reduced the authority of the tribal chieftains. It is probable that their authority in part depended on their ancestry, and on their native ability, but in order to gather a loyal following, it would be necessary for each chieftain to be generous with supplies and gifts. Only if by doing so he could hold on to his clients.[4] In social terms one may see, on the social summit, a small group of aristocrats, the 'chiefs', together with a wider set of their clients; these will have formed the landowners, and will have composed the cavalry in wartime; this force numbered 10,000 at Mount Magaba. The rest of the population were the peasantry, paying taxes in kind and accepting protection and receiving justice in exchange. These will have been the infantry at the battles, where they were clearly untrained, probably badly armed, if at all, and were all too willing to leave the battle line at the earliest opportunity. These were the main casualties, who were killed in the Roman pursuits, or captured to be sold as slaves. The wealthier men could probably ransom themselves. The loss of the public treasure and the extensive looting of private possessions after the lost battles therefore drastically impoverished both the tribal authorities and the individual lords, and this will have reduced their political authority as well. It amounted to the partial and temporary destruction of the political system as it had existed since the Galatian settlement in the 270s. Galatian society entered into a prolonged period of crisis from which it emerged much changed.

The first political result was the emergence of a single man of power. A shattering defeat is exactly the sort of occasion when this could take place, as the defeated rallied round a man of authority. The man was Ortiagon, who had been the leader of the Tolistobogii in the battle at Mount Olympos, a man already widely admired, and acknowledged as a notable warrior. Eposognatos may have aspired to the same position in the same tribe, but his pro-Roman policy had been unacceptable to other lords; after the defeats, this would be still less acceptable. Polybios provides a favourable portrait of Ortiagon (and another of his formidable wife), but this is only a partial view, from the point of view of a civilized and intelligent Greek. Within Galatia his achievement was to rally the remaining men of authority, presumably to exercise a powerful influence, and to implement some sort of coherent and no doubt careful foreign policy.[5]

The events of the Roman invasion and the defeats cast light on the Galatians' political system. The three states which had operated independently since the time of their settlement had, of course, also been linked by their common origins, and by the existence of the Council, which had some limited authority over all three. In the course of the Roman attack it was clear to all that, no matter how independent they had been, and had acted, the Romans and perhaps the Attalids and the Seleukids saw them simply as 'Galatians'. Vulso attacked them all, paying no heed to the separate states as political entities, and all had suffered indiscriminately from Roman savagery. The reduction in wealth and in the numbers of the male population was drastic; the military performance had been lamentable, even ludicrous. The loss of prestige of the aristocracy would take years to recover.

The emergence of Ortiagon as a single dominating man with some sort of state-wide authority apparently covering all three states implies the collapse of the existing governmental systems. There had been no place for single authority figures since the leaders of the original tribes in their crossing from Europe. The impact of war and the military defeats had in effect also nullified whatever treaty had been agreed by the Galatian lords with Eumenes before the crisis. This may explain the vague nature of the agreement, and the evident difficulty Vulso and Eumenes had in producing it – for who on the Galatian side could make an agreement which would stick? It is quite possible that Ortiagon had, perhaps ostentatiously, avoided participation in the peace process, such as it was; ratification, presumably something which should have been done by the several states individually, probably never took place in any meaningful way. Ortiagon's emergence as a leader and a rallying figure after the defeat and the humiliating peace, presupposes a loss of authority by the states. The casualties in the battles will have fallen heaviest on the aristocracy, whose task it was to stand in the front of the battle line; it is quite likely that many tetrarchs and chiefs had died, and governmental confusion will have followed.

The most aggrieved of the Pergamene enemies was King Prusias of Bithynia. He had been stripped of some Phrygian territory for Eumenes' benefit, but had failed to hand over all of it. Eumenes set about a campaign which was ostensibly designed to take over the disputed land, but his preparations and activities were so elaborate that rather more than a mere occupation of disputed territory was probably intended. He mobilized both his fleet and his army, took the fleet himself through into the Propontis, and his brother Attalos meanwhile took the army to take over the disputed land. Prusias had made himself disliked already by seizing the small cities of Kieros and Teion on the Black Sea coast from Herakleia Pontike, but Herakleia was itself unpopular for its general aggressiveness. In the face of Pergamon's attack, Prusias was able to gather support from his brother-in-law Philip V of Macedon (who himself was busy in a revisionist campaign in Thessaly) and from Ortiagon in Galatia. But the allies lost.[6] An inscription from Pergamon recorded Eumenes' military success, particularly a victory by Attalos at Mount Lypedron in Phrygia, and another, from Telmessos in the south, lists Pergamon's enemies as Prusias and Ortiagon, and adds 'and their allies', which means that several other rulers or cities – not necessarily large – were involved in the anti-Attalid coalition.[7]

Ortiagon therefore was able to bring a Galatian contingent into the war, one which was sufficiently large to allow him to be counted as an independent ally of Prusias, though he also shared in the general defeat, and the Telmessos inscription refers to his death. He is described by Polybios as being ambitious to rule all Galatia. This may well have been his ambition, but realizing it would be difficult. He had emerged as a war commander of the Tektosages in 189, and so had participated in their defeat by the Romans. He was prominent in the next years, and commanded the 'Galatian' contingents in the war with Eumenes. Once again the references are to 'Galatians'; it is evident that the internal arrangements in Galatia were either unknown to the rest of Asia Minor or something regarded as not worth knowing. We are not entitled to assume that Ortiagon was more than a war commander both against the Romans and against Eumenes. On the other hand, he was clearly a very prominent figure, and he may well have had ambitions. But the second defeat cannot have increased his support or prestige. His death followed and this ended his intentions; he had no political successor. His son was prominent later.

In 183 the new king of Pontos, Pharnakes I, seized control of the city of Sinope.[8] This was annoying, but it provoked no decisive response for the moment. Pharnakes apparently took this absence of a reaction as an encouragement for his wider ambitions. He made contact with at least two Galatian chieftains, Kassignatos and Gaizatorix.[9] The latter was of the Tektosages, though Kassignatos' tribe is not known; it is clear, however, that they could act on their own authority and without restraint by any higher authority. Kassignatos for one had a fairly lengthy career of command. Gaizatorix may have ruled a small region of Paphlagonia, perhaps an indication of the elasticity of Galatia's borders, or perhaps of the expansionism of these lords.[10] But the main point is that they could act independently, and were able to bring some military support to an alliance.

A dispute between Kings Pharnakes and Eumenes then boiled up into open war when Pharnakes sent one of his commanders into Galatia, ravaging the land. The Pergamene army marched against the Pontian, as far as the Halys River; this brought Kassignatos and Gaizatorix to offer to change sides, an offer which was rejected.[11] The war ended with Pharnakes' defeat, and one item in the peace treaty was that he cease intriguing in Galatia, which was thus clearly under Pergamene protection. The rejection of help from the two Galatian chiefs was also a rejection of Galatian independence; Eumenes had no wish to be beholden to any of those under his 'protection'.

The weakness and divisions of the Galatians are obvious from these events. Their central position in Asia Minor, however, made the country important, hence it was the prize for which Pharnakes and Eumenes were fighting. And yet no Galatian was involved in the discussion of the peace terms, nor probably in any preliminary discussions. Eumenes forced Pharnakes to retire, and extracted from him a substantial indemnity as compensation for costs and damages – but none of this, it seems, went to Galatia, which had probably suffered most from the fighting. Hostages and prisoners – who may well have been in part Galatian – were to be restored. The effect was to make all Galatia into an Attalid protectorate.

This was the nadir of Galatian fortune and power. Devastated by the Romans and by Pharnakes' invasion, chieftains such as Kassignatos and Gaizatorix, were divided and probably discredited after their conduct, and, an attempt at a near-kingship, or perhaps a tyranny, by Ortiagon having failed, the occupation and protection by an ancient enemy had brought the country to its lowest condition so far.

Eumenes used his domination of Galatia in part to recruit soldiers from the Galatian warrior class, which was always a useful way to defuse political opposition, though he probably did not do so until he was once again at war, and so needed the extra troops. His choice was always cavalry, that is, men from the Galatian aristocracy, the leaders of the society. He became involved in the third war of Rome against Macedon (171–167), and took part of his army to Europe. At one point he had a regiment of 1000 Galatian horse with him, commanded by Kassignatos,[12] while others were on board Attalid ships in the naval defeat of Chios.[13] One reason for recruiting such troops must have been to remove them from Galatia, since by the time of the war it must have been clear to Eumenes that the Pergamene domination was proving increasingly irksome to the Galatians. Sure enough, in 168, while Eumenes was in Thessaly supporting the Roman forces against Perseus of Macedon, a major rebellion against Pergamene authority began in Galatia. This compelled Eumenes to return home from the war in Greece, taking his Galatian cavalry with him, despite being requested to leave it in Europe to serve with the Roman forces – which was a considerable compliment to its quality.[14]

Eumenes appealed more than once to Rome for help in facing this Galatian uprising, a welcome indication of its seriousness and of the revived Galatian strength. Eumenes was defeated in one encounter and had to retreat, carried in a litter because he was ill. It would seem that he had been over-confident, a mistake he did not repeat, and on this occasion he escaped his pursuers by a simple ruse.[15] He sent his brother Attalos to Rome first, and later he went himself, but, in a notorious display of Roman ingratitude and political embarrassment, he was turned away by an invented law which was supposed to prevent Rome from accepting visits by any kings. The Senate did send a legate, P. Licinius, supposedly to mediate (which was hardly what Eumenes wanted) but he was less than successful in his negotiations with the Galatian commander Solovettios. As a result the Galatians, having thus defied Roman authority, were certainly encouraged still more in their defiance of Eumenes.[16]

Both sides retired to their homelands for the winter of 167/166. Eumenes was still ill, not for the first time in the midst of a war, but he organized a new muster of his own forces now that it had become clear that no help was to be had from Rome. He recruited extra mercenaries, possibly also receiving help from Ariarathes of Kappadokia, who may well have felt he was menaced by an independent Galatia, and from the Seleukid king Antiochos IV, whose reign marked a brief moment of Seleukid-Attalid friendship.[17] It is not known what became of the cavalry force he brought back from Europe.

In the spring of 166 the Galatian forces again moved out of their territory into Attalid Phrygia, camping at Synnada, where Licinius had met them the year before. Eumenes brought his army from Sardis, where it had mustered, to Apameia Kelainai. All this rather suggests that the Galatians, essentially on the offensive in the face of Eumenes' greater strength and potential, were aiming to campaign into the southern part of the Pergamene territories, possibly hoping for local support in some of the lands which had been transferred to Eumenes in the Apameia treaty. Eumenes advanced his army, however, and met and defeated the Galatians not far from Synnada.[18]

It is evident in all this that the Galatians had made a considerable recovery from their distraught condition in 179, when the whole territory was down and out. They had been able to muster a big enough army to face and defeat the Pergamene army at least once, and Eumenes' victory in the final battle was not decisive. He had been compelled to recruit a large mercenary force to achieve that victory, at great expense, and the Galatians had apparently succeeded in taking the fighting into Eumenes' territory. When the Roman Senate finally laid down the terms of peace, they did so by, in effect, repeating the terms of Manlius Vulso's treaty of 188, which declared that the Galatians should be autonomous, that Eumenes should not interfere in its affairs (a repeat of the condition Eumenes had imposed upon Pharnakes), and the Galatians should not raid beyond their borders.[19]

The Galatians were able to send an embassy to Rome during 166 to lay their complaints before the Senate, whose reply was simply to repeat the terms of peace. One wonders if this embassy had been one of the suggestions made to Solovettios by Licinius in their meeting – a meeting for which no first-hand evidence was available from either Livy or Polybios. Until then, of course, the Attalid version of affairs, despite the prohibition of Eumenes visiting Rome, had been the only one being presented to the Senate, and it was always Attalid practice to distort and propagandize. So being able to speak up for the Galatians and so achieve a public recognition of their autonomy by the Senate was worth an embassy. The absence of any serious reference to it in the major historians is perhaps a reflection of their heavy, and perhaps unhealthy, dependence on Attalid sources for Asian affairs.

Eumenes celebrated the battle as a victory and broadcast this interpretation throughout Asia and beyond. It was celebrated by his Greek audience and by his government. The range of relieved communities stretched from the Ionian league on the Aegean coast to the community of Amlada near the Taurus, which may be attributed to scare stories put out by the Attalids in their chosen role as defenders of Hellenic civilization.[20] This is, however, not necessarily to accept Eumenes' claim that it was an important victory, or that these relieved places were damaged or even threatened in the war, and all of them seem in some way dependent upon the Attalids.[21] The Roman embassy and the Senate's decision were not in fact an end to the war, and the celebrations in the Greek cities were perhaps as much due to the diversion of the Galatian invasion away from them as it was for the result of Eumenes' battle. If the Galatians were able to send an embassy to Rome in 166 or 165 they were still in a condition of effective independence and military defiance. Eumenes failed to restore his earlier domination of Galatia – that is, the Galatians by their combination of military aggressiveness and diplomacy, succeeded to some extent in their rebellion, though the defeat allowed Eumenes to continue his occupation and 'protection' of Galatia. Resentment at this also continued.

There was a story that the Galatians' general – presumably Solovettios – after a victory murdered his prisoners, sacrificing some and massacring the rest.[22] How correct and accurate this account was cannot be known. On the one hand, human sacrifice does appear to have taken place, according to evidence found at Gordion; on the other, it is quite possible that it was an invention or perhaps an exaggeration, an example of Attalid propaganda designed to influence both the Greek cities who were supposedly protected by Eumenes and his victory, or the Romans, with their ancient and continuing fear of Gauls of all sorts. Roman conduct in Greece in the Macedonian War (and their treatment of Perseus as a prisoner) was just as bad as anything the Galatians might have done, with the result that such stories probably lost much of their shock effect. It is related only in Diodoros, two centuries later, and may have not actually happened. If it did, it was no worse than the Roman conduct after the victories of Vulso.

The Galatian embassy in Rome had a degree of success, but Rome's alliance with Eumenes was too important to both sides to be seriously jeopardized, and so the terms the Galatians were given were a return to those which had been pronounced by Manlius Vulso in 188: autonomy and a prohibition to cross their borders in arms. This was a rebuff to the Galatians,[23] but, given that their uprising had been the result of Eumenes' domination of their country for the previous dozen years, the terms amounted to the achievement of the Galatians' main aim – a return to autonomy, even if Attalid forces remained in occupation of some parts. The problem of Galatia's overall weakness, however would always mean that the practice of such autonomy would be often at the mercy of its more powerful neighbours, and of their own divisions. The enforcement of the terms, both to restrain the Galatian activities (including, presumably, their service as mercenaries) and to prevent any intrigues and interferences by Eumenes or Pharnakes or Prusias was impossible, except by Galatian insistence. After all, none of the terms of the original peace of 188 had lasted more than a couple of years, and the Attalids had been serial breakers of the terms; there was no reason to believe that this new formulation of the same terms would last any longer.

In the midst of the senatorial discussions over the Galatian war, King Prusias had arrived in Rome, and during his visit he made a request that he should be allowed to take over an area of territory, formerly part of Antiochos III's kingdom, but which was now apparently occupied by the Galatians. The Senate refused, but politely, and did not finally close the door on his request, presumably wishing to keep the option open of rewarding Prusias if it seemed profitable.[24]

One of the results, therefore, of the peace terms of 166, was that the Galatians had moved politically out of Pergamon's shadow and had become independent diplomatic players. The embassy to Rome of 166/165 was followed by others. The Trokmoi were encroaching on Kappadokian territory, and King Ariarathes complained to Rome about it.²⁵ The Galatians 'continued to add to and further secure their liberties', is a curious formulation of Polybios which presumably means asserting their independence.²⁶ Prusias complained that Eumenes was interfering in Galatia contrary to the peace terms, and it seems clear from a set of letters exchanged between Attalid kings and the priests of Kybele at Pessinos that he was correct.²⁷ The Attalid king was therefore once again the main force undermining the peace settlement.

The crisis of the Roman invasion had changed the Galatian governing system of tetrarchs and chiefs, and the emergence of such men as Ortiagon had undermined it still more. Attalid occupation and protection, and the resentment it generated, appears to have had the effect of forcing the Galatians to think in terms of unifying their effort in resistance, and Solovettios seems to have been a war commander for all three states. And yet after the immediate crisis had ended, the three states re-emerged into 'autonomy', though still under Attalid dominance. But the change is clear: the 'autonomy' of the states had given way twice in two decades before the necessity of accepting a unified command. This would, of course, happen again.

Pessinos had been in the territory settled by the Tolistobogii when they arrived, but only just, and the arriving 'barbarians' respected its holiness and autonomy. It was semi-detached from the state, and was also bordered on two sides by Pergamene territory since the awards of the treaty of Apameia. The priest was clearly regarded by the Attalids as a near-independent prince, rather than as a part of the Tolistobogian state, and the Roman delegation in 205 had negotiated directly with the current priest over the transfer of the holy black stone to Rome. Yet when real information about the temple personnel is found, it is clear that the Galatians had established their influence firmly in the temple. Eumenes II and his brother and successor Attalos II corresponded directly with the temple priests. Attis was the main man, which may be a title or an assumed name, and his brother had a Galatian name, Aioiorix.²⁸ It emerges from a much later inscription that half of the priestly college consisted of men with Galatian names.²⁹ This may be assumed to be the result of a deliberate process of accommodation between the temple establishment and the Galatian, and it probably dated from soon after the Galatians' arrival. It is to be noted that all the urban centres in Galatia – there were not many – continued without interruption after the Galatians took over; this sheds a corrective light on the general methods of the Galatians from the start. The efforts of the Attalids were no doubt aimed at securing the temple's allegiance, but the evidence of the earlier encounters suggests that the priests were canny enough to avoid too great an acquiescence.

If this arrangement of half the priestly college being Galatians had operated in 205 on the Roman visit, the lack of reaction from the Galatians at this apparent encroachment into their area of influence can be explained by a Galatian decision not to make a fuss. That is, they were permitting the envoys to negotiate about the removal of the stone, seeing it as merely a private matter between the two. Of course, the Attalid king's letters pretended to a similar influence with the priestly college, but that does not prove that it existed. It has the air, once more, of the Attalid king seizing the chance of boosting their standing with Rome, even if it meant nothing in reality. In 189 the temple supported the Romans in their invasion, but not until the Roman army was well past Pessinos.[30] The priests were thus practiced at fastening their friendship onto the most powerful, first the Galatians, then Pergamon, then for the moment, Rome.

The Galatians' original settlement in what became known as Galatia may well have been seen as a preliminary to expansion, and a couple of items support this notion. The land they acquired was high and dry, cold in winter, and cultivable land was confined to the valleys, where water was available. This effectively dictated pastoral agriculture, sheep herding, which is probably what the native population already did. This pastoralism included the breeding of horses, and this is obviously one of the bases for the predominance of cavalry in the Galatian armies, quite apart from the universal propensity of an aristocracy to ride such beasts. The animals had to be moved, and the society was no doubt always in motion.[31] And more land was always needed. Hence the chieftain Gaizatorix, whose territory of Gangra was actually in Paphlagonia,[32] and the Trokmoi who in the 160s were complained about by King Ariarathes for encroaching into Kappadokian territory.[33] There was also the (unnamed) area which Prusias complained about, an unallocated, formerly Seleukid, territory, but which he claimed had been occupied by Galatians.[34] In the war of 168–166 it is noticeable that the Galatian armies moved out of their home territory into the south-east – the area of Amlada – and to the south-west towards Synnada. This could be attempts to annex new territory, rather than simply a campaign against Eumenes. (This was territory which was included in the Roman province of Galatia a century later.) Long ago, Ramsay pointed out that the Pontic, Bithynian and Pergamene kingdoms were all well organized and defended and alert, but to the south of Galatia the territory was, while technically Pergamene, actually scarcely controlled.[35]

This expansion was clearly undertaken quietly, slowly, and in an unorganized way. None of those who complained were ever able to do much about it other than complain to Rome, for Rome had guaranteed Galatian autonomy. There was clearly no Galatian central authority to whom they could complain or to which Rome could deliver instructions, and probably any complaint given to the tetrarchs of any of the three states would be useless – quite likely the tetrarchs were themselves involved in the Galatians' expansion. The explanation is the result of the concentration on pastoral farming, which, if there was a strong market, might well have been so developed as to leave the pastures worn out, so the search was on for more pasture land.

Amlada (Amblada to the Greeks) was in Lykaonia or Pisidia, a thinly populated region (like Kappadokia), and, as Ramsay pointed out, it was 'distant and defenceless' from the Attalid kingdom, which was so solidly based at the western end of the Asia Minor peninsula.[36] It had taken the opportunity to revolt when a Galatian force was operating in the area during the war of 168–166. From the Galatian viewpoint an expedition in this area might well produce dividends such as Amlada, by slicing off (and annexing) the eastern extension of the Attalid kingdom.

The connection between East and West, between Syria and the Aegean coastal cities, was the old Akhaimenian Royal Road, which had been fortified with cities by Antiochos I and II. The essential strategic point along that road was the city of Antioch in Pisidia, in the midst of the lakes of central Anatolia, with the turbulent and unsubduable Pisidians (such as Amlada) to the south and a range of mountains and then a desert to the north, beyond which was Galatia. And Antioch, which is described by Strabo as 'on a hill',[37] being a Hellenistic city, was walled. It had been colonized by a group from Magnesia, and in the Treaty of Apameia the

Roman Senate had picked it out and made it an autonomous city.[38] As such it neatly separated the Pergamene territories in western Asia Minor from those in the east, that is, in Lykaonia, leaving the latter vulnerable to the Galatian army from the north.

The Pergamene army could certainly reach as far as Lykaonia, as it did in the Pergamene-Pontic War in the 180s, but it seems probable that the Attalid kings paid little attention to their eastern province, outside the cities of the Royal Road, and perhaps tended to ignore even those – they did not control Antioch, for example, unless they had violated yet another of the terms of the Apameia treaty. Galatia and Kappadokia were both keen to expand into that southern area, and eventually it was Kappadokia which gained control of it for a time. The Galatians of the Trokmoi were expanding into Kappadokia itself in the 160s, according to King Ariarathes, and it is unlikely that they failed to take advantage of Pergamene neglect of the distant Lykaonian province. It would not need overt conflict for Galatian infiltration to take place, as flocks of sheep were grazed on both sides of the border, which was almost certainly not demarcated. This was all a very slow and insidious movement, liable to erupt into minor warfare; those who moved into Pergamene territory might even be accepted if they could be persuaded to pay the king's taxes; alternatively, by insisting on their status as Galatians or Kappadokians they might succeed in slicing off part of the Attalid territory for themselves.

The Attalid kingdom survived for only thirty years after the loss of its protectorate over the Galatians, and it appears that Attalos II, Eumenes' successor, abandoned the attempt to control Galatia. Its liberation was followed by the Galatian revival and expansion. Then in 133 the Attalid kingdom was bequeathed to Rome by Attalos III. The subsequent war to suppress a surviving Attalid claimant was followed by the deliberate break-up of the inheritance by Rome. In 129 the Roman commander Aquillius formed the province of Asia out of the richest (western) part of the kingdom, and awarded Great Phrygia, the territory west and south-west of Galatia, to King Mithradates V of Pontos, and Lykaonia to Ariarathes of Kappadokia.[39]

For Galatia this put Mithradates in control of lands on two sides of the country, north-east and south-west, and it is normally assumed that he therefore exercised some sort of protectorate over Galatia, in the same way as Eumenes II had done. Certainly he would have had influence there, since his lands boxed in Galatia relatively effectively, but how much influence, and what the supposed 'protectorate' consisted of – if either of these existed – it is not possible to say. Perhaps it was no more than the ability to recruit soldiers there. The memory of the success of the Galatian rebellion against Attalid influence and that kingdom's 'protectorate' may well have served to restrain Mithradates from anything too forceful. The award of Lykaonia to Ariarathes may have been a greater blow to the Galatians, since it could have restricted the possibility of expansion, which had probably been taking place. These awards caused trouble at Rome, becoming mixed up in that city's internal controversies.

These grants to Pontos and Kappadokia were soon revoked, when the recipient kings died – Mithradates V in 121, Ariarathes VII in *c.*116.[40] The lands awarded reverted to Rome, an arrangement which had possibly been understood from the start, since it would give Rome time to concentrate on organizing the province of Asia, while Great Phrygia and Lykaonia were much less valuable territories, and could be controlled in a rough and ready fashion by the kings. The urbanized area south of Great Phrygia, along the line of the road developed by the Achaimenids and now designated by Aquillius as the Via Aquillia, had remained part of the province all through, showing that strategic interests were as high in Roman considerations as was the possession of taxable territories.

The half-century or so following the defeat by Vulso's army, by damaging Galatia's governing system loosened any government control over the chiefs. A foreign controller, such as the Attalids or a Pontic king, would have great difficulty in exercising any real power. But it allowed some expansion of Galatian territory at the expense of the neighbours. The growing pressure of Rome after 129 BC was about to compel further changes, and further expansion, a process which would both force a change in its government yet reducing its independence, and still greatly expanding its reach.

Chapter 10

The End of the Scordisci

The defeat of King Perseus of Macedon in 167 by the Romans to end the final Romano–Macedonian War also destroyed the Macedonian kingdom and its system of royal government. The Roman settlement abolished the monarchy, and replaced it with four republics. These proved to be weak and quarrelsome, and incapable in the event of defending the Macedonian territory, a matter which had always required the resources of the entire united country led by the king. In 148 the pretender Andriskos succeeded, with Thracian help, in overthrowing the republics and reinstating the monarchy, calling himself Philip VI. This regime lasted only a few months, but in that time he also defeated a Roman army and killed its commander, P. Iuventius Thalma, and then had to be himself defeated by a consular force under Q. Caecilius Metellus. The whole affair caused a great shock in both Greece and Italy.[1]

A continuous Roman military presence in Macedon, which had not been thought necessary under the four republics, now followed. It was probably not originally intended to be continuous, but the frontier remained disturbed for several years, with copycat pretenders – an Alexander, another Philip, a Perseus – all of whom gathered barbarian support in the Balkans and had to be fought and defeated.[2] Andriskos' invasion had at first seemed like a barbarian attack of the traditional sort, with his use of Thracian forces, and the later pretenders worked in the same way, though using different barbarian auxiliaries. None of these invasions and threats, of course, convinced the Macedonians to support them, and Andriskos/Philip was not seriously given any help in the end. As a result of the continuing threat, which lasted eventually for seven years, the Roman military presence became in effect permanent, and Roman commanders, usually of praetorian rank, were appointed annually.[3]

Rome had become involved in wars in Dalmatia and Illyria in the 150s, and in 156 a Roman army penetrated as far as Siscia in the valley of the Sava River, where it defeated a Scordiscian force in an obscure battle.[4] This was at, or close to, the border of Scordiscian territory. It is tempting to link the two events, at Siscia and in Macedon, though they are really too far apart in time and space for any real connection. As far as the Scordisci were concerned they had no further repercussions for the moment. But in 141 a new raid against Macedon by a Scordiscian force was met by a Roman force and won the victory, though there is no further record of their actions on this occasion.[5]

Exactly what troops Rome maintained in Macedon is not quite clear. It is usually put at a legion, which is likely enough since this is the minimum Roman military formation which was usually employed, but this was not necessarily the whole force available to the Roman commander; and a legion would hardly be enough to defeat an invasion by the manpower of a whole Balkan tribe, who could usually muster perhaps 10,000 fighting men for an invasion. The Roman force, if it was kept concentrated, was in effect the reserve force backing up the local Macedonians, who would always turn out to combat a barbarian invasion. There were also forts, camps and posts at the frontier which were occupied by local forces, no doubt manned by rotating units, and it is probably with them that the first responsibility for the defence of the frontier lay. (This was, of course, the pattern of Vulso's army in the attacks on Mounts Olympos and Magada – put the allies/auxiliaries in the front of the battle, saving the Roman citizen manpower.) The Macedonian forces had in fact failed to block the invasion of Andriskos' forces in 148, undermined by a lack of organization in the rear and by the propaganda of a return to a monarchy put out by Andriskos. Now they were backed up by a Roman legion, so they were more likely to stand firm.

A second collision with the Scordisci came in 135, specifically in Thrace, and this time it was the Roman forces which scored a victory, under the command of C. Cosconius.[6] Again there seems to have been no follow-up; a defensive victory was probably sufficient to ensure the safety of Macedon; the fight is said to have been in Thrace, so Cosconius had certainly already moved out of Macedon, his province, perhaps in order to intercept a raiding party, or just possibly in alliance with the local Thracians.

The Scordisci operating in Thrace were not necessarily aiming to attack Macedon. It is possible that they were attempting to enforce their suzerainty over a variety of neighbours, Illyrians, Dalmatians, Thracians, and any others within reach – or possibly establish that suzerainty – and had assumed that the Romans would confine themselves to Macedon. They would understand enough about Roman attitudes and practices to know that launching a war against a Roman-occupied and defended region would be a major undertaking, not to be begun lightly – though the 140s and 130s would be a good time to try something, with Roman forces heavily engaged in Africa, Spain, and Asia at various times and occasionally all at the same time.

At some point in the period after 141, probably in the 130s, the praetor Cn. Egnatius spent three years organizing a new imperial Roman road, called the *via Egnatia* after him.[7] This was not so much a matter of physical construction, more a matter of occasional improvement, and mainly of marking the route by planting milestones with Latin inscriptions indicating distances; the aim of the road was to assist Roman military forces marching through on the way to somewhere else, hence the Latin. None of this would necessarily be of much local utility, for the locals already knew the way and the distances, and Latin would be of little use to them. The road already existed, of course as a traditional routeway, though perhaps only in local sections, but one can scarcely expect that the Macedonian kings would have ignored the need for roads leading to their dangerous frontiers, and especially this route, which facilitated travel behind the frontier line. Egnatius' work, therefore, was in part the designation of an imperial Roman road, and the result was a very obvious and permanent indication of the permanent presence of Rome in Macedon. Militarily it would provide an easy and well-known road all along behind the frontier, a means by which any Roman force could march quickly to the source of any trouble. (A few years later M. Aquillius in Asia Minor did the same, so that by the 120s there was a designated Roman road all the way from the Adriatic to southern Asia Minor.)

The ability of the Scordisci to campaign as far south as the northern border of Macedon in 141 and 135 presupposes the subjugation of, or possibly alliance with, the peoples of the territory between that frontier and the Scordiscian homeland in the Belgrade area and the Banat. In support of this it is noticeable that the name of the Dardanians disappear from all events from the 180s, though they were not destroyed as a people, for they re-emerged in the 90s; that is, they appear to have become part of the Scordiscian polity, no doubt by conquest and reduction to vassal status.[8] This would imply an extensive Scordiscian 'empire' stretching from the Macedonian frontier to the Drava–Danube junction, and from the Danube gorges to the site of Siscia, where they had clashed with another Roman force.

In 119 a new bout of Romano-Scordiscian warfare began, with another Roman attack on Siscia, which was apparently unsuccessful.[9] The cause of the war is not known, but the two states were neighbours and no doubt there were plenty of problems and hostile incidents which could be magnified if one or other wanted to make war. Both Romans and Scordisci were expansionist; the Romans in particular had a horror of any powerful state on their borders, paranoiacally always imagining an imminent attack. The result was a lengthy period of warfare. The attack on Siscia appears to have triggered a Scordiscian response with another attack on Macedon, a response the Romans perhaps did not expect. In alliance with at least one Thracian group, the Maedi, the Scordisci invaded Macedon by way of the town of Argos in Orestis, an interesting way of approaching the province, coming by way of the routes through the mountains which had earlier been utilized by the Dardani.

The praetor Sex. Pompeius was killed in the fighting, and command was taken over by M. Annius, his quaestor. From the account given in a decree from the town of Lete in Macedon, honouring Annius, it appears that he found the Scordiscian forces scattered after their victory, recovered the dead at the battlefield, and then defeated a new Scordiscian attack, presumably by the re-concentrated invaders. This was then followed by a victory over the Maedi, who had chosen the moment of the original Roman defeat to join in. It may be assumed that some of the fighting took place near Lete, which in turn was near Thessaloniki, for it was there that the thanksgiving inscription was erected – so the invasion had penetrated deep into Macedon. No doubt the unusual approach route created surprise. Annius certainly deserved his award of an olive wreath and commemoration in the equestrian games at Lete.[10]

It is also clear that the 'Gallic nation', as the inscription identified the Scordisci, was a largely mounted force. Annius several times captured horses and horse gear, and he refused to call up the local forces, giving as his reason his not wishing to burden the Macedonian cities with the soldiers' pay, but perhaps he also understood that a large infantry force would not be an appropriate counter to the Gallic cavalry; the Scordiscians scattering after the battle would be easier for cavalry than for infantry.

This fight and invasion in 119 was the beginning of a period of warfare lasting at least a decade. The Scordiscian territory and their area of suzerainty evidently covered a large part of the Balkans, from Siscia to the Macedonian border and into Thrace.[11] They were thus, as Pompeius discovered, a formidable power, and were also allied with the Thracian Maedi, who clearly in 119 acted independently. The Maedi also joined in the fighting in the next years, so alliance is perhaps the best word for their relationship, in that they continued to act separately but in accordance with the Scordisci.

To their north the Scordisci were in contact with the Boii of north Pannonia and Bohemia, with the Taurisci of the north-west Balkan area, and beyond that with Noricum and the Helvetii. When the tribes of the Cimbri and Teutones on their wanderings throughout Western Europe bumped into the Boii and were repulsed, they then met, in succession, these three Keltic states of the middle Danube, probably without fighting them, but certainly not being welcomed, and then they headed west into Gaul, all the time searching for a new homeland, and no doubt being repeatedly discouraged; they seem to have avoided the Norican kingdom.[12] The threat they posed was, however, as Rome discovered, powerful, and it may have helped to compel the Dacians to unite and to begin menacing their western neighbour, the Scordisci – whose own power may also have been one of the reasons forcing the Dacians to unite.

In the years immediately after the defeat of Pompeius and the expulsion of the Scordisci from Macedonia by Annius, there are records of several periods of fighting to the north of Macedon between the Scordisci and Roman forces. Details are absent in most cases, but it is known that there were battles, which presuppose both preliminary and succeeding campaigns, in 114, 113, 112 and 109.

These campaigns may well have been preceded, during the period between 119 and 114, by earlier campaigns (records are poor). In 114 the danger was sufficiently apparent in Rome to require the appointment of a consul, C. Porcius Cato, to the Macedonian command, possibly with increased forces, in place of the usual praetor. That the apprehension was correct is demonstrated by Cato's defeat in the subsequent fighting. This permitted another Keltic invasion of Macedon and Greece which reached as far as Delphi,[13] and next year the wandering Cimbri defeated another Roman consul, Papirius Carbo, in Illyria, also in the Balkan area.[14] The Scordisci attacked again, or were attacked, in 112–111. The consul of 113, C. Caecilius Metellus Caprianus, and that of 112, M. Livius Drusus, both celebrated triumphs over the Scordisci, but only the latter is credited with a serious victory.[15] The final fighting took place probably in 110 or 109, when the Roman forces under the consul (for 110), M. Minucius Rufus, defeated a Scordiscian invasion of Thrace – that is, Roman forces were again operating to the north of the Macedonian frontier. This took place at some point in his extended term of office as consul and proconsul, from 110 to 106.[16]

This was a major conflict, lasting at least a decade and probably more, but one which in the Roman sources is largely overshadowed by the contemporary wars in North Africa against Jugurtha, and against the Cimbri and Teutones, not to mention the ongoing internal political crisis within the city. But the Scordisci clearly mounted a major threat to the Macedonian frontier, and penetrated through the defences at least twice, in 119, and most spectacularly, in 114, when they reached Delphi. The reaction of the Greeks to this renewed Keltic spoliation of their major sanctuary was much less vehement than it was in 278, no doubt because of their consciousness of their military weakness, and their own inability to mount any sort of defence; Minucius Rufus, whose victory seems to have finally brought the war to an end, at least for the moment, was honoured with a statue at Delphi, or rather perhaps claimed the credit for the victory. The inscription lists his enemies as Gauls, Scordisci, Bessi, and 'the remaining Thracians', a catalogue amounting to the whole of the central and south-eastern Balkan peoples.[17] The attack was clearly a major invasion.

The record of this war, thin and fragmentary as it is, does reveal that the Scordisci were the dominating power in the southern Balkans at the time. They had subdued the Dardanians of the Scopje basin, and this gave them access to the Macedonian frontier. They were also allied, it seems, with the Maedi in Thrace, again a neighbour of Macedon. To the north their territory extended along the Sava River valley at least as far as Siscia which they controlled in 156 and 119; along the Danube northwards they appear to have controlled, or dominated, the river and its banks as far as a boundary with the Boii, which was at some indeterminate distance north of the junction of the Drava and the Danube – if Siscia is a guide, the border was probably about a hundred kilometres beyond the junction. In this territory not only the Dardanians were under Scordiscian control, but also most of the Pannonians, who lived in the Sava valley, south of the later Roman province which was named after them; other Pannonians were part of the Tauriscian and Boiian states.

This was an extensive territory. To the west the Romans were in control of most of the Adriatic coast, and were allied with the Keltic kingdom of Noricum; there were probably a series of small independent groups between the Roman and the Scordiscian territories, which were useful buffers between them, and likewise were their occasional victims. The Romans also controlled Macedon to the south, and so, apart from the small 'buffer' tribes, the Scordisci had Roman territory as their neighbour all the way around from Thrace to the northern Balkans, and the two were in direct contact in the south and in the Save Valley, and perhaps elsewhere. The geography may explain the Scordiscian ability to exert pressure on the Romans at several points, using their control of internal routes – notably at Siscia and on the Macedonian frontier almost simultaneously in 119. They had other Keltic states to the north, the Boii, and the north-west, the Taurisci, with which they were at least friendly and possibly even allied – there is never any suggestion of conflict with these states. To the east were the Dacians, who by the end of the first century BC were becoming increasingly organized and powerful.

The domination which the Scordisci exercised over their subject tribes was somewhat tenuous. The Dardani, the Pannoni, and the other tribes under them – the Moesi and probably the Andizetes of the lower Sava and Drava valleys, for example – were not disturbed in their homelands, but were subjected by Scordiscian control in some way, and were no doubt compelled to pay tribute and to supply troops on demand. It was therefore not too difficult for them to detach themselves from the Scordisci when they got the chance – and it is by their later appearance in the records that we know of them. The Romano-Scordiscian conflict which continued from 119 (or before) to about 106 quite possibly resulted in a decisive weakening of the Scordiscian state and the dissolution of its empire. It would certainly be a sensible political move by the Roman commanders to encourage independence among the Scordiscian subjects. This Scordiscian 'empire' essentially consisted of the domination of a relatively small Keltic-Illyrian group which had become the Scordisci over its tribal neighbours, and the Scordisci may well have suffered severe casualties in the Roman wars. The account of the fighting preserved in the inscription from Lete describes the Scordisci as a cavalry army, and such a force is always expensive to maintain, and therefore somewhat deficient in numbers – the infantry will have been largely supplied by the subject peoples, and will have probably been untrained and unenthusiastic, just as were the Galatian armies facing Vulso in 189. In the 119-106 war the Scordisci probably suffered considerable losses, and their empire and dominating authority was no doubt weakened by their ultimate defeat.

The peace with the Scordisci after 106 or so was firm enough that the praetor T. Didius in 101 or 100 directed his military strength to the conquest of a Thracian tribe called the Caeni in the Chersonese area,[18] and the next praetor had the task of sorting out and establishing the government for the conquered territory, according to a decree of the Senate which regulated the conquests.[19] The peace on the Macedonian frontier did not actually last long, but when fighting took place again, in 97 or thereabouts, the Romans' enemies were the 'Dardani and the Maedi'.[20] That is, on this occasion the Dardani were fighting on their own behalf, and not as Scordiscian clients, and they had apparently inherited the alliance with the Maedi. However, this is in the note by an excerptor, who was essentially not much interested in Rome's wars, and it is quite possible that the name of the Scordisci was either omitted or otherwise dropped out of the record. But naming the Dardani as a participating tribe implies its independence, when for the previous century it had been under Scordiscian power. If the notice is in error or perhaps incomplete in not naming the Scordisci (for there is evidence that the three tribes were later allied), then it could be that as late as 97 the Scordisci were still active in the South Balkans, and in good relations with the other two peoples named. Nevertheless, the separate mention of the Dardani does indicate that they were now independent, just as the Maedi had been all along. The invasion of 97 was apparently defeated, but the praetor C. Sentius was himself defeated by the Maedi alone at some point in his extended governorship between 93 and 87. This was probably in 92, but he later recovered and won a victory.[21]

The collapse of the Roman state into civil warfare in the 80s inevitably tempted the Balkan tribes and Roman victims into a new invasion. The Scordisci, Dardani, and Maedi were allied in an invasion of Macedonia and Greece in 85 or thereabouts, during which, once again, a (part-) Keltic army reached and looted Delphi. The temple and shrine would seem to have become a fixation among the barbarian tribes.[22]

L. Cornelius Sulla in 85 or 84 attacked 'the Thracians', or maybe just the Maedi,[23] which notice is sufficiently vague to imply only a Roman raid, but it may well have stirred them up sufficiently to reply. While in Macedonia, Sulla also made war on the Dardani and two more tribes, the Emeti and the Sinti, presumably Thracians. The reason, according to Appian, is that he wanted to 'exercise his troops and enrich them'.[24] There is no sign of any Scordiscian involvement in this conflict. Either these tribes were now wholly independent of the Scordisci (as the Maedi always were) or the Scordisci deliberately stayed out of the fighting – either way it surely meant the end of any Scordiscian authority over those peoples.

At about the same time, but in a direct reply to the raid which reached Delphi, the praetor L. Cornelius Scipio Asiagenus (who was consul in 83, and so probably praetor in 85), conducted a major campaign which brought a decisive defeat upon the Scordisci.[25] Assuming that Asiagenus was operating from Greece with the Roman army stationed there, and assuming also that the Scordisci were defeated in their home territory, this must mean that the Roman forces were able to march through the territories of the southern Balkan tribes in order to reach the Scordisci; no fighting in Thrace or against the Dardani implies that they permitted the Roman forces to march through their territory to fight the Scoedisci.

These two military crises, coming in the same year, but from different Roman commanders (who were no doubt on different sides in the Roman civil wars) would be the moment for those tribes to reach finally for their independence. The result would seem to have been that the Scordiscians' tribal subjects all finally broke free from their domination. The relationship between these campaigns is not at all clear, but from the Scordiscian point of view the result is perfectly clear. After their defeat by Asiagenus, their empire collapsed and they are scarcely heard of again for the next seventy years. And just in case the southern tribes facing the Macedonian province felt called on to celebrate their freedom from domination by a raid into Greece, Sulla's cynical campaign to exercise his troops as their expense will have stopped them.

The Scordisci did not actually disappear, of course, any more than their earlier tribal subjects had disappeared. They were, however, stripped of those subordinates, reduced, says Appian, to living on some islands in the Danube.[26] This is clearly a curious exaggeration, or diminution, but they were certainly confined to their core territory in the Banat from then on. Their decline was illustrated in 74 when C. Scribonius Curio, commanding against the Dardani in a war which lasted from 76 to 73, marched his army all the way to the Danube, the first time a Roman force had reached that river, or so it was claimed. He arrived in the land of the Moesi, recently released from Scordiscian overlordship, and so becoming known to Rome for the first time also.[27]

In about 60 BC (or between 56 and 50, perhaps) the Scordisci were defeated by the Dacians, who were now powerfully united under their King Burebista. His power, which reached south by the 50s to threaten the Macedonian frontier, was clearly replicating that of the former Scordiscian empire, but with a larger, richer base – like Noricum, Dacia was wealthy in metals. The Roman war against the Dardani no doubt sufficiently weakened that people that they were, like the Scordisci, relatively easily dominated.[28] In their easy submission, the Scordisci were perhaps fortunate. The Dacians also fought the Boii, who had combined in some way with the Taurisci under a single king called Kritasirs; but they were so damaged and frightened that they fled from their lands, and headed west, where they helped push the Helvetii westwards; it was stopping this movement which in turn gave Julius Caesar his excuse to begin his conquest of Gaul. The former Boiian lands were left as 'desert', though in fact, as ever, the removal of the overlords merely revealed the existence of their subjugated tribal subjects, who were Pannonians. The Boii who fled were no doubt the aristocracy, their overlordship having collapsed at their defeat, just as had that of the Scordisci a generation earlier.[29]

Strabo gives a clue to the fate of the Scordisci in commenting that though Burebista 'destroyed the Boii and the Taurisci, he used the Scordisci as allies'.[30] This must mean that the Scordisci submitted quickly when attacked, like their own former subjects the Dardani. They therefore survived and kept their homeland, but it looks as though both of these tribes were demoralized – it was unlike either of them to submit easily.

It is from this period that the evidence begins to appear which suggests that the Kelts of the Scordisci had become a population better described as Keltic-Illyrian or Keltic-Pannonian. Studies of the surviving names of the people in the area are generally from this period those of the underlying populations; the Kelts had thus been absorbed, or at least had amalgamated with their subjects.[31] In fact, it seems likely that the frequent wars they had fought had helped reduce the numbers of the aristocracy drastically. They certainly lost their empire, and then their independence. The Dacians' empire broke up after Burebista's death in 44, and so once more the Scordisci, the Dardani, and other tribes or states, re-emerged from the ruin of a brief empire, some in Dacia itself, while others emerged from the wreck of the Boiian state, at least a dozen peoples in all, not counting the Thracians.

The political situation in the Balkans, therefore, for the first time in well over a century, was now one where no overarching inland Balkan power exercised control over many of the tribes, and so was powerful enough to confront Rome. The Scordisci had exercised some control over the southern Balkans for a time, and their successor, Burebista's empire, lost its peripheral conquests, in the north and in Thrace. This included the Scordisci themselves, while Burebista's own homeland territory was divided among several separate kingdoms. No new greater power emerged to take control of the situation, though the Romans, with their Civil War winding down and ending in 31 BC, were beginning to scent the possibilities of decisive conquests in the Balkan area beyond the Adriatic coast and the northern Macedonian frontier.

Julius Caesar as dictator between 48 and 44 spread rumours that he intended to attack Dacia,[32] in part because Burebista had offered to join Pompey in his dispute with Caesar, back in 48,[33] but then both Caesar and Burebista fell to assassins in 44, and Caesar's carefully circulated rumour was not put to the test. Burebista's power had been essentially personal, however, while Caesar's, also in many ways personal, was based on seizing control of the well-organized Roman Republic, and the state even survived yet another and worse civil war. Caesar's grandnephew, who eventually changed himself from the teenage terrorist Octavian to the mature statesman Augustus, inherited Caesar's personal legacy, his wealth, his clients, his position, and much of the political authority he had wielded. Octavian had, of course, to prove himself as Caesar's heir, and he did so by a political ruthlessness, by gathering competent men around him, by playing on his adoptive father's legacy, and by using his clever political sense; rumours of a Dacian war lasted well into his personal rule, before fading away. Yet Caesar's ambitions and plan were part of his legacy.

Octavian/Augustus was not himself a very competent military commander, but he and his circle could spot strategic opportunities and possibilities with clarity. One of these was the necessity for Italy (his essential power base) to be properly defended if his political support was to be maintained. In the Balkans this meant controlling the passageway from the northern Balkans into northern Italy and its approaches, through the Julian Alps. One of the keys to this was the former Scordiscian town at Siscia, which controlled the Sava River route from the Banat westwards. This had become Pannonian territory with the collapse of the Scordiscian domination, and in 35 BC the town was taken by an army under Octavian's ultimate command. This, of course, was also, if anyone in Rome remembered, a place where a Roman army had earlier suffered defeat, which Octavian could, once he had taken the place, make claim to be avenging; the main result of the conquest, however, was to set up an advanced defence for Italy, while at the same time acquiring for Rome an advanced base from which further Balkan conquests could be prepared and begun. He left a major force of 25 cohorts – over 10,000 men if the cohorts were fully manned – in garrison in the place. This force became useful as soon as the main Roman force withdrew, when it had to put down a rebellion in the winter of 35-34.[34]

As it happened, it was not from Siscia that the decisive Balkan campaign by Roman forces was launched, though the place did function as a major base in later stages of the war of conquest. Instead the campaign came, appropriately, out of Macedonia. After defeating his opponents, Octavian gave the governorship of Macedonia to M. Licinius Crassus, who had switched sides in the Civil War at a crucial moment. Whether it was realized just how ambitious Crassus was is not known – though he was a grandson of the Crassus who had been a triumvirate colleague with Caesar and Pompey, and in those years, any Roman governor was inevitably ambitious – but it was perhaps not expected that he would launch himself into a major war of conquest.

The condition of the Macedonian frontier had not essentially changed since the time of the death of Alexander the Great. The line of control of the Roman garrison was much the same as that from which Philip II had headed north in his temporary conquest of the lands as far as the Danube in the 330s. Since then, on at least three major occasions, the northern barbarians – Thracians, Scordisci, Dardani, and others – had penetrated that defence line, in some cases to reach and loot the sanctuary at Delphi, and on several other occasions had raided into Macedon. Previous Roman governors had defended the frontier either by fighting inside Macedon when an invasion came, or marching beyond it to intercept a raiding party somewhere in Thrace and Dardania, or to pre-empt a planned invasion. There had been no attempt to move the frontier forward, in part because there was no obvious line of defence before one reached the Danube, except perhaps the line of the Haemos Mountains (Philip's forward defence line in Thrace), and the conquest of the Balkan Peninsula was unlikely to be welcomed in Rome – successful competitors with Octavian/Augustus were not needed; and no governor would usually have the time in office to achieve much more than the defence of the existing line. Now, however, for the first time, a Roman commander was aiming to shift the Roman-Macedonian frontier well forward. One might expect that the Greeks and Macedonians who had recently suffered from the campaigns of Roman armies fighting a Roman civil war – the various battles concluding each section of that war had been fought at Pharsalus in Thessaly, Philippi in Macedonia, and at Actium, with the accompanying ravaging and military damage – would be only too happy to see Crassus moving that frontier well away from their settled lands, and Crassus himself and his soldiers as well.

The object of Crassus' conquests were some of the Thracians and the Getai, but also the Bastarnae of the Danube mouth and delta, and the groups and tribes between the Macedonian frontier and the Danube, a whole area of minor states, tribes, and the occasional city. These groups could not resist a Roman army consisting of considerable numbers of war-hardened soldiers. The conquests of the eastern Balkan area was completed in two years, by 28 BC,[35] although risings and rebellions did follow. As a result of these campaigns in the north and south-east, there was left outside Roman control just the central Balkans, the valley of the Morava River, the area which later became the province of Upper Moesia, sandwiched between the Romans along the Adriatic and Crassus' conquests in Thrace and the lower Danube area. This was the territory of the Scordisci and the Dardani and some others, not recorded as being active in any way since Burebista's time; it was in fact roughly the area which had been the Scordiscian 'empire' two generations before. Crassus had come close to the Scordisci in his campaigns, for he operated in the land of their neighbours the Moesi, further along the Danube[36] – and Augustus' conquest of Siscia was of a place of proud memory for Scordiscian warriors. The Scordisci no doubt felt threatened from both sides, but were given a reprieve, and Crassus returned to Rome to celebrate a triumph.

It may be assumed that these various conquests in the Balkans had led to the 'pacification' of the conquered peoples – or their 'subjection' – but this did not necessarily mean that there had been any serious campaigns against them.[37] When he had acquired Siscia, Octavian accepted the submission of the local Pannonians, but did nothing more.[38] This may have been what happened to the other groups who were not campaigned against; the presence of a victorious Roman army in the region might well have persuaded them simply to render a formal submission and so to avoid a serious ravage by an army which was all too competent at such activity.

This situation held for over a decade. Then in 16 BC an attack by the Scordisci and the Denthelitai against Macedonia is recorded; Dio's words imply that they broke through the frontier defences and ravaged widely, though this may be either his guesswork or an exaggeration (or both).[39] These were two of the Balkan peoples who had not been noted as either conquered or subdued during Crassus' campaigns, though the Denthelitai had been Roman allies and had been defended by Crassus against attacks by, for example, the Bastarnae.[40] The Scordisci, rather surprisingly, are not mentioned at all in either Octavian's campaign in 35, or Crassus' in 29–28. But it seems evident from events in 16–15 that the apprehensions and the tensions amongst both groups had been growing. In 16 the two launched a joint attack on Macedonia; and in the same year the Pannonians, only theoretically subdued by Augustus in 35, attacked the Roman position in Istria, at the gateway into Italy. These Pannonians were apparently allied in this enterprise with the Noricans, whose kingdom has been a Roman ally for a century or so.[41]

This was evidently a coordinated attack by these several peoples, who must all have felt under an urgent and immediate threat from Rome. That one of them was a Roman subject tribe – the Pannonians – and two were Roman allies – the Denthelitai and Noricum – only emphasizes that they feared something, which could only be a Roman campaign of conquest. So the three who were in treaty relationship with Rome were pre-empting an apprehended attack, which they must have expected, by their ally, and their object was presumably to drive the Romans back to the borders of Italy. By attacking first, of course, they could be accused of bad faith, whereas in fact it was their perception of Roman bad faith which had provoked them. Noricum had been a Roman ally for a century, and the Denthelitai had been saved from their enemies by Crassus, so both clearly owed Rome a major political debt. The Pannonians had the well-garrisoned Siscia, a town taken from them, in their midst. All three of these peoples in their rebellion could be accused – and no doubt were guilty – of faithlessness, but none of them would be likely to undertake a rebellion against their powerful protector without a very good reason. The only possible reason is that they feared that that protector, Rome, intended them harm.

The status of the Scordisci at the time is, however, unknown. The absence of notices of the Scordisci in the events in the Balkans since Burebista's assassination is uncharacteristic. For two centuries and more they had been a warrior people, and for a time they had controlled an unsteady local empire for rather longer than had Burebista. They were long familiar with Rome and its wars and methods. Their subjection to, and then alliance with, Burebista suggests that they had been so weakened by rebellions and defeats by his time that they were not capable easily of continuing in independence. Yet they held the most important strategic position in the Balkan region, and they had bold relations with all the peoples around them. Possibly their protection against trouble was that very strategic position, which none of their potential enemies would wish to see fall into other hands. It is evident in this connection that they were about the only Balkan state which was still without any political relationship with Rome other than old conflicts. This may well be the clue to the events of 16-15.

The pattern of the attacks launched in 16 by the Pannonians to the north-west and by the Scordisci and the Denthelitai to the south is very reminiscent of those which had been sent by the Scordisci alone in 119 and after, when they were at the height of their power. Then they had launched simultaneous attacks against the two areas of Roman power they could reach, out of Siscia and on Macedonia, no doubt in the hope of unbalancing the whole Roman defensive system. Further, the Pannonians were former Scordiscian subjects whose city had been taken from them, the Noricans were fellow Kelts, and the Denthelitai were their immediate neighbours. It seems obvious that the outbreak of attacks on Roman positions all around the Balkans in 16 was coordinated and pre-planned, and it may be plausibly suggested that the central element in the alliance would seem to have been the Scordisci.

It is almost needless to say that the allies' attacks failed, assuming that their purpose was in some way to disrupt the Roman positions and intentions, or to drive the advanced positions of the Romans back. Instead it provided a stimulus for what they had probably feared – widespread and permanent Roman annexation of their lands. The participation of the Noricans might suggest a hope that other peoples, perhaps in Gaul, might join in, or perhaps in the Alpine regions; the participation of the

Denthelitai might suggest that a successful raid into Macedonia might persuade some of Crassus' Thracian victims to join in the war. To some degree the allies did stimulate others – two Alpine tribes, the Cammuni and the Vennii, did join in[42] – but in the Balkans the recent Roman campaigns had been all too successful, and Crassus' old victims remained at home.

It was almost as if the Romans were waiting for this war to begin. Augustus sent his militarily-capable stepson Tiberius to command, and he, with characteristic military precision, located the heart of the problem as the Scordisci country. P. Silius Nerva defeated the Pannonian attack, and then went on next year (15) to annex Noricum.[43] Tiberius then attacked the Pannonians and the Scordisci.[44] And while the Pannonians rebelled again soon afterwards, and gave their name to the succeeding war, the Scordisci are not mentioned again. It has been suggested that, having been crushed by Tiberius, they then became faithful Roman allies.[45] It is perhaps more likely that, given the important strategic position they occupied at Singidunum/Belgrade and in the Banat, their country would now be heavily garrisoned and their young men forcibly recruited into the Roman forces, the traditional, and effective, Roman methods of holding down conquered territory. The land had certainly been badly damaged in the course of the war.

Whatever the fate of the people or their country, this was the end of the Scordisci as a political entity. The population was already less than purely Keltic, according to the recorded names, and it would not be difficult to classify the remaining people as Illyrian or as Thracians. The surviving Scordiscian aristocrats could be subverted into Roman citizenship. In the event, when the Roman province system was delimited, they put the Scordiscian territory into Pannonia, named after their former subjects; it was the final extinction.

Chapter 11

The Kingdom of Galatia

The Scordisci of the Balkans seem to have played the game of diplomacy well during the first century BC, keeping themselves clear of any involvement for or against any of the Roman or Dacian warriors who were active in the region, or carefully submitting to one of them when there was no alternative. This worked until 16 BC, when their participation in the First Pannonian War brought final defeat and annexation. In Asia Minor, the same canny behaviour by the Galatians is evident, in a more dangerous situation, and ultimately with a good deal more success, even though it also ended in annexation, but, whereas the Scordisci effectively disappeared after their conquest by Rome, the Galatians of Asia had an afterlife as a Roman province. First, however, they went through the grinder of the Roman civil wars, and the capricious attentions of a series of unscrupulous, greedy, and brutal Roman politicians.

The arrival of direct Roman control in the province of Asia in 133, formed out of a large part of the former Attalid kingdom, brought a new and greater political power to Galatia's western border. At the same time, to the north was the growing power of the kingdom of Pontos, which from 120 was under the rule of the highly capable – and highly ambitious – King Mithradates VI. For the next seventy years, after the Roman acceptance of the legacy of Asia, the Galatians' international relations lay in deciding how to exist between these two powers. The new crises forced another decisive change in the Galatian governing system, the emergence of a Galatian kingdom.

Needless to say, the sources for this period concentrate overwhelmingly on the two greater states rather than on the Galatians, and it is therefore difficult, as usual, to adopt a viewpoint which centres on the subject of this book, so that the result has to be highly impressionistic at times. One of the major issues was that Rome had taken over only part of the Attalid inheritance, and the rest of their territory had disintegrated into minor states. Mithradates of Pontos saw this as an opportunity for extending his control over them (rather as the Scordisci had done in the Balkans), and Galatia was either in the way of his ambitions or was simply one of his victims.

Mithradates, in 108, moved to annex part of Paphlagonia. By arrangement Nikomedes III of Bithynia took the other part. This would have removed a solid block of territory which partly separated Pontos from Galatia. Mithradates had been forbidden to do this by the Romans, but he ignored their prohibition, and followed it up by moving further south into Galatia, which he dominated.[1] (Nikomedes set up a local king, his son, in his part of the annexed country.) This was a Pontic advance which took advantage of Roman preoccupations with events elsewhere, in particular with the crisis in Africa, the war in the Balkans, which lasted perhaps until 106, and with the wandering threat of the Teutones and Cimbri, which was not scotched until 101. He must have hoped that the passage of time would let the Romans ignore his advances, but he also claimed it was part of his inheritance; the Romans did not believe him, taking it as an obfuscatory ploy. Mithradates presumably considered it reasonable, but it seems that later he withdrew the claim once more.

Southeast of Galatia was Kappadokia, where Mithradates' sister Laodike had been married to King Ariarathes VI.[2] In 116 or thereabouts Mithradates procured the murder of Ariarathes by a disaffected Kappadokian noble, Gordios. Laodike, his widow, therefore acted as regent for Ariarathes VII, who was apparently too young to rule himself.

Mithradates and Gordios were associated later, and it is usually assumed that Gordios acted with Mithradates' encouragement, if not his actual instigation, in committing the murder. With Laodike as regent for Ariarathes VII, Mithradates had some influence in Kappadokia,[3] or at least he had a friend on his southern border. In 103, however, Nikomedes III invaded Kappadokia, in which enterprise he had the assistance of Laodike; the boy Ariarathes VII was dethroned, but then Mithradates retaliated and drove out both the Bithynians and Laodike. Ariarathes VII was returned, but then Mithradates tried to get him to accept the return of Gordios. This Ariarathes refused, and he was then murdered at Mithradates' instigation. This extinguished the ancient

Kappadokian royal line; Mithradates renamed his eight-year-old son as Ariarathes, and installed him as king (Ariarathes VIII).[4]

These coups and murders were spread over a period of almost two decades. The net result in Asia Minor was that Mithradates controlled in various ways Pontos, Galatia, and Kappadokia; outside, another result was that their continual disputes eventually came to the attention of the Senate in Rome, which was free from major distractions after the defeat of the wandering tribes in 102 and 101. The Senate ordered all the disputing rulers out of the kingdoms they occupied, and Mithradates and Nikomedes were to relinquish their control over Paphlagonia and Kappadokia. These places were declared free, though the Kappadokians used their freedom, to Roman surprise, to insist on having a king, choosing a man called Ariobarzanes, a prominent Kappadokian noble.[5] The earlier dynasty had, after all, become so incompetent and stained by treachery that any collateral living representative of the family had to be rejected. The only other candidate was Gordios, who soon conspired to get the Armenian King Tigranes (Mithradates' son-in-law) to drive out Ariobarzanes. The plotters were unlucky in that a Roman propraetor of unusual capacity and steeliness, P. Cornelius Sulla (the future dictator), was in the area. He was diverted from his allotted task and instructed by the Senate to restore Ariobarzanes, which he did with dispatch.[6]

In all these plots and murders Galatia is not mentioned. Mithradates' occupation of Paphlagonia had been at once followed by his occupation of Galatia, and his repeated interference in Kappadokia suggests that he was in control of Galatia all the way through until 95 BC. (But Nikomedes III, in invading Kappadokia, had probably sent his army through Galatia.) That control was probably less than onerous, and there is no record that he interfered in any way with the government of the country, though he certainly became familiar with how it worked. It seems from later events that the ruling class in Galatia – that is, the tetrarchs and the judges – continued to be wealthy and to maintain local control; Mithradates, in fact, is usually assumed to have been only selective in the parts of Galatia he chose to control, but this is only an assumption, for there is no clear evidence either way.[7] Galatians were recruited into Mithradates' armies,[8] though he did not do much fighting in the first part of his reign, preferring intrigue and assassination as his imperialistic methods. Some selected Galatians were recruited as officers and then entrusted with relatively important commands.

The political condition of Galatia has been described as a protectorate of Mithradates,[9] but from the few details we know about the country at this time it looks much more likely that the Galatians were eventually fairly well integrated into Mithradates' kingdom, which had also been his aim in seizing control of his part of Paphlagonia. The failure of his bid to control Kappadokia was largely due to the existence of the monarchy, which stood in his way, and around which the loyalties of the Kappadokians could coalesce, a factor which the Kappadokians clearly understood when they insisted on choosing a new king rather than presumably being divided into a series of independent city-states or chieftainships. Without their own focus of loyalty, they would have been as vulnerable to Mithradates' control as Galatia had been. Neither the Paphlagonians nor the Galatians had such a central political figure, and this was one of the elements which made it relatively easy for Mithradates to impose his own control. One of the results of the intrusion of Sulla into Kappadokia and Paphlagonia in 95 seems to have been that Mithradates' control of Galatia was reduced, though he had no doubt numerous ties of obligation with the tetrarchs and the chiefs. At any rate when in 86 he commanded the Galatian tetrarchs to meet him at Pergamon, most of them came.

This condition did protect Galatia from the attentions of the rapacious Roman tax gatherers, whose activities in the Asian province became steadily more offensive and notorious. Galatia itself was hardly wealthy enough to attract such tax men, and perhaps its powerful local lords could resist the tax men's importunities. Its main usefulness to Mithradates, as later to the Romans, was its human population. It was a continual source of slaves throughout the Roman period, and so no doubt earlier,[10] though not to the extent of wholesale rural depopulation which took place in Bithynia, or to the destruction of its military manpower – the chiefs and the aristocracy were not subject to enslavement and sale. But it is to be noted that those who sold 'Galatians' (usually, it seems, of Phrygian descent and with Phrygian names) were the Galatian lords, just as in Bithynia it was the king. No doubt a legal process was devised to permit a Galatian aristocrat to sell his own people, or they may have undertaken cavalry raids against their Galatian neighbours – we do not know enough about Galatian internal affairs to decide, and these are only speculations.

The instructions of the Senate and the actions of Sulla compelled Mithradates to withdraw from Kappadokia in 95. This left Galatia without a powerful protector, and in the next ten years, both Mithradates and the Romans used its military potential for their own benefit. This was the result of the activities of Sulla, but the Roman intervention in Kappadokia in 95 had at last fully involved Rome and the Senate in the affairs of central Anatolia for the first time since the wars of the 160s.

Mithradates had been successfully blocked by Sulla, but he was also stimulated to develop his military and naval strength, which, according to one source, amounted to 200,000 men, and to another to 300,000 soldiers – figures as usual to be treated with the utmost scepticism.[11] These were troops recruited from Bithynia, Kappadokia, Paphlagonia, the Bosporan kingdom, from the Galatians, and from the available mercenaries. An increase in the minting of coins for the kingdom which took place was possibly to pay for these men, most of whom will have been mercenaries. It is worth recalling that Mithradates was a very wealthy ruler.[12] The recruits were probably not raw soldiers. Roman control of Asia was based on the use of local Asian forces under Roman command in any military emergency; after 129 and until the 80s there were no Roman forces in Asia.

By his military preparations, Mithradates clearly assumed that the removal of Kappadokia and Galatia from his control was the diplomatic precursor for a Roman attack on his weakened kingdom. He may well have been simply planning for defence, and his abandonment perhaps of his parts of Kappadokia, and probably of Galatia, were intended to remove any obvious pretext for a Roman attack on him. In the event, he resolved to take the initiative himself when the opportunity arose with the outbreak of civil war in Italy (the 'Social' War) in 91. The war must have seemed to many observers to represent a terminal collapse of the fragile Roman political system.

He moved against Kappadokia and against Bithynia. Ariobarzanes was driven out of Kappadokia, and Mithradates' son, Ariarathes VIII, was installed there once more.[13] In Bithynia, however, Nikomedes IV survived both an assassination attempt and a pretender's invasion, both of which were organized by Mithradates.[14] Perhaps to Mithradates' surprise, the Roman reply seemed to indicate a resolve to act decisively: Ariobarzanes was restored, and Nikomedes was given support.[15] This was done by armies which the Roman officials recruited from the Anatolian populations: 'Bithynia, Kappadokia, Paphlagonia, and the Galatians' provided the troops, perhaps readily enough since Mithradates was an even greater menace to his neighbours than he was to Rome; three of the contributing territories were those which Mithradates had recently ruled and had then been freed by Roman pressure. Both sides in the coming war therefore had armies recruited from the same countries – it was, in a way, an Asia Minor civil war.

The recruits were organized as three armies, each said (no doubt with some exaggeration) to be about 40,000 strong; Nikomedes also commanded an equivalent army, and used it to invade Pontos.[16] He was not opposed, and after looting his way over the western part of the kingdom he withdrew back to Bithynia. Mithradates now had his clear excuse for war.[17] It was later claimed that Nikomedes had been urged on by the Roman officials, and that he agreed when they pressed him for the repayment of debts he had contracted with them; the loot, by implication, went largely to the Romans. They were now all faced by Mithradates' newly recruited force of '250,000' troops.[18]

Mithradates had a clear grievance with Rome and its officials. He had not contested their latest restorations of territories at his expense, but he had still been subjected to Roman intrigues which were designed to make him take the first hostile steps, thereby permitting Rome to claim that its territories, their people, and their allies were being attacked. The threat that this was his intention was certainly the later and repeated Roman justification for the war, and the Romans were all the more insistent on it as the disasters to their forces multiplied. It was a known Roman method, and Mithradates was canny enough – he had used the method himself – to avoid falling into the trap. The war therefore began with Nikomedes' extensive invasion of Pontos, which was not resisted, and which produced for Nikomedes, and supposedly for the Roman officials, large quantities of loot. Behind Nikomedes were the three locally-recruited Roman armies in theoretical support, stationed outside Pontic territory, but available if Nikomedes needed help. When Mithradates' army did not retaliate, it was all too obvious that the war had been begun by Nikomedes, and the Roman forces had no obvious excuse to intervene.

Of the three armies under Roman command, one, under Q. Oppius, had moved into Kappadokia, a second, under M. Aquillius, who had been instrumental in restoring the kings, was in Bithynia, clearly intended to act as the first support for Nikomedes, and the third, under the governor of Asia, C. Cassius, had advanced 'along the boundary of Bithynia and Galatia'.[19] All three were thus outside Pontos, but so close to Mithradates' borders that they were clearly threatening to invade. In keeping with the employment of local forces, these were to be the supporters of the main attack, but not the spearheads. Presumably the idea was that they were to move in to assist if Nikomedes was defeated, or even if he became involved in fighting, or perhaps to separate the competitors, on a pretence of neutrality. But his withdrawal without having fought anybody sabotaged the plot. Mithradates now, after Nikomedes' ravaging and withdrawal, advanced to seek revenge for the attack, presumably clad in the armour of righteousness, not having been the first to begin the fighting for a change. This all was fairly nonsensical, of course, given his propensity for assassination and the subversion of his neighbours – Nikomedes' invasion was actually a response to Mithradates subversion of Bithynia earlier. His huge army and fleet were fully prepared, but he was clearly acting in an equivalent way to the Romans and using their methods.

The Romans not only miscalculated Mithradates' political response, but the effectiveness of his military response as well. He advanced against Nikomedes, who was in Paphlagonia, inland from Sinope, in territory theoretically neutral, though claimed by Mithradates. The Bithynians were rapidly defeated, and at once the whole Roman position collapsed. Nikomedes went to join Cassius. Mithradates' victorious army met and defeated Aquillius, who fled – his army was no doubt disintegrating – first to Pergamon, then to Rhodes. Cassius withdrew first into Phrygia, then south to Apameia. Oppius pulled out westwards from Kappadokia as far as Laodikeia-ad-Lykon, only seventy kilometres, or two days' march, from Apameia. This looks rather like an attempt to combine their forces, but Mithradates chased Cassius away (to Rhodes, again). Oppius, however, installed his army in Laodikeia-ad-Lykon, and then resisted for a time, until Mithradates persuaded the Laodikeians to hand him over, on a promise of no harm to the city. He had carefully released all his prisoners so far – all local men, of course – and had established a reputation for generosity, so the Laodikeians were confident enough to trust his promises.[20]

Many other places either welcomed Mithradates or surrendered to his forces, and this may have included Galatia after the withdrawal of Oppius' army. Others, particularly in the south – Lykia, Karia, Pamphylia, all regions with reputations for independence – resisted and were in contact by sea with Roman naval forces in the region. So far Mithradates had been conciliatory, even generous, in his relations with the cities he captured. It was also in this spirit of capturing the allegiance of the cities by policy that he ordered the murder of the Romans who were in Asia, said to be 80,000 (or 150,000) in number – both figures probably well exaggerated by Roman sources in order to justify their later permanent enmity towards the king. This enabled him to confiscate their wealth, simultaneously filling his war chest and relieving the cities of Asia of the oppressive presence of the Roman tax gatherers; one victim was Aquillius, captured and then killed.[21]

Mithradates' armies invaded and overran Macedonia and Greece, but the Romans had been able to overcome their internal difficulties sufficiently to send an army to fight him. The policy of murdering Romans and Italians ultimately failed, partly because Rome's determination to gain revenge for the murders was steeled even in the time of its own Civil War, but also because the apparent early success of the murder policy seems to have persuaded Mithradates to use the same policy and method elsewhere. Once his military fortunes began to decline, with the siege and capture of Athens by L. Cornelius Sulla (who took over Cassius' post as governor of Asia), Mithradates' supporters, who had been only opportunistic in their acceptance of his rule, became antagonistic. He saw his position crumbling. Sulla conquered Athens in 86 after a long siege, and then defeated two successive Mithradatic relief armies in Greece, at Chaironeia and at Orchomenos. And it seems to have been at this point that Mithradates' temper gave way.

At Pergamon he summoned the collective aristocracy of Galatia to meet him. The news of his armies' disasters in Greece had forced him to recruit a new army, and one of the main sources of recruitment was

Galatia. He already had some Galatians in his army in Greece, but Oppius had had Galatians in his forces earlier. It may be that the news of defeats in Greece had firmed up the pro-Romans in their loyalties, and this made those favouring Mithradates less vocal. Probably finding new recruits had suddenly become more difficult. The chiefs will have been in charge of the process, and maybe it was this prospect which soured the Galatian relationship with the king. It seemed likely also that the Galatians, who had been under less than full Pontic control since 95, were undergoing a long-term change of political attitudes. The country had been relatively controlled, so it seems, under Pontic protection before 95 for two decades, and before that for several decades under Pergamene control or influence. Then renewed independence, brought about by Sulla on the Pontic withdrawal, had been followed by a renewed subjection to Pontos when Mithradates became successful in 89/88; this may have fed further Galatian discontent as the preceding independence was snatched away. And it was Rome which had brought that independence to Galatia in the person of Sulla, who was currently defeating Mithradates' armies.

Mithradates evidently understood this reaction, and moved to forestall it. The summons to the Galatian tetrarchs and chiefs, sixty in number, was the first move in a new campaign to re-establish his much fuller control on Galatia. But his method was a disaster, both for him and for the Galatians. At a banquet he had those who were attending killed. Those who did not attend were sought out and murdered, as were their wives and children. Appian notes that he made no distinction between his 'friends' and 'those who are not his subjects', a sign of the division amongst the Galatians. It is not altogether clear if Appian's words refer only to Galatians or perhaps to others who were not Galatians, but were caught up in his campaign of murder, but it does seem to mean that parts of Galatia were not under his control, and yet the lords had obeyed his summons and had been killed.[22]

The Galatian society of lords and peasants, living close together, with very few towns, but perhaps with no great gradient of wealth or lifestyle, made for a symbiotic social relationship between the classes. This is not to be idealized, but by removing at a stroke the tetrarchs and other lords of the country, Mithradates was also removing the main social glue of the country. (One wonders if he knew of the collapse which had followed a similar slaughter by Vulso's army in 189.) Mithradates' action damaged the whole Galatian society, and destroyed its political and economic organization and cohesion. The peasantry, for example, suddenly found that their judges and their sources of economic organization had both disappeared. It is also very likely that Mithradates understood what the consequences of his actions would be before he undertook it.

The main point and result of all such campaigns of killing, however, is that no matter how thorough the murderer aims to be, he always misses some of his victims – in this case three men in particular. Either they had not been at Pergamon or they had escaped from the massacre. They were hunted, and a new governor, Eumachos, was appointed as Mithradates' satrap in Galatia. This would seriously tighten his grip on the region, and was another stimulus to Galatian resistance. The removal of the tetrarchs and chiefs was clearly designed not just to disrupt the social organization of the country, but to open the way for Eumachos to plant Pontic control firmly in the place of the tetrarchs, acting as an all-powerful governor. Eumachos was probably therefore accompanied in his appointment as satrap by an army of occupation, and a flock of Pontic officials. So we may assume that, to the earlier increasing discontent, the loss of independence after a brief and tantalizing period of freedom, and the murder of the aristocracy, we may add agents hunting for the escaped Galatian lords and a new and more rigorous governmental and perhaps taxation control under a single governor; all this can be added to the roster of annoyances. It is a classic cases of the mishandling of a sensitive province. There is thus quite enough in all this to provoke a rebellion.

And that is what Mithradates got, a Galatian rebellion. The memory of the Galatians' partial success in rebelling against the Attalid domination seventy years ago may not have faded very much. Three men had escaped and they roused their fellow Galatians – though one must doubt that only three were involved, or had survived. The number of tetrarchs and chiefs attending the fatal banquet is said to be sixty, which seemed rather low compared with earlier similar numbers (up to 183). It is unlikely that all the chiefs attended at Mithradates' summons, and certainly there were enough men of officer material to organize an army afterwards. They recruited that army, and quickly drove Eumachos out, along with his presumed officials and any garrisons he had installed.[23] The Galatians from now on were at permanent enmity towards Mithradates, and that meant they were loyal to Rome (since there was no alternative source of power strong enough to protect them). Their territory was repeatedly traversed by Roman armies in the wars against Mithradates and Tigranes which followed during the next two decades, apparently without resentment at their presence. So the Galatians, having had Mithradates as their protector against Roman exploitation from 120 to 95, now from 86 had Rome as their protector against Mithradates. The alliance with Rome was permanent – after all, any such relationship with Mithradates was now out of the question on both sides, since neither could any longer trust the other, not to mention the clear and decisive supremacy of Roman power once Mithradates had been beaten and driven back to Pontos; it was a permanent alliance because Rome now were so clearly predominant, and had the power to insist on compliance.

The internal results inside Galatia were also decisive. The three chief men who had survived, became the senior political figures of the states. As it happens, three men who are known by name dominated affairs in the period after 86, and it is tempting to assume that these were the three survivors, but there is no proof. What is clear is that the massacre of the tetrarchs destroyed the previous political and social system in Galatia, which must have been effectively a fairly wide oligarchy, with the tetrarchs, four to a state, and so twelve altogether, at the social peak, and these tetrarchs will have necessarily been present at Pergamon. It did not eliminate the arrangement of the three states, but the individual states became politically much less significant.

What new arrangements developed after the massacre and the removal of Mithradates' people are not known. On the analogy of the emergency after 189, single prominent men took charge in each of the states. We know of three of these men, Deiotaros of the Tolistobogii, Brigotaros of the Trokmoi, and Kastor of the Tektosages. As earlier, the absence of the murdered tetrarchs, and of their heirs, enabled single men such as these to establish their own power, and presumably to permit the emergence of other new chiefs and tetrarchs. The fact that this happened suggests that Galatian society had already changed sufficiently to be able to accept a monarchic system in place of the old tetrarchs. The past experience of the emergence of men like Ortiagon must have been in many minds as this was happening.

The emergence of this small group of powerful rulers was assisted at first, of course, by the murder of their rivals and colleagues, but the continuing warfare between Romans and others was probably just as instrumental in maintaining their local power, though their positions were hardly secure in the first years after the defeat of Mithradates.

It was the international emergency affecting all Asia Minor which allowed these men to consolidate their positions, and the practice of Roman commanders of using them to mobilize support within Galatia. There is no sign that other tetrarchs existed, and the title became fixed on the three individual rulers. Over the next generation, by a mixture of intermarriage and murder, one man emerged as the Galatian monarch, though he kept the title tetrarch. This was Deiotaros.

Any attempt to maintain the peace between Rome and Mithradates was doomed by their continuing mutual suspicion, and by the maverick behaviour of Roman officers. Aquillius was conveniently dead and so could easily be blamed for the Roman conduct before the war, and for the war itself, but this did not entirely rein in his successors; also the continuing wars in Italy clearly loosened the Senate's control over these men.

In 85, returning to Pontos after making a peace treaty with Sulla, Mithradates had to mobilize his forces to put down a rebellion. Rome was instantly suspicious, and L. Licinius Murena, in command of an army stationed in Kappadokia, launched an attack into Pontos. He may have marched through Galatia to reach Pontos, though he seems to have aimed at the eastern part of the kingdom, which he could reach without going through Galatia.[24] A second attack, in which Murena crossed the Halys River, and so was moving through Galatia, persuaded Mithradates to appeal to the Senate, whence came a messenger from Sulla with oral instructions for Murena to desist, though Mithradates was not informed, and it was reported that Murena and the messenger conferred secretly after the message had been delivered. (Sulla had not provided a written version of the peace agreement he and Mithradates had made, and now he was using secret oral messages; no wonder Mithradates was suspicious.) Murena, whatever orders he had received, pushed on with a new attack, but in this advance he was met and defeated by Mithradates' army. Surprisingly, Sulla, in power in Rome, now refused to support Murena, even though Mithradates had gone on to annex parts of Kappadokia.

This was turning to his own advantage the orality of his proceedings. He sent a new envoy to make peace between the kings of Pontos and Kappadokia, successfully.[25]

Mithradates had been accused of holding on to parts of Kappadokia in violation of the peace treaty he had agreed with Sulla, and this was part of Murena's pretext for his war. It may even have been true, for as part of the peace agreed between Mithradates and Ariobarzanes in 82, the former took over some other parts of the Kappadokian territory; this was part of the betrothal agreement of his infant daughter with Ariobarzanes.[26] However, he withdrew later from that territory, perhaps impressed by the presence in the south of Anatolia of an army of four legions under P. Servilius Vatia, the governor of Cilicia, who was campaigning in the Taurus Mountain region. This was the largest Roman army (apart from the armies of local levies under Aquillius, Cassius, and Oppius) which had yet campaigned in Asia Minor, and was a sign of Roman earnestness in dominating the region. Vatia, however, also campaigned in Phrygia Paroreois, perhaps as a warning to Mithradates to keep the peace. At least he seems to have kept clear of Galatia in his campaigning.[27]

L. Licinius Lucullus was appointed to the province of Asia and then to Cilicia as well in 74. These were in reality commands against Cilicians and others, particularly Pisidians, who threatened Roman territory and its friends, not a command with control of Cilicia itself, yet. Lucullus had succeeded to it on the death of the previous proconsul, Cn. Octavius, Vatia's successor, and was given the task of the 'war against Mithradates', even though Sulla's peace agreement still stood. This was the result of a complex political intrigue at Rome, in which it was casuistically argued that the war with Mithradates had not actually ended with the peace of 82/81, but still continued, thus giving Lucullus the opportunity for wealth and glory. The contriver of the intrigue, his colleague, M. Aurelius Cotta, secured Bithynia as his province, which King Nikomedes IV of Bithynia, who died in 74, had left to Rome in his will. The prospect of acquiring wealth in organizing the new province attracted Cotta as much as the war attracted Lucullus, and Rome speedily took possession.[28] But Mithradates acted first, before the Roman commanders (coming out from Rome) could move. He invaded Bithynia, but, going further, he moved on towards the province of Asia, where he had reason to think he would be welcomed,[29] but he was held up at Kyzikos, which he had to besiege. On the way a revolution in Herakleia Pontike produced the murder of Romans in the city, a clear warning of what might happen in the Asian cities.[30] The resistance of Kyzikos, however, held up the whole of Mithradates' campaign, for it became clear that only when his forces were actually present would the cities of Asia openly join him, and not all of them then. Hence the war revolved around the result of the siege.

Lucullus organized a relief expedition with care, knowing that the siege meant that Mithradates was prevented from moving on. He marched his force of five legions from Kappadokia (where he had been planning an invasion of Pontos, as Murena had), but took his time, partly because he had to arrange for the defence of Kappadokia and Galatia first. No doubt he recruited auxiliaries from the local population, but he certainly conscripted 30,000 Galatians to help transport food and other supplies towards Kyzikos to feed his own army, which was destined to besiege the besiegers. Mithradates had brought such a huge army with him to the siege (which, of course, he had not expected) that the critical point of the campaign had become logistics, food for the troops in particular. The army which could feed itself the longest would win.[31] Lucullus' measures were successful. Mithradates, after several defeats and after being trapped in the counter-siege, broke out and returned to Pontos, having lost much of his army. This time he found that the enemy followed him, supplied by the Galatian logistics system, defeated his forces, and gained control of the whole Pontic kingdom; Mithradates took refuge with his son-in-law Tigranes of Armenia.

So far so good, but Lucullus then became entangled in a new war against Tigranes, until in 67 his command was transferred to Cn. Pompeius Magnus (Pompey), who eventually finished off the war. Mithradates briefly returned to Pontos, having worn out his welcome with Tigranes, but was driven out again in Pompey's campaign; Tigranes lasted another decade and died in his bed. Mithradates took refuge in his subsidiary kingdom of Bosporos where he ruled for another three years, planning a riposte by invading Italy through the Balkans (aiming to persuade several Keltic states, including the Scordisci, to join him, or so the Romans believed),[32] but eventually he committed suicide in 63, assisted in the act by one of his Galatian officers, Bituitus.[33]

These wars swirled about Galatia, though the country itself is seldom referred to. It may be assumed that Galatian help was available to all these Roman commanders, given Galatian attitudes towards Mithradates, though in what form is not known. 30,000 porters with Lucullus in 72 is about the one concrete detail we know; they were no doubt detailed to the task by their chiefs, and by the new single tetrarchs. On the other hand, the known predilection of Galatia for Rome must have been the excuse for the deposed Mithradatic governor Eumachos in that same year to launch an attack on Pisidia and Cilicia, which he may well have reached by a march through Galatia. This was the second attempt by Mithradates to distract Lucullus by attacking his base, in this case in the east. The first had been an expedition commanded by Diophantos at the same time as the invasion of Bithynia; he had been sent into Kappadokia.[34] Eumachos' campaign went further, but was stopped by a force commanded by Deiotaros, the tetrarch of the Tolistobogii, who had survived Mithradates' massacres.[35] It would therefore seem that Lucullus was relying on the Galatians, not only is porters, but more certainly to keep Pontic forces out of Kappadokia and other regions of eastern and central Anatolia. There are occasional other items which indicate the recruitment of Galatians, such as the force of Galatian cavalry with Lucullus in 69 – but they turned aside to loot some treasure, where they had been close to capturing Mithradates.[36] The use of Galatian territory by the Romans is highlighted by the fact that when Pompey finally caught up with Lucullus in 67 to take over the command, the Roman army was camped at the town of Posdala in the Trokmoi country.[37]

Pompey quickly finished off the war with Mithradates, and then organized Pontos and Bithynia as Roman provinces, and so took the glory for the achievement, even though the earlier commanders, from Sulla to Lucullus, had actually done most of the hard work. The inland area of Anatolia, south of Pontos, and north of the Taurus – that is, principally Kappadokia and Galatia – were rearranged as several states which were Roman allies but were under their own rulers – client kingdoms. Ariobarzanes returned once more to his kingdom and received extensions of territory; the Paphlagonians were organized into two small kingdoms; Galatia was recognized as a trio of states, each with its own single tetrarch.[38]

The three tribes had in fact been emerging as quasi-monarchies for the previous twenty years, following Mithradates' massacres. During the wars Galatian help had been useful to the Roman commanders and was provided whenever it was asked for, and two of the Galatian tetrarchs had proved themselves fully capable as rulers already: Deiotaros of the Tolistobogii had taken the lead in defeating Eumachos in 72 when he emerged to campaign in the Taurus and Pisidia. He was recognized as a king, though not of the Galatians, but his title was attached to his rule of some other sections of Anatolia; to the Tolistobogii he remained as tetrarch. Brogitaros was tetrarch of the Trokmoi, and was also later given the royal title, though his exact contribution to the war effort is not known. He was assigned also a great fortress which Mithradates had built; it was somewhere east of the Trokmoi lands at Mithradateion, which therefore represented an extension of Brogitaros' Galatian lands, and was perhaps the reason for his royal title. These two men were linked by the marriage of Brogitaros with Deiotaros' sister. Later Deiotaros' nephew Kastor was installed as the Tectosages' ruler, and his father (Deiotaros' brother-in-law) may well have been his predecessor as tetrarch of the Tectosages.

The new tetrarchs had power and wealth. Their power made them vulnerable to rivals (which included the other tetrarchs) and their wealth involved them in Roman politics. In Galatia Dioetaros is known to have built himself castles, one at Blukion, which was his palace, another at Peion, which was his 'treasury'.[39] These two have been examined with an archaeological eye. They proved to have been earlier buildings which Deiotaros expanded, strengthened, and modernized. Since they already existed it is reasonable to assume that one at least, and perhaps both, were the castles of earlier tetrarchs of the second century BC.[40] They are certainly sites which were carefully chosen and defensible places, which suggests that the period of their original building was less than peaceful. This is hardly surprising, given the Galatian political system.

The recognition of these places as Tetrarchic castles (if that is what they were) has suggested that there would be other such places. With four tetrarchs per state, the hunt was on for the others; that there would be a set of four in each state can be tentatively identified.[41] The problem is, of course, that the office of tetrarch was not necessarily hereditary, and in that case the death of one tetrarch might result in a man from a different part of the state emerging as the new man. We know, in fact, of only two inheritances of influence – the son of Ortiagon is known by name, though whether he was a tetrarch is not known, and the father of Deiotaros, Sinorix, may have been one. In such circumstances identifying places as Tetrarchic seats is not a productive exercise.

These men acted as did other contemporary kings, disputing with each other, intriguing to transfer territories to themselves, looking for advantage. Brogitaros, for example, for a time secured control of Pessinos from Deiotaros by intriguing at Rome, but Deiotaros (the Tolistobogii usually had the privileges at Pessinos) drove him out.[42] The essence of the problem was the susceptibility of political Romans to corruption; inevitably the kings used their subjects' tax contributions to attempt to bolster their own positions.

These new arrangements were incorporated in the *Lex Julia* in 59, and supplemented by a *Lex Pompeia* a little later, though they were actually in place from 67/66; the bitter disputes in Roman politics had delayed the legalization of Pompey's measures until Caesar drove them through as a plebiscite during his consulship. Yet they were hardly set in stone, and the territories of Deiotaros in particular were expanded and shifted repeatedly over the next twenty years. Even so the Galatian territories always remained at the heart of these kings' lands. Deiotaros was wary enough to organize his army on the Roman fashion and lend it to Roman governors at need – for example, to Cicero in Cilicia in 51,[43] and to Cn. Domitius against Mithradates' son Pharnakes in 47[44] (though they suffered a total defeat).

The recurring civil warfare amongst the Roman warlords caught up the Galatians as usual, but their leaders' political instincts failed them in choosing sides, for they regularly found themselves supporting the defeated, though in truth their geographical position in the east scarcely allowed them any choice at all; but their relatively small military contributions may have been the least they could provide, so attempting to limit their responsibility, just in case. If so, this was good politics, for the Romans based in the east all lost. Deiotaros was with Pompey with 600 horse at Pharsalos in 48, and then commanding 5000 cavalry with Brutus and Cassius at Philippi in 42, and then there were more Galatian cavalry with Antony at Actium in 31.[45] Brogitaros had died before these difficult decisions had been necessary, but Deiotaros survived until 40 BC or so, dying at a great age – he had first been politically active in about 90 BC.

He had been as ruthless as any Hellenistic king (or Roman emperor), murdering sons and daughters when they seemed to threaten him. Partly as a result of the various marriages he came to rule all three of the Galatian tribes, the first time they had been united under a single ruler. When he died the central monarchy was inherited by his nephew Kastor, and then by Amyntas, one of his officials, who was appointed king by M. Antonius in 37, and held the post under Augustus, as well as other lands and areas, until his death fighting in Pisidia in 25.

At that point Augustus was compelled to make a new decision on the status of the whole area. Perhaps Amyntas had no obvious successor, and certainly Deiotaros' family were no longer considered, though his descendants were active in the area during the next two centuries. But Galatia (like the Scordisci in the Balkans) had now become a much more important strategic location, when the Parthian frontier was in Armenia. Amyntas' territories were annexed and converted into a Roman province. (This, however, was not the end of the juggling of territories, and the province of Galatia at times included Pamphylia and Kappadokia, which was annexed when its last king died in AD 17.) Deiotaros' army was eventually converted into a Roman Legion, *legio XXII Deiotariana*. The kingdom of Galatia, as you may call it, had lasted about forty years.

Like the conquest of the Scordisci in 15 BC, the annexing of Amyntas' kingdom in 25 BC marked the end of any independence for the Galatians of Asia, though it cannot have been much of a surprise to them. It was, in fact, one more political upheaval to add to those over the past two centuries, during which the country had gone from a free land to dependence on a series of 'protectors', or more accurately oppressors, to a triple kingdom, then a single kingdom at the disposal of a series of Roman warlords, and now a Roman province under a Roman governor. Henceforth they remained as part of the Roman Empire, which they had been happy to join after their treatment at the hands of their earlier protector in 86. As speakers of a Keltic language their descendants can be found in the area into the sixth century AD, but only as a minor, even exotic, group of people in the rural half of central Anatolia, a distinctly curious home for a Keltic people.

Chapter 12

A Roman Province

The kingship of Amyntas was decisive for Galatia because of his vigorous expansion of his territory southwards, the move which had been signalled by campaigns and infiltrations during the previous century and was now accomplished with success. The peoples of Pisidia and the Taurus Mountains were resistant to any outside authority, and Amyntas became very busy in enforcing his own authority, and by extension, that of the Roman Empire, of which his kingdom was a part, over this region. He had been appointed as king by Mark Antony, but deftly changed sides before the Battle of Actium, and so retained his kingship. Indeed, he was killed in 25 BC, either by an enemy ambush or by assassination, while attempting to continue this process.[1]

At that point the Emperor Augustus determined that the region needed a Roman administration, Amyntas having done much of the necessary hard work. Amyntas' kingdom was annexed whole and made into the province of Galatia.[2] By this time the kingdom had grown so large, and Amyntas had been so militarily successful, that a certain suspicion probably existed in Rome over the intentions of any of Amyntas' possible successors; his son Pylaemenes was deemed to be too young to rule, which was a perfect excuse to convert the land into a new province. This was to be the fate of many client kingdoms of Rome: if one was successful it would be annexed to prevent its king becoming too powerful; if it was not successful, of course, this was a different problem, and it would be annexed to reform it. There was also the issue of Parthia, looming from the east; more than one client kingdom of Rome took Parthia's side in a war; therefore, so the thinking went, none of them could be trusted.

The result was a curious provincial region, for the kingdom's boundaries became those of the province for the next century, but were then extended even further. It included the original three states of Galatia in the north-centre of Anatolia, which had been extended southwards under Deiotaros and then under Amyntas, to take over Lykaonia and eventually even Pamphylia on the south coast. This meant it also included considerable parts of Pisidia as well, those at least which were conquered by Amyntas. The mountainous area had hardly been 'pacified', as the Romans might have put it, and it remained a constant problem for any Roman governor for centuries yet, though an early campaigner, P. Sulpicius Quirinus, suppressed the Homodanenses effectively.[3]

The main solution, partial at any rate, was the same as that adopted by the early Seleukid kings: to develop a system of fortified cities which hemmed in the Pisidian region. Pamphylia was already an urban region with a string of half a dozen cities on or close to the coast who between them occupied the whole region. Along the old Persian Royal Road there were also several cities, mainly founded or developed by Antiochos I and Antiochos II in order, it seems, to control the Galatians, but just as much to hem in the unruly Pisidians – one of the cities, Antioch, was always distinguished from others by the name of 'towards Pisidia'. Several of these places were now denominated as Roman *coloniae*, and a whole series of other places were developed to the same status.[4] They were settled by detachments of Italians, mainly from provincial areas of Italy, and mainly discharged soldiers, who as Roman citizens in a Roman colony, automatically became the civil rulers, a Roman practice which imitated the Seleukid system.

The province of Galatia therefore developed unevenly, adding Pamphylia in about 6 BC, and was later united with Kappadokia in a large, surely unwieldy, double province. Galatia had a heavily, and increasingly urbanized southern part, which was not really 'Galatian' at all, but Greek, and a rural area in the north with only a few cities – the old Galatian territory in the north. The old urban centres of old Galatia – Pessinos, Ankyra, Tavium – all became Roman *coloniae* as well.[5] But this produced a curiously-shaped province; the governors will have necessarily paid most attention to the cities of the south, and to the restless Pisidian borderlands; the old Galatia in the North was perhaps somewhat neglected, which will, no doubt, have suited the chiefs well enough.

The other major imperial concern in Asia Minor was external, in that the empire of the Parthians had expanded into Armenia and now was closer to the province on the east. The border between the Roman and the Parthian Empires in that mountainous area was uncertain, as was the allegiance of Armenia, particularly Armenia Minor.[6] A peace with Parthia which was negotiated by Augustus in 20 BC held for a time, but control of Armenia tended to fall into the hands of members of the Parthian royal family, to whom the Armenians felt culturally attracted, and this the Romans inevitably did not like. Armenia's geographical position in relation to Asia Minor made it seem a constant threat. The mountainous nature of the country made it difficult to campaign in and it was also awkward to discover what was going on there.[7]

The upland plains of Galatia, Lykaonia and Kappadokia, on the other hand, were largely open country, and so were just the sort of land over which the Parthian cavalry would be able to campaign successfully. This was probably the main reason for uniting them into a single province, the decision of the militarily-alert emperor Vespasian in about AD 71. In addition, this was just the sort of territory, pastoral, poorly urbanized, with a mobile population, which the Romans were at somewhat of a loss to rule successfully. Their governing system was based on cities, which governed themselves and their nearby countryside, distantly supervised by the provincial governors, and in central Anatolia the cities were far apart. At the same time that Galatia and Kappadokia were joined, Pamphylia and Pisidia and the southern cities were separated off into a new province, and joined with Lykia. The governor of the new Galatia-and-Cappadocia province could therefore concentrate his attention on the military frontier, where a distinct and enforceable line of control, the *limes*, was developed, based on the legions stationed at Satala and Melitene.[8] This was a belated recognition that the two parts of Galatia, south and north, were incompatible in social terms.

After the hyper-activity of the Republican civil wars and Augustus' period of power, events moved much more slowly in the early Imperial period. Partly this was because the east was rarely at the head of concerns for the emperors, who rarely moved out of Rome. It was the internal developments – city founding, Italian immigration, new army garrisons, and so on, and eventually the rearrangement of the provinces – which marked the changes in the Galatian province. But all these developments largely bypassed old Galatia (as opposed to the extensions brought about by Amyntas' conquests and Augustus' fiddling.)

Through all the changes, however, the three Galatian states continued as distinct sections of the provinces as they had in the kingdom. Their central cities had their tribal names included in their titles – Ankyra was 'the Metropolis of Galatia, city of Augustan Tektosages Ankyra'[9] – and their highest offices, such as the priests of the imperial cult, were often occupied by men who bore Galatian names. The prime example is the cult at Ankyra, where a list of the priests of the reign of Tiberius is preserved.[10] They include Kastor son of King Brigatorius, and Pylaemenes, son of King Amyntas, and four or five men with Galatian names and/or fathers with Galatian names – this out of twenty names, several of which are repeated. The Galatian aristocracy, that is to say, lived on and flourished.

The same is the case with the lords of the countryside, who were partly Italian in name, partly Roman, but often could and did boast of Galatian descent, especially descent from Galatian royalty. These were the successors and descendants of the chiefs and tetrarchs of the previous three centuries. These men (and some women), like Deiotaros and his family, continued in power and wealth and intermarried, so that the rulers of the whole region were connected to each other, and will have had much more influence locally than the Roman governors, who were posted in the province for two years at most.[11] They may not have ruled as kings or tetrarchs, but they extolled and controlled the region – that is, most of Asia Minor – as an aristocratic network. These connections and marriages began in Augustus' reign (though some connections no doubt existed among the Galatian lords earlier), and were fully functional by the time of Claudius and Nero; they remained in existence for at least the next two centuries, and one family eventually reached the rank of emperor (see Appendix). In other words, the order of society which had existed in the time of the independent Galatian states, and was damaged in 189 and in 86 and suffered under Deiotaros, reconstituted itself each time, and flourished again in the Roman Empire, extending itself into neighbouring regions, but still being anchored in Galatia.

Appendix

Three Roman Emperors from Galatia

Every Roman commander in Asia Minor in the late Republic conferred Roman citizenship on selected local supporters, and each of them took the commander's names as his own, usually tacking on his original name as his *cognomen*. So there are plenty of Pompeii, Julii, and Antonii in the east, and rather fewer of those of other less generous or less prominent men; the Antonii normally had the *praenomen* and *nomen* Marcus Antonius.

A Roman's citizen name, at least in the elaborating form which became all too common in the early Empire, describes his ancestry. So a Marcus Antonius in the third century AD was descended from a Marcus Antonius who had been awarded the Roman citizenship by Mark Antony in the 30s BC. It had become common, at least among the wealthy and senatorial classes, to include also a reference to his maternal family, so a Sempronianus had a grandfather called Sempronius (and a mother called Sempronia). A further *cognomen* might describe a physical peculiarity (Rufus for a man with red hair, for example), or it might indicate his geographical origin – 'Gallus' for a man from Cisalpine Gaul, for example.

So M. Antonius Sempronianus Gordianus Romanus was descended from a man who was given the Roman citizenship in the 30s BC by Mark Antony, his maternal family name was Sempronius, with the *cognomen* Romanus, as an emphasis on his citizenship, perhaps, and his second *cognomen* Gordianus indicates that he came from Gordion in Galatia. Too many Roman families' names are common with too many others – there were tens of thousands of Julii, the family name of Julius Caesar and Augustus, both very free with their awards of citizenship, so individuality mandated still more elaborate *cognomina* to distinguish oneself from others of the same name. 'Gordianus' was virtually unique in the names of prominent men of the empire, though it was not uncommon in Asia Minor; 'Romanus' was the proclamation of an ancestor's loyalties in

Asia Minor where Roman citizenship was rare and adhesion to Rome equally so.

As if to make up for this deficiency, three men of that name appear in the records in the short period between 238 and 244. The first, or eldest, had a long slow career as a Roman official. He was born a little before 160, and commanded the *legio IV Skythica* in Syria, possibly during the reign of Septimius Severus (by which time he was almost 50 years old – the normal age for such a command would be the early 40s), and was serving as the propraetorian governor of Britannia in 216. The delay in reaching the legionary command could have been due to dislike by the Emperor Commodus (180–192); his promotion to the post by the Emperor Septimius Severus could be because the emperor wanted a man of little energy or ambition in a sensitive area. He was suffect consul during the reign of Elagabalus, between 218 and 222, long past the normal age for the post. He was governor of Africa in 238 at the age of eighty, which would almost certainly have been his final post – but he surprised everyone.[1]

He had clearly been caught up in a violent changes in Roman imperial politics which came after the accession of Commodus; his offices were mainly held under Severan emperors (Septimius and Elagabalus), and his last (but one), as governor of Africa, was reached automatically. His politics would seem to be revealed in his career.

The governorship of Africa was a post to which ex-consuls went in rotation, if they lived long enough, and so it was an honour, not necessarily a working post but then, after such a slow and less-than-distinguished career, Gordian suddenly had himself proclaimed as emperor, along with his eldest son, also Gordian (II).[2] The precise personal reason or reasons for his action is not known, but the general political condition would be detestation of the Emperor Maximinus Thrax. This coup set off an extraordinary series of events during which, in 238, the Roman Empire had six emperors, five of whom died violently, leaving Gordian's teenage nephew, Gordian III, as the sole surviving emperor. The political reverberations of Gordian's rising then lasted for over thirty years, until a new soldier emperor, Diocletian, clamped his iron grip on the empire and began a new sequence of political and administrative changes.

Gordian himself was a cultured man, the author of a long epic poem addressed to the Emperor Caracalla, though Caracalla was hardly the most suitable recipient for anything cultural, and one doubts he ever read it. Philostratus in turn dedicated his *Lives of the Sophists* to one of the Gordians, presumably as a recognition of the future emperor's cultural eminence.[3]

From his name Gordian's family came from Galatia. It seems very likely that he was born there, and his mother is recorded in an inscription from Ankyra.[4] He would need to move to Rome in his teens to pursue his political career; his father is said to have been a senator, reaching the rank of praetor, but he died young. He was therefore rich, and possessed large estates, probably in Galatia, but also no doubt in Italy if he was to qualify for the Senate. He was connected in various ways with other families in the region, with Herodes Atticus, for example, and the rhetor Aquila, who was perhaps Sempronia's father.[5] He was, that is, a member of the Asian aristocratic network. His career was cautious and careful, subject to the interruptions due to the political perturbations of the times. He would be eligible for the consulship (having been through the preliminary stages of aedile (during which he gave public games of a memorable extravagance) and praetor by about the year 200, but he did not reach the consulship until, probably, shortly before 222. In his governorship of Britain he was still at praetorian rank. In fact, he does not seem to have actively sought administrative posts, though to qualify for the governorship of Britain he must have had some experience beyond holding the offices in the city of Rome and commanding a legion for a couple of years. One source says he had been governor of several provinces, but apart from those in Britain and Africa none are securely known.[6] This is not a man one would expect to grasp at the imperial office under any circumstances, still less from the base in a province which had no Roman troops stationed in it, other than the governor's own bodyguard. At a guess he was progressively disgusted at having to serve under such emperors as Commodus, Elagabalus, and Maximinus Thrax, and took the opportunity of a riot in his province to make a final damaging protest. However, it is also possible he was part of a conspiracy which stretched into the Roman Senate, which reacted suspiciously quickly to his *pronunciamento*.

It ended in tears for Gordian and his son within three weeks. The commander of the *legio III Augusta* in the neighbouring province of Numidia, a man called Capellianus, was a personal enemy (though he is not known of in any other way). He seized the opportunity to invade Africa; illegally – he was not supposed to leave his own province – unless he had instructions to do so from the Emperor Maximinus. He moved with such speed that the younger Gordian was killed in the subsequent fight, and then the elder Gordian committed suicide.[7]

This was a period, after the eastern expedition of the Emperor Julius Verus in the 160s, when the eastern provinces of the empire were bestirring themselves. For the first time they began producing men who took an active part in the imperial government.[8] Easterners reached the level of the imperial family with Septimius Severus' wife Julia Domna from Emesa in Syria, and so their son Caracalla was half-Syrian. From Caracalla's succession in 211 to the death of Philip the Arab in 249, all the emperors but one came from an eastern province. Gordian I therefore was part of a clear pattern, and it may well be that it was in part this atmosphere of eastern revival which propelled him up the career ladder, even though he seems for a long time to have been reluctant, or at least unambitious. It certainly brought him to imperial power – and to his death.

So far as can be seen, he, his son, and his nephew, were the only men from Galatia ever to become emperors. They were hardly shining monuments of decision or the exercise of power, but the old man and his son were directly instrumental in bringing about a political earthquake. It is unfortunate, however, that there is nothing in their Galatian ancestry to suggest that it had anything to do with this result. But this Galatian family, at least, was clearly thoroughly Romanized.

Notes and References

Introduction
1. Barry Cunliffe, *The Ancient Celts*, 2nd ed., Oxford 2018, ch 5; also M. Diepeveen–Jansen, *People, Ideas, and Goods: New Perspectives on 'Celtic Barbarians' in Western and Central Europe (500–250 BC)*, Amsterdam 2001.
2. Any book on the Roman Republic must discuss the Gallic invasions, but all too many confine it to a few pages, since it interrupts the flow of constitutional discussion. Cunliffe, *Ancient Celts*, 131–142 is also fairly brief; similarly, Henri Hubert, *The History of the Celtic People*, 2 vols, London 1934, ch. 1; Kathryn Lomas, *The Rise of Rome*, London 2017 167 – 169 and other references.
3. Livy 5.34; Pliny, *NH*, 12.5.5; H.D. Rankin, *The Celts and the Classical World*, London 1987.
4. E.T. Salmon, *Samnium and the Samnites*, Cambridge 1967, 35.
5. E.T. Salmon, *Roman Colonisation under the Republic*, London 1969; Lomas, *Rise of Rome*, chapter 13.
6. Cunliffe, *Ancient Celts*, 76–82.
7. A coincidence rarely noted – the invasion of Italy began about 400 BC, the sack of Rome was in 390 or 387.
8. Cunliffe, *Ancient Celts*, 198–202.
9. The Hylli: *Etymological Magnum*, 776, 39; Skylax 33; Strabo 7.1.1.
10. Apparently taking the name – or being given their name – from Mons Scordus, south of their new homeland: Hubert, *History of the Celtic People*, 2.123.

Chapter 1
1. N.G.L. Hammond and G.T. Griffith, *A History of Macedonia*, vol 2, Oxford 1979, ch. XVII.
2. Zofia Archibald, *The Odrysian Kingdom of Thrace*, Oxford 1998, 235–236.
3. Nicholas Hammond, *Philip of Macedon*, London 1994, 135–139.
4. Justin 9.3.1–2; Demosthenes 13.3–7; Frontinus, *Stratagems* 2.8.14.
5. Arrian, *Anabasis* 1.1–6.
6. Strabo 7.3.8; Arrian, *Anabasis* 1.7.8; both of these are quoting from Ptolemy's lost account.
7. Arrian, *Anabasis* 1.7.8; Strabo 7.3.8.
8. Diodoros 17.113.3; Arrian, *Anabasis* 7.15.4; this is only a vague, geographically indistinct notice; which Gauls were meant is not specified, though the Scordisci are one of the most likely groups.
9. Peter Beresford Ellis, *Celt and Greek*, London 1997, 63–64.
10. Diodoros 17.1 15.1–5; Plutarch, *Alexander*, 72.5; Arrian, *Anabasis* 7.14.8; Justin 32.12.12; these included extensive, but vague, intentions of conquest in the West; there is considerable scholarly scepticism here, but the extravagances of the plans fall in well with Alexander's mood in his last days.
11. Cunliffe, *Ancient Celts*, 140–142.
12. Strabo 4.1.13.
13. Strabo 5.1.6; though Strabo claims the Balkan Boii were refugees from the defeated Boii in Italy.
14. Polybios 2.22.1; they were prominent in the Battle of Telamon against Rome in 225 BC (2.30.4–5).
15. Cunliffe, *Ancient Celts*, map 6.2.
16. Andras Mocsy, *Pannonia and Upper Moesia*, London 1974, 2–7.

17. Cunliffe, *Ancient Celts*, map 21, page 452, showing the distribution of 'La Tène finds'; there are strong indications along the river, one in the region around Budapest, the other in the region of the Banat, about Belgrade – the territory of the Scordisci.
18. Appian, *Illyrian Wars* 5.
19. Onomaris is probably no more than a legend, based on some action which took the local imagination. She is said to have led the Galatians across the Danube, but in what direction is not known: Ellis, *Celt and Greek*, 64, expands this to leading them in the campaign of conquest.
20. *Etymologicum Magnum*, 776, 39; Hubert, *History of the Keltic People*, vol 2, 42.
21. Hubert, *History of the Keltic People*, 60–62 is an example, but more recent discussions, as by Cunliffe, *Ancient Celts*, 192, are much more restrained, indeed minimal.
22. Cunliffe, *Ancient Kelts*, map 21, page 452.
23. Ibid, map 22, page 453; M.J. Treister, 'The Kelts in the North Pontic area: a Reassessment', *Antiquity* 67, 1993, 789–804 and M. Shchukin, 'The Kelts in Eastern Europe', *Oxford Journal of Archaeology* 14, 1995, 201–227.
24. Arrian, *Anabasis* 7.15.4.
25. Diodoros 20.19 (the date is 310 BC).
26. Polyainos, *Stratagems* 7.42; Athenaios, 10.443H (from Hermippos).
27. This is Pompeius Trogus' explanation for Gallic expansion; as a Vocontian Gaul himself his testimony is valuable: Justin 34.4.1–7, and 44.5.11.
28. Ellis, *Celt and Greek*, 64–65; Cunliffe, *Ancient Celts*, map 21, page 452, for the distribution of these finds.
29. *Ibid* 66; Daphne Nash, *Coinage in the Keltic World*, London, 1987.
30. 3000 in the original invasion force in 334, brigaded with a smaller set of Triballi and Illyrians (Arrian, *Anabasis* 1.28), 3500 joined at Susa (Quintus Curtius 5.1.41), 5000 joined at the Hydaspes in India in 326 (Quintus Curtius 9.3.21); the return from India was disastrous, and the army suffered many casualties; see also Donald W. Engels, *Alexander the Great and the Logistics of the Macedonian Army*, Berkeley and Los Angeles 1976, tables 4–6.
31. Engels, *Alexander/Logistics, passim*; J.D. Grainger, *Antipater's Dynasty*, Barnsley 2017.
32. At Kypsela, in south-west Thrace, and at Kabyle: Archibald, *Odrysian Kingdom* 307.
33. *Ibid*, 309–315.
34. Strabo 7.5.12.
35. Diodoros 19.7 3.7–9; Pausanias 1.10.4; Helen S. Lund, *Lysimachos*, Oxford 1992, 40–43.
36. Archibald, *Odrysian Kingdom*, 308–309.
37. Pausanias 10.19.4.
38. Plutarch, *Demetrios* 30.1; Appian, *Syrian Wars* 55; Polybios 5.67.4–10.
39 Archibald, *Odrysian Kingdom* 316.
40. Diodoros 21.2.1–3.

Chapter 2
1. Pausanias 10.1.4.
2. Helen S. Lund, *Lysimachos, a Study in Hellenistic Kingship*, London 1992.
3. Polybios 2.19.7–8.
4. Suetonius, *Tiberius* 8.
5. Rankin, *Celts*, 87.
6. John D. Grainger, *Seleukos Nikator, Building a Hellenistic Kingdom*, London 1990, ch. 10; Lund, *Lysimachos*.
7. Appian, *Syrian Wars* 56 and 63; Memnon *FGrH* 434 F 11.
8. Memnon 13; Justin 24.1.8.
9. Trogus, *Prologue* 24; Justin 17.2.13–14; 24.2–3.
10. Trogus, *Prologue* 17; Justin 17.2.13–15.
11. Trogus, *Prologue* 24; Justin 24.2–7.
12. The main modern discussions of the invasions of Macedon and Greece is by G Nachtergael, *Les Galates en Grece et les Soteria a Delphes*, Brussels 1977; see also Karl Strobel, *Die Galater, Geschichte und Eigenart des Keltisches Staatenbildung auf den Boden deseHellenistischen Kleinasian*, Berlin 1996, 186–226.

13. Pausanias 10.1.4.
14. The force commanded by Brennos in the next year (279) is stated by Pausanias to have had 152,000 infantry and 20,400 cavalry, but the cavalry was really 61,200, since each cavalryman was accompanied by two grooms who could take his place if he fell (Pausanias 10.1.6). This was in fact the full force in 279, and so each of the three forces in 280 was apparently a third of the whole, though the number was clearly exaggerated.
15. Pausanias 10.1.4.
16. Pausanias 10.14.4.
17. Archibald, *Odrysai*.
18. Justin 24.4.9.
19. Appian, *Illyrian Wars* 5.
20. Justin 24.5.1–4.
21. It is worth recalling that he had recently handed over a considerable force to Pyrrhos, who had taken it to Italy. Presumably these were mercenaries or volunteers, but it was still a considerable reduction in his available force.
22. Justin 24.5.5–7; Pausanias 10.1.4; Diodoros 22.3.2; N.G.L. Hammond, *The Macedonian State, the Origin, Institutions, and History*, Oxford 1989, 299.
23. Justin 24.5.8–11.
24. Pausanias 10.1.4.
25. Plutarch, *Pyrrhos* 22; Eusebios, *Chronographia* I, 233; A.J. Sachs and H. Hunger, *Astronomical Diaries and Related Texts from Babylonia*, Vol. I, Vienna 1988, 281.
26. Plutarch, *Pyrrhos* 22.1; for a discussion see F.W. Walbank, *A Commentary on Polybius*, vol. I, Oxford 1957, 49–51.
27. For the succession of these brief kings see N.G.L. Hammond and F.W. Walbank, *A History of Macedonia*, vol III, Oxford 1988, appendix 2; the sources are there detailed and discussed.
28. Diodoros 21.7.
29. See John D. Grainger, *Antipater's Dynasty*, Barnsley 2019, 208–214.
30. Plutarch, *Moralia* 851e; see also Pascalis Paschidis, 'Between City and King: Prosopographical Studies on the Intermediaries between the Cities of the Greek Mainland and the Aegean and the Royal Courts in the Hellenistic Period (322–190 BC)', *Meletemata* 59, Athens 2008, 153–159.
31. Justin 24.5.12–14.
32. Eusebius, *Chronographia* 1.235.
33. This is the suggestion of W.W. Tarn, *Antigonos Gonatas*, Oxford 1911, 167.
34. Pausanias 10.19.5–6; for a comment on the numbers see note 14 in this chapter.
35. Pausanias 10.20.1 lists Paionia alongside Macedon and Thrace as specific victims of the previous attacks.
36. This is the route claimed by Hammond, *Macedonian State*, 200.
37. Justin 24.6.1–3.

Chapter 3
1. Pausanias 10.20.1.
2. Justin 24.7.2.
3. Sources for these events: Pausanias 10.19.5–23.9; Justin 24.6 – 8; Diodoros 22.9; of modern accounts, Tarn, *Antigonos Gonatas* 148–157; Nachtergael, *Galates*, 140–164; Strobel, *Galater*; R. Flaceliere, *Les Aitoliens a Delphes*, Paris 1937, 93–104.
4. Pausanias 10.20.3.
5. Pausanias 10.21.1.
6. Pausanias 10.20.4–21.2; Justin omits the Thermopylai fight; Nachtergael, *Galates* 140–150.
7. Pausanias 10.22.1, though this part of the text has gaps.
8. Pausanias 10.22.4 puts their number at 40,000, which is not believable; still less is Justin's figure of 65,000 (24.7.9).
9. Pausanias 10.22.1–4.
10. The Aitolians put up statues of Apollo, Artemis, and Leto at Delphi later; these were possibly the divinities who 'appeared'.

11. Pausanias 10.23.11; their availability suggest that these contingents had not retreated very far from Thermopylai after the joint army broke up; with the pass open their own danger was increased, of course.
12. Pausanias 1.4.4 and 10.23.1–6; Pausanias claims 16,000 killed in the fight – again not a believable figure; Justin 24.7.1–15 gives all the credit to the Delphians, and does not once mention the Aitolians; certainly Pausanias implies that the fighting was done by Delphi and the Phokians.
13. The evidence is a decree of Kos of the next year (276) – Austin 66 – which celebrates Apollo's inviolate status, but Livy, Appian, and Diodoros all say the sanctuary was looted. These are, of course, all much later sources.
14. Pausanias 10.23.7–8.
15. Pausanias 10.23.8.
16. Pausanias 10.23.8; Justin 4.8.16; Diodoros 22.9.3.
17. Scordisci: Justin 32.3.6–8; Nachtergael, *Galates* 164–172.; see chapter 4.
18. Complaints about this by Lykiskos the Akarnanian, Polybios 9.35.1; the absence of any mention of the Aitolians in Justin's account is perhaps a sign of the antagonism they had provoked by their harping on the matter; cf C. Champion, 'Polybius, Aetolia, and the Gallic attack on Delphi (279 BC)', *Historia* 45, 1996, 315–328 for a study of the 'legend' of the Aitolian defence which developed afterwards.
19. Austin 66, for the inscription from Kos; for the *Soteria*, Nachtergael, *Galates*, 295–382 and Burstein 62.
20. Pausanias 10.23.8.
21. Pausanias 10.15.2 and 18.7.
22. A.J. Reinach, 'Un Monument Delphien: l'Aitolie sur les Trophees Gaulois de Kallion', *Journal International d'Archeologie Numismatique* 1911, 177–240, lists these coins on 187–203.
23. Pausanias 10.16.2.
24. Pausanias 1.3.5.
25. *Syll* (3) 398.
26. Strabo 4.1.3; Justin 33.3; Cassius Dio 37, *fr*. 90; Orosius 5.15.25: see also A.L.F. Rivet, *Gallia Narbonensis, Southern Gaul in Roman Times*, London 1988, 45; C. Champion, 'Polybius, Aetolia, and the Gallic attack on Delphi (279 BC)', *Historia* 45, 1996, 315–328.
27. Justin 3.3.6–8.
28. Livy 38.16; Memnon *FGrH* 434 F 19.
29. Memnon *FGrH* 434 F 18; Polyainos 6.7.2.
30. Justin 25.1–2; Trogus, *Prologue* 25; Diogenes Laetius 2.141.
31. Tarn, *Antigonos Gonatas*, ch 7.
32. Burstein 100 = *OGIS* 55 = Austin 270.
33. *P. Cairo Zen* 1.59019, line 6; Porphyry, *FGrH* 260 F 3.10
34. Plutarch, *Pyrrhos* 26.
35. *Ibid* 34; Pausanias 1.13.8 and 2.2250 1.4.

Chapter 4
1. Livy 38.16.1; Diodoros 22.9.3; one of those occasions when the Galatians were said to be annihilated.
2. Livy 38.16.3.
3. Justin 32.3.8.
4. Apart from Justin's comment, the name is used by Livy referring to 197 BC, by which time they were a fully-organized and mature state; Livy was writing, like Trogus, two or more centuries later than his reference.
5. Archibald, *Odrysian Kingdom*, 302–309.
6. *Ibid*; one of these men claimed the title of *basileus*.
7. Arrian, *Anabasis* 1.
8. Appian, *Illyrian Wars* 3; Appian says the tribe was extinct in his day.
9. This, of course, was the position of the Galatians in the Sordiscian kingdom, as lords controlling their non-Galatian subjects, the descendants of the previous inhabitants; it may not be the position of the rulers of the Tylis kingdom.

228 The Galatians

10. Summary accounts are in Hammond, *Macedonian State*, part XII, and R. Malcolm Errington, *A History of Macedonia*, Berkley and Los Angeles 1990, 162–190; see also Tarn, *Antigonos Gonatas*.
11. Justin 32.3.9–12; Strabo 4.1.13.
12. Athenaios 6.234b–c.
13. Ibid.
14. Hubert, *History of the Celtic People*, vol. 2, 60–61; there are archaeological indications of Celtic settlements such as burials and metalwork. Dacia was not, it seems, an organized state until the mid-second century BC.
15. Athenaios 6.234b–c.
16. Strabo 7.5.12.
17. Mocsy, *Pannonia and Upper Moesia*, 60–66.
18. D. O hOgain, *The Celts, a History*, Woodbridge 2002, 60.
19. Cunliffe, *Ancient Celts*, 319–321; G. Alfoldy, *Noricum*, London 1974.
20. Mocsy, *Pannonia*, 66.
21. Justin 32.3.5; Livy 33.1 9.1–5.
22. Alfoldy, *Noricum*; Cunliffe, *Ancient Celts*, 319–320.
23. Mocsy, *Pannonia* 10.
24. Cunliffe, *Ancient Celts*, maps 20 and 21.
25. Polybios 4.46; Trogus, *Prologue* 25.
26. Polybios 4.46; Justin 32.3.6.
27. Justin 25.2.
28. The main studies of the Tylis state are by G. Mihailov, *Trakite*, Sofia 1972 (in Bulgarian), and the several essays in L.F. Vagalinski (ed.), *In Search of Celtic Tylis in Thrace (III C. BC)*, Sofia 2010.
29. Pausanias 10.2 3.4.
30. Justin 25.2.
31. Memnon *FGrH* 434 F 11.20; Livy 38.16.2–3.
32. Hubert, *History of the Celtic People*, 43.
33. Archibald, *Odrysai*, 313–314.
34. L. Lazarov, 'The Celtic Tylate Style in the Time of Cavaros' in Vagalinski, *Search*, 97–117.
35. Suggested by more than one contributor in Vagalinski, *Search*.
36. K D 'Celts, Greeks and Thracians in Thrace during the third century BC', in Vagalinski, *Search*, 57–66.
37. Polybios 4.46.3–4.
38. F.W. Walbank, *A Commentary on Polybius*, vol. 1, Oxford 1957, 499 – 500.
39. Polybios 4.38.1–10, and 46.3–4; Thomas Russell, *Byzantium and the Bosporus*, Oxford 2017, 94–98.
40. Polybius 4.32; Walbank, *Commentary* 1.506–507; Sheila L. Ager, *Interstate Arbitrations in the Greek World, 337–90 BC*, Berkeley and Los Angeles 1996, no. 51.
41. Polybios 4.46.4–5; 8.22.1.
42. Antiochos III took over the ruined city in 196 and restored it; its destruction is attributed to the Thracians, but how long before is not clear: Polybios 18.51.7.
43. Polybios 8.22.1.
44. A summary account is in Cunliffe, *Ancient Celts*, 151–152, 198–202; Hubert, *History of the Celtic People* 2.44–45; Ellis, *Celt and Greek*, 59–60.
45. This distribution is based in part on map 22 in Cunliffe, *Ancient Celts* (page 453), and on a similar map in 'Galatians', Wikipedia, oddly entitled, 'Lugii–Trokmi').
46. This is the sort of construction which would have been built in Asia Minor as bases for the three raiding tribes, but which have not been located; the tribes certainly built them in Galatia once they had settled there.
47. M.J. Treister, 'The Celts in the North Pontic Area, a Reassessment', *Antiquity* 67, 1997, 789–801.
48. Austin 115.

Chapter 5

1. The only source for the events at the Straits is Livy 38.16.1–9.
2. Appian, *Syrian Wars* 63; for Philetairos' relationship with Seleukos I and Antiochos I see R.E. Allen, *The Attalid Kingdom, a Constitutional History*, Oxford 1983, 11–14, and Roger B. McShane, *The Foreign Policy of the Attalids of Pergamon*, Urbana IL 1964, 32–35.
3. Antigonos and Antiochos fought a small naval war: Memnon *FGrH* 434, F 10.
4. The Northern War: Memnon *FGrH* 434 F 9.
5. Crossing the Bosporos: Memnon *FGrH* 434 F 11.10–11; Livy 38.16.7–9.
6. Memnon *FGrH* 434 F 11.11; clearly a paraphrase, since the term 'barbarians' would hardly have been included in the original.
7. I have discussed this matter in John D. Grainger, *Great Power Diplomacy in the Hellenistic World*, London 2017, especially chapter 1.
8. Memnon *FGrH* 434 F 11.11; H.H. Schmitt, *Die Staatsvertrage des Altertums*, vol. III, Munich 1969, 469; Austin 159; Burstein 16.
9. Livy 38.16.9: Henri-Louis Fernaux, *Notables et elites des cites de Bithynie aux epoques hellenistique et romaine*, Dijon 2004, 59–60; G. Vitucci, *Il regno di Bitinia*, Rome 1953, 35; Stephen Mitchell, *Anatolia, Land Men and Gods in Asia Minor*, 2 vols, Oxford 1993, 1.15–16.
10. Livy 38.27.7.
11. Livy 38.16.11–14.
12. Memnon, *FGrH* 434 F 11.11.
13. Christian Marek, *In the Land of a Thousand Gods, a History of Asia Minor in the Ancient World*, trans. Steven Rendall, Princeton NJ, 2016, suggests 30,000–35,000 men overall (p. 204), though I feel this is too high, and it omits dependants.
14. Livy 38.16.10 – 12.
15. *OGIS* 748; M. Launey, 'Un episode oublie de l'invasion galate en Asie Mineure', *Revue des etudes anciennes* 66, 1944, 217–236; the celebratory relief is reproduced in a rather dim photograph in F. W. Hasluck, *Cyzicus*, Cambridge 1910, and in *Bulletin de Correspondemce Hellenique* 56, 1932, plate xxv; K.M.T. Atkinson, 'The Seleukids and the Greek Cities of Western Asia Minor', *Antichthon* 2, 1968, 32–57.
16. Strabo 13.1.27 (from Hegesianax); J.M. Cook, *The Troad*, Oxford 1973, 100 and 364.
17. Xenophon, *Hellenica* 7.20 – 22; Ellis, *Celt and Greek*, 52–54.
18. For an idiosyncratic account of the relationship of Massalia with the neighbouring Kelts, see Arnaldo Momigliano, *Alien Wisdom, the Limits of Hellenization*, Cambridge 1975, 50–73.
19. Parthenios 8; I. Lampsakos 4; Austin 197.
20. Strabo 4.1.13 (from Timagenes); Justin 3.3.36.
21. Diodoros 22.9.1.
22. *I. Didyma* 426.
23. C.B. Welles, *Royal Correspondence of the Hellenistic Period*, London 1934 (reprinted Chicago 1974) no. 5; for Seleukos' patronage of Didyma see Susan Sherwin-White and Amelie Kuhrt, *From Samarkhand to Sardis, A New Approach to the Seleucid Empire*, London 1993, 24–26.
24. *I. Didyma* 479, 480; G.E. Bean, *Aegean Turkey*, London 1966, 195.
25. Bean, *Aegean Turkey*, 195.
26. See note 13, and *Palatine Anthology* 7.492.
27. Burstein 17.
28. Plutarch, *Parallela minora* 15.
29. *I. Erythrai* 24 and 28.
30. *IG* XI.4.1105; Austin 228.
31. *TAM* V.2.881.
32. Welles, *Royal Correspondence* 10–13 = Austin 21; Cook, *Troad* 365–366.
33. See, for the history of Karia, Richard A. Billows, *Kings and Colonists, aspects of Macedonian Imperialism*, Leiden 1995, 81–84 and 90–96; for Pleistarchos see John D. Grainger, *Antipater's Dynasty*, Barnsley 2019, 207–208.
34. Appian, *Syrian Wars* 65.
35. Livy, 38.16.10.

36. Austin 168; Burstein 19; see also M. Worrle, 'Antiochos I, Achaios der Altere, und des Galater', *Chiron* 5, 1975, 59–87.
37. See John D. Grainger, *The Syrian Wars*, Leiden 2010, 83 – 84.
38. Pausanias 10.3 2.4; Mitchell, *Anatolia* 1.17.
39. Pausanias 10.30.9.
40. Stephanus of Byzantion sv. *Agriai*.
41. *Journal of Hellenic Studies, Archaeological Reports* 1989/1990, 118; rejected by Karl Strobel, 'State Formation by the Galatians of Asia Minor', *Anatolica* 28, 2002, 1–46.
42. Grainger, *Syrian Wars*.
43. Getzel M. Cohen, *The Hellenistic Settlements in Europe, the Islands, and Asia Minor*, Berkeley and Los Angeles 1995.

Chapter 6
1. Diodoros 15.70.
2. Plato, *Laws*, 637de.
3. Memnon *FGrH* 434 F 11, 5.11; Austin 159; Burstein 16; Schmitt, *Staatsvertrage*, 469.
4. Polyainos 4.6.17; Tarn, *Antigonos Gonatas*, 169.
5. M. Launey, *Recherches sur les armees hellenistiques*, 2nd ed., Paris 1987, discusses Galatians as soldiers pp. 490–534, but only incidentally as mercenaries; Angelos Chaniotis, *War in the Hellenistic World*, Oxford 2005; and G.T. Griffith, *The Mercenaries of the Hellenistic World*, Cambridge 1935.
6. Plutarch, *Pyrrhos* 26; Diodoros 22.12.
7. Plutarch, *Pyrrhos* 26.2.
8. Pausanias 1.7.2.
9. Polyainos 4.6.17; Antigonos paid at the rate of one stater per man.
10. Polyainos 2.29.2.
11. Tarn, *Antigonos*, commented that they 'stood by their salt', a very British imperial sentiment (written just pre-Great War).
12. See note 5.
13. Gunther Holbl, *A History of the Ptolemaic Empire*, translated by Tina Saavedra, London 2001, 38–40; Grainger, *Syrian Wars*, 83–84.
14. Pausanias 1.7.2.
15. *Ibid*.
16. Pausanias 1.7.2; Kallimachos, *Hymn to Delos*, 4.185–187; H.P. Laubscher, 'Ein Ptolemaischer Gallierdenkmal', *Antike Kunst* 30, 1987, 131–154.
17. Justin 26.2.1–6, an imaginative account which actually says little about either Antigonos or the mutineers. Tarn, *Antigonos Gonatas*, 300, claims that they were 'a new tribe' recruited as a whole, but this is not evident in Justin's account.
18. Justin 27.1.1–2; Porphyry *FGrH* 260 F 43; Polyainos 8.50; Grainger, *Syrian Wars*, 155–160.
19. Austin 267.
20. Appian, *Syrian Wars* 66; Polybios 4.48.8; Trogus, *Prologue* 27.
21. Polybios 5.40–60; E. Will, *Histoire Politique du Monde Hellenistique*, vol. 2, Nancy 1982, 17–18; Grainger, *Syrian Wars*, 183–198.
22. Polybios 5.59.3.
23. Polybios 5.59.8.
24. Livy 37.40; Appian, *Syrian Wars* 32; B. Bar-Kochva, *The Seleukid Army, Organisation and Tactics in the Great Campaigns*, Cambridge 1976, 163–173.
25. Griffith, *Mercenaries*, notes these Gauls at various points, but does not consider them as a distinctive set of mercenaries.
26. Polybios 5.82.5.
27. Polybios 2.65.2; Griffith, *Mercenaries*, 69–70.
28. Polybios 5.3.2 ('some Gallic horse').
29. Not noted in Schmitt, *Staatsvertrage*.
30. Justin 32.3.5; Livy 40.57.5.
31. Livy 42.51.
32. Livy 44.26.2–27.7.

33. Polybios 30.25.
34. Cunliffe, *Ancient Celts*, 208–209.
35. Polybios 5.77.2–4; 78; 111.2–4; Griffith, *Mercenaries*, 173–174.

Chapter 7
1. Appian, *Syrian Wars* 62.
2. A treaty between Mithradates and the Tektosages must be assumed. The fragment of the *Karike* of Apollonios of Aphrodisias which notes that Ankyra was assigned to the Galatians before 266 implies such a formal agreement (Stephanos of Byzantion, sv Ankyra, *FGrH* 740 F 14).
3. Strobel, 'State Formation'; Jeremiah R. Dondey *et al*, 'Celtic Sacrifice in Gordion', *Archaeology* 55, 2002.
4. The territories of the three tribes vary with authorities; for a reasonable map see Stephen Mitchell, *Anatolia, Land, Men, and Gods in Asia Minor*, vol. I, Oxford 1993, maps 4(a) and (b), pages 52–53; the land of the Trokmoi is described by Christopher Garber, 'New Insight into the Settlement History of the Tavium Region', in K. Strobel (ed.), *New Perspectives on the Historical Geography and Topography of Anatolia in the II and I millennium BC*, Florence 2008.
5. The raids into Lykia can be easily argued to be undated, or misinterpreted (see chapter 5).
6. Strabo 12.5.1.
7. Strabo 12.5.1–3; his placement of the tribes is not generally accepted, but his indication of the evolution of the Galatian government system is convincing.
8. Anne Ross, 'Ritual and the Druids' in Miranda J. Green (ed.), *The Celtic World*, London 1995, 423–444, at 437 in a very speculative paragraph; Strabo discussed Pessinos in the next chapter of his work, so why he should fail to identify it as Drunemeton is surprising; I conclude they were not the same place.
9. For more details see Mitchell, *Anatolia*, 1.51–58; K. Bittel, 'Die Galater in Kleinasien, archaeologisch geschen', in D. Pippida (ed.), *Assimilation et Resistance à la culture Greco-Romaine dans le Monde Ancien*, Bucharest and Paris 1976, 241–249. There is little on this in Green, *Celtic World*, or in Rankin, *Celts and the Classical World*.
10. Mitchell, *Anatolia*, 50–51.
11. Lynn E. Roller, 'Hellenistic Epigraphic Texts from Gordion', *Anatolian Studies* 37, 1987, 103–133; *OGIS* 757.
12. Justin 25.7.8–9; Livy 38.16.13.
13. Mitchell, *Anatolia*, 20; this is the underlying sentiment in other descriptions of Galatian conduct, also often simply an assumption.
14. Memnon, *FGrH* 434 F 14.
15. *Ibid*; Justin 27.3.
16. BC McGing, *The Foreign Policy of Mithradates Eupator, King of Pontus*, Leiden 1986, 20–21, states that 'when Ariobarzanes died he was at variance with the Galatians', but no authority is given for this statement, nor is there any evidence for it; it is in fact only an assumption from the fact that war followed his death.
17. Austin 168, in which the villages are said to be part of the estates of Akhaios.
18. Memnon, *FGrH* 434, F 15; Polyainos 4.16.
19. Grainger, *Syrian Wars* 153–170.
20. Details can be found in R.S. Bagnall, *The Administration of the Ptolemaic Possessions outside Egypt*, Leiden 1976.
21. R.A. Billows, *Kings and Colonists, Aspects of Macedonian Imperialism*, Leiden 1995, 94–96.
22. Allen, *Attalid Kingdom*; McShane, *Foreign Policy*.
23. Justin 27.2.10–11; Polyainos 4.9.6; Athenaios 13.593e (from Phylarchos); Plutarch, *Moralia* 489a–b. The status of the Galatians in this war is widely assumed to be as mercenary hirelings, but since Antiochos was allied with Mithradates and the battle took place deep in Galatian territory it is more reasonable to count them as independent allies. It would be highly unusual to make war on the state simply because some of its people were serving as mercenaries on the other side; I conclude the 'Galatians' were the Tektosages; they may also, of course, have had assistance from the other states.
24. Justin 27.2.11.

25. McGing, *Foreign Policy*, 22.
26. Justin 27.2.
27. This was the policy which was the foundation of McShane's theory of Pergamon as the centre of a symmachy: McShane, *Foreign Policy*.
28. This truce is not recorded, but the fact that Seleukos marched off to Iran after the defeat rather suggests that one existed.
29. Justin 41.4.8–9; Strabo 11.8.
30. *OGIS* 273–279; E.J. Bikerman, 'Notes on Seleucid and Parthian Chronology', *Berytos* 8, 1943–1944, 73–83 at 76–78; Austin 231; Burstein 85; discussed with a variety of conclusions by David Magie, *Roman Rule in Asia Minor*, Princeton NJ 1950, 2.737–739; E.V. Hansen, *The Attalids of Pergamon*, Ithaca NY, 1971, 34–38; Allen, *Attalid Kingdom*, 28–38 and 195–199: McShane, *Foreign Policy*, 59–61; Will, *Histoire Politique* 1.296–301.
31. Justin 27.4.9–10; Aelian, *In Animaliam* 6.44; Pliny *NH* 7.158.
32. Trogus, *Prologue* 27.

Chapter 8
1. *OGIS* 277 (= Austin 231).
2. R.A. Billows, *Kings and Colonists, Aspects of Macedonian Imperialism*, Leiden 1995, 90–91, 99–100, 110.
3. John Ma, *Antiochos III and the Cities of Western Asia Minor*, Oxford 1999, 54–63.
4. Polybios 4.48.5–12.
5. Polybios 5.57.4–6; this may be one of the reasons Antiochos Hierax had failed in his attempt to overthrow his brother; both he and Akhaios were using an army recruited mainly in Asia Minor.
6. Polybios 7.15.1–18.10, 78, 8.15.1–21.10.
7. *OGIS* 275 and 276 (= Austin 231).
8. Justin 27.2.11.
9. Polybios 5.107.4.
10. This is the interpretation of the sculptures of handsome Galatians fighting and dying on the altar of the sanctuary of Athena at Pergamon, generally dated to the late third century.
11. Polybios 5.77–78.
12. Mitchell, *Anatolia* 1.22.
13. Polybios 5.111.1–7.
14. Livy 38.7.10.
15. Livy 29.10.4–8 and 11.3–8.
16. John D. Grainger, 'Antiochos III in Thrace', *Historia* 45, 1996, 329–343.
17. Austin 197.
18. Appian, *Syrian Wars* 6.
19. In John D. Grainger, *The Roman War of Antiochos the Great*, Leiden 2002, 80–82, I favoured local recruitment within Thrace; John Ma, *Antiochus III and the Cities of Western Asia Minor*, Oxford 1999, 92, claims them for the Asian state.
20. Livy 37.40–41.
21. Livy 38.18.1–3 and 7.
22. Livy 38.12.2–4; a later speech, chiefly composed by Livy rather than Vulso, goes into more local detail.
23. Livy 38.12.5–17.11; John D. Grainger, 'The Campaign of Cn. Manlius Vulso in Asia Minor', *Anatolian Studies* 54, 1995, 23–42, for a discussion of the intricacy of the route, and its purpose.
24. Livy 38.18.1.
25. Livy 38.19.1–2.
26. Livy 38.19.6–20.1.
27. Livy 38.20.1–23.11; Polybios 21.37.3.1–39.14; there are considerable difficulties with the route of the army, discussed by Mitchell, *Anatolia* 1.23–24 and Magie, *Roman Rule* 1.1307.
28. Livy 38.25.1–3.
29. Livy 38.26.3.
30 Livy 38.2 6.1–27.

31. Livy 32.27.7; this is not proof that the Galatians indulged in raids for 'many years'.
32. Livy 38.27.1 – 9; Vulso carried the loot away on his journey towards Rome, but lost a lot of it in an ambush by Thracians. He was lamentably liable to fall into ambushes.
33. Livy 38.40.1–2.

Chapter 9
1. Livy 38.38.2–17.
2. Livy 38.40.1–2; Polybios 21.40.6.
3. Livy 38.18.11 and 13.
4. This is not really all that different from the Roman social-political system of patrons and clients.
5. Livy 38.19.2 (at Mount Olympos); Polybios 22.21 (a brief portrait).
6. Memnon 28.1; Polybios 23.1.4 and 3.1; Livy 46.9; Justin 32.4.2–3 and *Prologue* 32; Cornelius Nepos, *Hannibal* 10–11; McShane, *Foreign Policy*, 159–160; Mitchell, *Anatolia* 1.24.
7. *OGIS* 298; M. Segre, 'Due nuovi testi storica', *Rivista de filologia*, 60, 1932, 446–452; Magie, *Roman Rule* 2.1194, 1196.
8. Polybios 23.9.2; Strabo 12.3.11; Livy 40.2.6; McGing, *Foreign Policy* 25.
9. Polybios 24.14.6; McShane, *Foreign Policy*, 161, expands this to 'a number of Gallic tribes', which is not justified.
10. Strabo 12.3.41.
11. Polybios 24.14–15 and 25.2; Mitchell, *Anatolia* 1.25; McShane, *Foreign Policy* 161 – 163; McGing, *Foreign Policy* 26–29.
12. Livy 42.57.7.
13. Livy 44.28.12–12.
14. Polybios 29.22.4; and 20.1.2–3; Livy 45.19.3 and 12.
15. Polyainos 4.8.1.
16. Polybios 30.3.7–8; Livy 45.3 4.12–14; some believe that Licinius was sent to encourage the Galatians, but Polybios was reporting on the result of the embassy and then reading back to assume that that result explained what happened in the meeting. This is not evidence.
17. This aid from Kappadokia and Syria is only vaguely apparent in the sources (Polybios 30.3 4.4 and 31.8.2), but it fits with the wider diplomatic situation.
18. Livy 45.34.11–14 and 44.21.
19. Polybios 30.28 and 30.6.
20. Polybios 31.2: Welles, *Royal Correspondence* 54 (Amblada), 52 (Ionian League); *Milet* 1.9.307 (Miletos).
21. It is all too easy to take the celebrations as evidence of the places being under direct threat, but the written evidence does not extend Galatian military activity beyond Synnada.
22. Diodoros 31.13.
23. Mitchell, *Anatolia* 1.26; Will, *Histoire Politique* 2.246; Walbank, *Commentary* 3.454.
24. Polybios 30.18.
25. Polybios 37.2.13.
26. Polybios 30.30.6.
27. Austin 244; Welles, *Royal Correspondence* 61.
28. Welles, *Royal Correspondence* 61.
29. Sir William Ramsay, *A Historical Commentary on St Paul's Epistle to the Galatians*, London 1900, 62.
30. Livy 38.8.9.
31. A century later King Amyntas is said to have owned 300 flocks of sheep.
32. Strabo 12.5.41; Mitchell, *Anatolia* 1.23.
33. Polybios 31.8.1–2
34. Polybios 30.30.2–3.
35. Ramsay, *Historical Commentary*, 45–46.
36. Welles, *Royal Correspondence* 54.
37. Strabo 12.8.14.
38. *Ibid.*

39. Justin 37.1.2; the settlement as a whole is discussed by Robert Kallet-Marx, *Hegemony to Empire, the Development of the Roman Imperium in the East from 148 to 62 BC*, Berkeley and Los Angeles 1995, 109–122.
40. Mitchell, *Anatolia*, 1.29, note 23.

Chapter 10
1. Zonaras 9.28.3–7; Livy, *Per.* 50; Diodoros 31.9a; Polybios 36.17.15; Strabo 13.4.2; for modern accounts, Kallet-Marx, *Hegemony to Empire*, 31 – 37; Erich Gruen, *The Hellenistic World and the Coming of Rome*, Berkeley and Los Angeles 1984, 431–433; John D. Grainger, *Rome, Parthia, India*, Barnsley 2000, 30 – 38 for a more extensive account of Andriskos' adventure.
2. Livy, *Per.* 53.
3. Kallet-Marx, *Hegemony to Empire*, 40–41; Gruen, *Hellenistic World*, 435: 'the Republic accepted responsibility for the defence of Macedonia'.
4. Julius Obsequens 16.
5. Livy (Oxy) 54.
6. Livy, *Per.* 56.
7. Kallet-Marx, *Hegemony to Empire*, 347–349; F.W. Walbank, 'The Original Extent of the via Egnatia,' *Liverpool Classical Monthly* 2, 1977, 73–74; W.L. Adams, 'Polybius, Pliny, and the via Egnatia', in W.L. Adams and E.N. Borza (eds), *Philip II, Alexander the Great and the Macedonian Heritage*, Washington DC 1982, 269–302.
8. Mocsy, *Pannonia and Upper Moesia*, 12.
9. Appian, *Illyrian Wars*, 22.
10. Sherk, 48.
11. Mocsy, *Pannonia and Upper Moesia*, 10–13.
12. Strabo 7.2.3.
13. Livy, *Per.* 63; Eutropius 4.24; Appian, *Illyrian Wars* 6; Florus 1.3 9.3–4.
14. Livy, *Per.* 63; Strabo 5.1.8; Appian, *Gallic Wars* 1.13; Plutarch, *Marius* 16.
15. Livy, *Per.* 63; Florus 1.39.5.
16. Sherk 52; Frontinus, *Stratagems* 2.4.3; Kallet-Marx, *Hegemony to Empire* 223–225.
17. Sherk, 52.
18. Cicero, *in Pisonem* 61; Ammianus Marcellinus 27.4.10.
19. *Lex de Cilicia Macedoniaque provinciis*; see M. Hassall, M. Crawford, and J. Reynolds, 'Rome and the Eastern Provinces at the end of the Second Century BC', *Journal of Roman Studies* 64, 1974, 195–220.
20. Julius Obsequens 44.
21. Livy, *Per.* 70; Cicero, *in Pisonem* 84, and *in Verrem* 3.217.
22. Appian, *Illyrian Wars* 5.
23. Thracians: Livy, *Per.* 83; Maedi: Plutarch, *Sulla* 23.
24. Appian, *Mithradatic Wars*, 55; it is possible that this is the same as the war on the Thracians or the Maedi (previous note), but the names of the victims are clear, distinct, and different, and it would seem therefore that this was a different war, though perhaps aimed at the same purpose.
25. Frontinus, *Stratagems* 4.1.43; Sallust, *Histories* 2.80 and 4.18; Rufus Festus, *Breviarum* 7; Eutropius 6.7.
26. Appian, *Illyrian Wars* 5.
27. Frontinus, *Stratagems* 4.1.43; Sallust, *Histories* 2.80; Livy, *Per.* 2, 95; Kallet-Marx, *Hegemony to Empire* 297.
28. Mocsy, *Pannonia and Upper Moesia*, 18; the dating is highly speculative.
29. Strabo 7.5.2; Pliny *NH* 3.147.
30. Strabo 7.5.2.
31. Hubert, *History of the Celtic People* 2.59–60.
32. Strabo 7.3.5; Livy, *Per.* 117; Suetonius, *Caesar* 44, and *Augustus* 8.
33. Sherk, 71.
34. Appian, *Illyrian Wars* 23; Cassius Dio 49.3 6.1–38.1.
35. Cassius Dio 51.23; Livy, *Per.* 134 and 135; Horace, *Carmina*, 3.8.18.

36. In fact, the Moesi had fought harder against being conquered than almost any other of Crassus' victims: Livy, *Per.* 134; Cassius Dio 51.23.5–24.1; Strabo 7.3.4.
37. Mocsy, *Pannonia and Upper Moesia*, 32–33.
38. Cassius Dio 49.3 7.6.
39. Cassius Dio 54.20.3.
40. Cassius Dio 51.2 3.4 and 25.3.
41. Cassius Dio 54.20.2.
42. Cassius Dio 54.2.1.
43. Cassius Dio 54.20.2. This separated the two northern allies, and provided the Roman military with access to the Danube lands, and a second way to the Pannonian country.
44. Cassius Dio 54.3 1.3; attributed to 15 BC by Mocsy, *Pannonia and Upper Moesia* 23.
45. Mocsy, *Pannonia and Upper Moesia* 34; 'their services were for sale', he says, clearly disapproving, but it is only his interpretation.

Chapter 11
1. Justin 37.4.3–6; McGing, *Foreign Policy*, 68–70.
2. Justin 38.1.1; the date of the marriage is not known, though it was probably before Mithradates became king.
3. How this army travelled from Bithynia to Kappadokia is not known, but it seems probable that, geographically, the troops must have marched through Galatia.
4. For a clear account of these events, see McGing, *Foreign Policy* 75–77.
5. Justin 38.2.8; Strabo 12.2.11.
6. Plutarch, *Sulla* 5.3; Magie, *Roman Rule* 1.206 and 2.1163; E. Badian, 'Sulla's Cilician Command', *Studies in Greek and Roman History*, Oxford 1964, 157–178 (from *Athenaeum* 1959).
7. McGing, *Foreign Policy*, 71; Mitchell, *Anatolia* 1.30.
8. Appian, *Mithradatic Wars*, 41; this is a reference to the army in Greece in 86; but it may be assumed that Mithradates recruited Galatians at any time during his reign, at least after 108.
9. Mitchell, *Anatolia*, 30.
10. Mitchell, *Anatolia*, 1.47, citing in particular manumissions at Delphi; Ramsay, *Historical Commentary*, 81–85, based on much the same evidence.
11. Appian, *Mithradatic Wars* 17; Memnon, *FGrH* 434 F 31 and 37.
12. These figures seem enormous, but some historians more or less accept them: Griffith, *Mercenaries*, 190–193; McGing, *Foreign Policy*, 85, accepts them by implication; A.N. Sherwin-White, *Roman Foreign Policy in the East*, 1983, considers them 'not [a] gross exaggeration'. Sheer numbers, of course, do not equate to high quality.
13. Appian, *Mithradatic Wars* 15.
14. *Ibid*, 10.
15. *Ibid*, 11.
16. So much for Nikomedes complaint that his kingdom was depopulated by the actions of Roman slavers.
17. Appian, *Mithradatic Wars* 11.
18. *Ibid* 17.
19. *Ibid* 17; Magie, *Roman Rule* 2.1101.
20. Appian, *Mithradatic Wars* 27-19; McGing, *Foreign Policy* 109–112.
21. Justin 38.3.9; Appian, *Mithradatic Wars* 22-23; McGing, *Foreign Policy* 113–118.
22. Appian, *Mithradatic Wars* 46.
23. Appian, *Mithradatic Wars*, 46.
24. Appian, *Mithradatic Wars*, 64; he attacked Komana.
25. Appian, *Mithradatic Wars*, 65–66.
26. *Ibid*, 66.
27. For Servilius' campaign see Sherwin-White, *Roman Foreign Policy*, 152–158.
28. Plutarch, *Lucullus*, 5.1–6.5, and *Pompeius*, 20.1–2.
29. Plutarch, *Lucullus*, 7.5.
30. Memnon 27.5–6.

31. Plutarch, *Lucullus* 14.1.1.
32. Appian, *Mithradatic Wars*, 109.
33. *Ibid*, 111.
34. Memnon, *FGrH* 434 F 27.2.
35. Appian, *Mithradatic Wars*, 75.
36. Memnon, 44; Plutarch, *Lucullus*, 28.2.
37. 'Posdala' in Mitchell, *Anatolia* 31; the Loeb Strabo (15.2.1) has 'Damala'; Plutarch, *Pompeius*, 31 is content with 'Galatia'; whatever the precise name of the place, it was clearly in Galatia.
38. Sherwin-White, *Roman Foreign Policy*, 226–234; Kallet-Marx, *Hegemony to Empire*, 325–331.
39. Strabo 12.5.2.
40. Stephen Mitchell, 'Blucium and Peion; the Galatian Forts of King Deiotaros', *Anatolian Studies* 24, 1974, 61–75.
41. Mitchell, *Anatolia*, 84–86; Strobel, 'State Formation', is particularly definitive in his choices of the sites, without direct evidence.
42. Mitchell, *Anatolia*, 1.34, and references there.
43. Cicero, *ad Atticum* 6.1.14.
44. [Caesar], *Bellum Alexandrinum* 34.
45. Pharsalos: Caesar, *Civil War* 3.4.5; Philippi: Appian, *Civil War* 4.88; Actium: Plutarch, *Antonius* 63, Vellius Paterculus 2.84.1; Cassius Dio 50.13.8.

Chapter 12
1. Strabo 12.6.3 and 5; the date of his death is not wholly certain; see Barbara Levick, 'The Beginning of Tiberius' Career', *Classical Quarterly*, 1971.
2. Cassius Dio 53.21.2.
3. Strabo 12.6.3; Tacitus, *Annals* 3.48.2; Ronald Syme, *Anatolica, Studies in Strabo*, Oxford 1995, ch. 23, 'The Homonadensian War'.
4. Barbara Levick, *Roman Colonies in Southern Asia Minor*, Oxford 1967.
5. For Pessinos, M. Waelkens, 'The Imperial Sanctuary at Pessinos', *Epigraphica Anatolica* 7, 1986, 37-74, and Angelo Verlinde, *The Roman Sanctuary Site at Pessinos*, Leuven 2015; for Ankyra, Stephen Mitchell and David French, *The Greek and Latin Inscriptions of Ankara*, Vol. I, Munich 2012; for Tavium, Christophe Gerber, 'New Insight into the Settlement History of the Tavium Region', in Karl Strobel (ed.), *New Perspectives on the Historical Geography and Topography of Anatolia in the II and I Millennium BC*, Florence 2008.
6. Syme, *Anatolia*, ch. 12, 'The Status of Armenia Minor'.
7. The campaign of C. Domitius Corbulo during Nero's reign is the classic case.
8. The provincial shuffle is summarized by Christian Marek, *In the Land of a Thousand Gods*, Princeton NJ, 2016, 338–343; see also R.K. Sherk, 'Roman Galatia: the Governors from 25 BC to AD 114', *Aufstieg und Niedergang des Romische Welt*, II.7.2, Berlin, 1980, 954–1052. For the best discussion of the Roman period in Galatia, see Mitchell, *Anatolia*; Syme, *Anatolica*, has many essays in individual issues and subjects.
9. Mitchell and French, *Inscriptions of Ankara*, no. 10, e.g.
10. Mitchell, *Anatolia* 1.108.
11. John D. Grainger, *Nerva and the Imperial Succession Crisis of AD 96–99*, London 2003 ch.≈7, map p. xxiv and tables on p xxvii, for the situation in the 90s.

Appendix
1. Britain: A. Birley, *The Fasti of Roman Britain*, Oxford 1981, 181–186.
2. Herodian 7.5.2; *Historia Augusta*, 'The Three Gordians'.
3. *Historia Augusta*, 'The Three Gordians'; Philostatos, *Lives of the Sophists*.
4. E. Bosch, *Quellen zur Geschichte des Stadt Ankara*, Munich 1967, n. 203.
5. Mitchell, *Anatolia*, 2.85.
6. Birley, *Fasti*, 181–186.
7. Herodian 7.5.8.
8. For the Eastern reluctance to be involved in the Roman governing system, see John D. Grainger, *Syrian Influences in the Roman Empire to AD 300*, London 2018, ch. 1.

Bibliography

Abbreviations
Austin – *The Hellenistic World from Alexander to the Roman Conquest*, 2nd Ed., Cambridge 2006.
Burstein – Stanley M. Burstein (ed.), *The Hellenistic Age from the Battle of Ipsus to the Death of Kleopatra VII*, Cambridge 1985.
FGrH – F. Jacoby, *Die Fragmente der greichischen Historiker*, Berlin from 1923.
I.Didyma – A. Rehm, *Die Inschriften, Milet*, vol 3, Berlin 1914.
I.Erythrai – H. Engelmann and R. Merkelback, *Die Inschriften von Erythrai und Klazomenai*, Bonn, 1973.
IG – *Insciptiones Graecae*.
I.Lampsakos – P. Frisch, *Die Inschriften von Lampsakos*, Bonn 1978.
OGIS – *Orientis Graeci Inscriptiones Selectae*.
Sherk – R.K. Sherk, *Rome and the Greek East to the death of Augustus*, Cambridge 1984.
TAM – *Tituli Asiae Minoris*. Okay

Books and Articles
Sheila L. Ager, *Interstate Arbitrations in the Greek World, 337–90 BC*, Berkeley and Los Angeles 1996.
G. Alfoldy, *Noricum*, London 1974.
R.E. Allen, *The Attalid Kingdom, a Constitutional History*, Oxford 1983.
Zofia Archibald, *The Odrysian Kingdom of Thrace*, Oxford 1998.
K.M.T. Atkinson, 'The Seleukids and the Greek Cities of Western Asia Minor', *Antichthon* 2, 1968, 32–57.
E. Badian, 'Sulla's Cilician Command', *Studies in Greek and Roman History*, Oxford 1964, 157–178.
B. Bar-Kochva, *The Seleukid Army, Organisation and Tactics in the Great Campaigns*, Cambridge 1976.
R.S. Bagnall, *The Administration of the Ptolemaic Possessions outside Egypt*, Leiden 1976.
G.E. Bean, *Aegean Turkey*, London 1966.
E.J. Bikerman, 'Notes on Seleucid and Parthian Chronology', *Berytos* 8, 1943–1944, 73–83.
Richard A. Billows, *Kings and Colonists, aspects of Macedonian Imperialism*, Leiden 1995.
A. Birley, *The Fasti of Roman Britain*, Oxford 1981.
K. Bittel, 'Die Galater in Kleinasien, archaeologisch geschen', in D. Pippida (ed.), *Assimilation et Resistance à la culture Greco-Romaine dans le Monde Ancien*, Bucharest and Paris 1976.
E. Bosch, *Quellen zur Geschichte des Stadt Ankara*, Munich 1967.
C. Champion, 'Polybius, Aetolia, and the Gallic attack on Delphi (279 BC)', *Historia* 45, 1996, 315–328.
Angelos Chaniotis, *War in the Hellenistic World*, Oxford 2005.
Getzel M. Cohen, *The Hellenistic Settlements in Europe, the Islands, and Asia Minor*, Berkeley and Los Angeles 1995.
J.M. Cook, *The Troad*, Oxford 1973.
Barry Cunliffe, *The Ancient Celts*, 2nd ed., Oxford 2018.
Karen Dimitrov, 'Celts, Greeks and Thracians in Thrace during the third century BC', in Vagalinski, *Search*, 57–66.
M. Diepeveen–Jansen, *People, Ideas, and Goods: New Perspectives on 'Celtic Barbarians' in Western and Central Europe (500–250 BC)*, Amsterdam 2001.
Jeremiah R. Dondey *et al*, 'Celtic Sacrifice in Gordion', *Archaeology* 55, 2002.

Peter Beresford Ellis, *Celt and Greek*, London 1997.
Donald W. Engels, *Alexander the Great and the Logistics of the Macedonian Army*, Berkeley and Los Angeles 1976.
R. Malcolm Errington, *A History of Macedonia*, Berkley and Los Angeles 1990.
Henri-Louis Fernaux, *Notables et elites des cites de Bithynie aux epoques hellenistique et romaine*, Dijon 2004.
R. Flaceliere, *Les Aitoliens a Delphes*, Paris 1937.
Christopher Garber, 'New Insight into the Settlement History of the Tavium Region', in K. Strobel (ed.), *New Perspectives on the Historical Geography and Topography of Anatolia in the II and I millennium BC*, Florence 2008.
John D. Grainger, *Antipater's Dynasty*, Barnsley 2019.
John D. Grainger, *Seleukos Nikator, Building a Hellenistic Kingdom*, London 1990.
John D. Grainger, *Great Power Diplomacy in the Hellenistic World*, London 2017.
John D. Grainger, *Syrian Influences in the Roman Empire to AD 300*, London 2018.
John D. Grainger, *The Syrian Wars*, Leiden 2010.
John D. Grainger, 'Antiochos III in Thrace', *Historia* 45, 1996, 329–343.
John D. Grainger, *The Roman War of Antiochos the Great*, Leiden 2002.
John D. Grainger, 'The Campaign of Cn. Manlius Vulso in Asia Minor', *Anatolian Studies* 54, 1995, 23–42.
John D. Grainger, *Nerva and the Imperial Succession Crisis of AD 96–99*, London 2003.
G.T. Griffith, *The Mercenaries of the Hellenistic World*, Cambridge 1935.
N.G.L. Hammond and G.T. Griffith, *A History of Macedonia*, vol 2, Oxford 1979.
Nicholas Hammond, *Philip of Macedon*, London 1994.
N.G.L. Hammond, *The Macedonian State, the Origin, Institutions, and History*, Oxford 1989.
N.G.L. Hammond and F.W. Walbank, *A History of Macedonia*, vol III, Oxford 1988.
E.V. Hansen, *The Attalids of Pergamon*, Ithaca NY, 1971.
F.W. Hasluck, *Cyzicus*, Cambridge 1910.
Gunther Holbl, *A History of the Ptolemaic Empire*, translated by Tina Saavedra, London 2001.
Henri Hubert, *The History of the Celtic People*, 2 vols, London 1934.
Robert Kallet-Marx, *Hegemony to Empire, the Development of the Roman Imperium in the East from 148 to 62 BC*, Berkeley and Los Angeles 1995.
H.P. Laubscher, 'Ein Ptolemaischer Gallierdenkmal', *Antike Kunst* 30, 1987, 131–154.
M. Launey, 'Un episode oublie de l'invasion galate en Asie Mineure', *Revue des etudes anciennes* 66, 1944, 217–236.
M. Launey, *Recherches sur les armees hellenistiques*, 2nd ed., Paris 1987.
L. Lazarov, 'The Celtic Tylate Style in the Time of Cavaros', in Vagalinski, *Search*, 97–117.
Barbara Levick, 'The Beginning of Tiberius' Career', *Classical Quarterly*, 1971.
Barbara Levick, *Roman Colonies in Southern Asia Minor*, Oxford 1967.
Kathryn Lomas, *The Rise of Rome*, London 2017.
Helen S. Lund, *Lysimachos, a Study in Hellenistic Kingship*, London 1992.
John Ma, *Antiochos III and the Cities of Western Asia Minor*, Oxford 1999.
Roger B. McShane, *The Foreign Policy of the Attalids of Pergamon*, Urbana IL, 1964.
David Magie, *Roman Rule in Asia Minor*, 2 vols, Princeton NJ 1950.
Christian Marek, *In the Land of a Thousand Gods, a History of Asia Minor in the Ancient World*, trans. Steven Rendall, Princeton NJ, 2016.
G. Mihailov, *Trakite*, Sofia 1972.
Stephen Mitchell, *Anatolia, Land, Men, and Gods in Asia Minor*, 2 vols, Oxford 1993.
Stephen Mitchell, 'Blucium and Peion; the Galatian Forts of King Deiotaros', *Anatolian Studies* 24, 1974, 61–75.
Stephen Mitchell and David French, *The Greek and Latin Inscriptions of Ankara*, Vol. I, Munich 2012.
Arnaldo Momigliano, *Alien Wisdom, the Limits of Hellenization*, Cambridge 1975.
G. Nachtergael, *Les Galates en Grece et les Soteria a Delphes*, Brussels 1977.
Daphne Nash, *The Coinage of the Celtic World*, London 1987.
D. O hOgain, *The Celts, a History*, Woodbridge 2002.

Pascalis Paschidis, *Between City and King: Prosopographical Studies on the Intermediaries between the Cities of the Greek mainland and the Aegean and the Royal Courts in the Hellenistic Period (322–190 BC)*, Meletemata 59, Athens 2008.
Sir William Ramsay, *A Historical Commentary on St Paul's Epistle to the Galatians*, London 1900.
H.D. Rankin, *The Celts and the Classical World*, London 1987.
A.J. Reinach, 'Un Monument Delphien: l'Aitolie sur les Trophees Gaulois de Kallion', *Journal International d'Archeologie Numismatique* 1911, 177–240.
A.L.F. Rivet, *Gallia Narbonensis, southern Gaul in Roman Times*, London 1988.
Lynn E. Roller, 'Hellenistic Epigraphic Texts from Gordion', *Anatolian Studies* 37, 1987, 103–133.
Anne Ross, 'Ritual and the Druids', in Miranda J. Green (ed.), *The Celtic World*, London 1995.
Thomas Russell, *Byzantium and the Bosporus*, Oxford 2017.
A.J. Sachs and H. Hunger, *Astronomical Diaries and Related Texts from Babylonia*, Vol. I, Vienna 1988.
E.T. Salmon, *Samnium and the Samnites*, Cambridge 1967.
E.T. Salmon, *Roman Colonisation under the Republic*, London 1969.
H.H. Schmitt, *Die Staatsvertrage des Altertums*, vol. III, Munich 1969.
M. Segre, 'Due nuovi testi storica', *Rivista de filologia*, 60, 1932, 446–452.
M. Shchukin, 'The Kelts in Eastern Europe', *Oxford Journal of Archaeology* 14, 1995, 201–227.
R.K. Sherk, 'Roman Galatia: the Governors from 25 BC to AD 114', *Aufsteig und Niedergang des Romische Welt*, II.7.2, Berlin, 1980, 954-1052.
A.N. Sherwin-White, *Roman Foreign Policy in the East*, Norman OK 1983.
Susan Sherwin-White and Amelie Kuhrt, *From Samarkhand to Sardis, A New Approach to the Seleucid Empire*, London 1993.
Karl Strobel, *Die Galater, Geschichte und Eigenart des Keltisches Staatenbildung auf den Boden deseHellenistischen Kleinasian*, Berlin 1996.
Karl Strobel, 'State Formation by the Galatians of Asia Minor', *Anatolica* 28, 2002, 1-46.
Ronald Syme, *Anatolica, Studies in Strabo*, Oxford 1995.
W.W. Tarn, *Antigonos Gonatas*, Oxford 1911 (reprinted 1969).
M.J. Treister, 'The Kelts in the North Pontic area: a Reassessment', *Antiquity* 67, 1993, 789–804.
L.F. Vagalinski (ed.), *In Search of Celtic Tylis in Thrace (III C. BC)*, Sofia 2010.
Angelo Verlinde, *The Roman Sanctuary Site at Pessinos*, Leuven 2015.
G. Vitucci, *Il regno di Bitinia*, Rome 1953.
F.W. Walbank, *A Commentary on Polybius*, vol. I, Oxford 1957.
M. Waulkens, 'The Imperial Sanctuary at Pessinos', *Epigraphica Anatolica* 7, 1986, 37–74.
C.B. Welles, *Royal Correspondence of the Hellenistic Period*, London 1934 (reprinted Chicago 1974).
E. Will, *Histoire Politique du Monde Hellenistique*, vol. 2, Nancy 1982.
M. Worrle, 'Antiochos I, Achaios der Altere, und des Galater', *Chiron* 5, 1975, 59–87.

Index

Abydos, 133, 152
Achaian League, 44–5, 74
Actium, battle, 194, 214, 216
Adriatic Sea, 4, 11, 16, 21, 32, 183, 187, 194
Aegean Sea, 2, 33, 120, 124, 141, 154, 174, 178
Agathokles, tyrant of Syracuse, 16, 107
Aigai, 53, 108, 110, 121
Aigosages, Galatian tribe, 90, 117, 123, 133–4, 150–2, 155–6, 167
Ainianians, 41, 43–5
Aioiorix, 176
Aiolis, 151
Aitolian League, 20, 41, 43–9, 54
Akhaios I, 105, 116–18, 120, 123, 139, 148, 150, 165
Akhaios II, 148–9, 153
Akichorios, xi, 24, 27, 29, 31, 37, 45–7, 50, 55, 61, 63, 69, 80
Alexander III the Great, 1, 3, 56–7, 193
  Galatian embassies to, 3–6, 8–9, 12, 18
Alexander, Macedonian pretender, 181
Alexandria Troas, 90, 97, 152
Allobrix, 78
Alps, vi, 192
Ambitouti, Galatian clan, 132
Amisos, 138
Amlada, 174, 178
Amphissa, 43, 45
Amyntas, king, 215–17
Ananes, 7
Andizetes, 187
Andriskos, Macedonian pretender ('Philip VI'), 181–2
Ankyra, xii, 125, 127, 141, 143–4, 146, 161–2, 217, 219, 222

Annius, M., 184–5
Antigonos I, king, 16, 21, 23, 32, 103
Antigonos II Gonatas, Macedonian king, 2, 24, 41–2, 44, 51–4, 58–9, 67–70, 81–4, 86, 98, 107–109, 114–16, 118, 121, 137
Antigonos III Doson, Macedonian king, 121
Antioch (Syria), 105, 115, 140
Antioch-in-Pisidia, 178–9
Antiochos I, Seleukid king, 24, 42, 51–2, 83–5, 87, 91, 97, 99–102, 104, 108–10, 112–14, 124, 126–7, 129, 135–6, 138, 178, 217
Antiochos II, Seleukid king, 115–16, 128, 134, 138, 144, 156–8, 178, 217
Antiochos III, Seleukid king, 116–18, 120–1, 123, 132, 148–50, 153, 155, 162, 165, 166, 175
Antiochos IV, Seleukid king, 122–3
Antiochos Hierax, 116, 120, 140–6, 148–50, 165
Antipater, Macedonian Regent, 13–14, 33
Antipater, son of Kassandros, Macedonian king, 36
Antipater, son of Philip, Macedonian king, 33–6, 51–2
Antipatros, Seleukid governor, 82–3, 85
Antonius, M. (Mark Antony), 214–16, 220
Antonius Sempronianus Gordianus Romanus, M. (Emperors Gordian I, II, III), 220–3
Apama, wife of Magas, 102, 110

Apameia-Kelainai, 103, 105, 173, 204
  Treaty of, 166, 168, 176, 178
Apatourios, Galatian assassin, 120, 148–9
Apollonia, 105
Aquillius, M.,
  (1), 179–80, 183
  (2), 204–205, 209
Arabs, 120
Argos, 53, 58
Argos, Orestis, 184
Ariarathes I, Kappadokian King, 139, 143
Ariarathes IV, Kappadokian King, 157–8, 167, 173, 175, 177
Ariarathes VI, Kappadokian King, 199
Ariarathes VII, Kappadokian King, 179–80, 199
Ariarathes VIII, Kappadokian King, 200, 202
Ariobarzanes, son of Mithradates VI, 136–8
Ariobarzanes I, Kappadokian King, 200, 202–203, 210, 212
Arisbe, 152
Armenia, 124, 215, 217–18
Arrhidaios, Macedonian king, 37
Arsinoe II, 22–3, 52
Artigniakos, 132
Asia, Roman province, 198
Asia Minor, vi, 7, 16, 20–2, 55, 82, 140–1
Assyrians, 125
Athens, 23, 35, 41, 47, 49, 58, 147, 205
Attalid kingdom, 20–1, 178, 198
Attalos I, King, 117–18, 120, 123, 133, 142–52, 154–5, 159, 162, 165, 167

Attalos II, king, 74, 170, 172, 176, 179
Attalos III, king, 161, 179
Attica, 15
Attis, 176
Augustus, Emperor, 192, 197, 216, 218, 220
  see also Octavian
Aurelius Cotta, M., 210
Austria, ix
Autariatai, 10–11, 14
Axios River, 14, 27, 38
Azov, Sea of, 78

Balkans, vi–vii, ix, 18, 55
Babylon, 5–6, 9
Baktria, 83, 141
Balkans, vi–vii, ix, 18, 55
Banat, ix, 4, 15–16, 24, 55–6, 60–3, 66, 80–1, 183, 192
Bastarnai, 122, 194–5
Bathanattos, 61–3, 68, 70
Bavaria, 7
Belgrade, ix, 63, 183
  see also Singidunum
Berenike, wife of Antiochos II, 115, 138–40
Berenike, wife of Ptolemy III, 140
Bessi, 186
Bithynia, xii, 69, 74–5, 84–7, 91–2, 98–9, 101, 127–8, 130–1, 138, 168, 201–203, 210, 212
Bituitus, 211
Black Sea, 1, 5, 21, 64, 77–8, 130, 136, 138, 156, 170
Blukion, 213
Bohemia, vi–vii, ix, 6–7, 12, 77, 165
Boii, vii, ix, 4, 6–7, 20, 185, 187, 190–1
Boiotia, 41, 47, 50
Bolgios, xi, 24, 27–32, 34–6, 38
Borysthenes River, 64, 77
  see also Bug
Bosporan kingdom, 202, 211
Bosporos, 69, 73–4, 81, 83, 84, 87, 107
Bratislava, 8
Brennos, 24, 27, 29, 31–2, 35, 37, 40, 43–7, 55, 59, 62–3, 68, 80, 91, 113
Brigotaros, chief of Trokmoi, 208, 213–215, 219

Britolagi, 77
Bug River, 77–8
  see also Borysthenes
Burebista, Dacian king, 190–2, 194, 196
Burgas, Gulf of, 70–2
Byzantion, 1, 29, 71–5, 82–7, 92, 96, 101, 137, 139

Caballum, 161
Caecilius Metellus, Q., 181
Caecilius Metellus Caprianius, C., 186
Caeni, 188
Capelianus, 223
Caracalla, Emperor, 222
Carpathian Mountains, 8, 70, 77
Carthage, 153
Cassius, C., 204–205
Celtiberians, viii
Chaironeia, battle, 205
Chersonese, 70, 81–2, 115, 156, 188
  see also Thracian Chersonese
Chios, 172
Cicero, 214
Cilicia, 140, 210, 212, 214
Cimbri, 20, 185–6, 199
Cisalpine Gaul, vii, 12, 64
Claudius, Emperor, 219
Coins, as evidence, 13
Commodus, Emperor, 221–2
Corinth, 49
Cornelius Scipio Asiagenus, L., 189–90
Cornelius Sulla, L., 189–90, 200, 202, 205–206, 209
Cosconius, C., 182
Costobogi, 77
Crete, Cretans, 120
Crimea, 10, 64, 77
Culloden, 42
Cummuni, 197
Cyrene, Cyrenaica, 102, 110–11, 114, 140

Dacia, Dacians, 8, 10–12, 63–4, 66, 77, 187, 190–1, 193, 198
Dalmatia, 181, 183
Danube River, vi–vii, 1, 4, 8, 12–13, 17, 25, 48, 61, 64, 66, 185, 187, 190
Daphne, 122

Dardanians, xi, 1, 14, 28–30, 32, 40, 55, 58–60, 64–6, 81, 121–2, 184, 187, 189–91, 193, 195
Deiotares, chief of Tolistobogii and tetrarch, 208–209, 213–16, 219
Delos, 96, 147
Delphi, vi, xi, 41, 43, 45–6, 48, 50, 61, 69, 80–1, 85, 92, 100, 114, 147, 186, 189, 193
Demetrias, 42
Demetrios I Poliorketes, King, 17, 19, 21, 23, 35–6, 53
Demochares, son of Laches, 35–6, 40
Demosthenes, 35
Dentheletai, 195, 196–7
Didius, T., 188
Didyma, xii, 35, 92–3, 97, 101
Diocletian, Emperor, 222
Dionysius I, tyrant of Syracuse, 107
Diophantos, 212
Dniepr River, 10, 64, 77
Dniestr River, 10, 77
Dokimeion, 105
Domitrios, Cn., 214
Doris, 43
Drava River, ix, 63, 66, 184, 187
Dromichaites, Getai king, 17
Drunemeton, 131

Egnatius, Cn., 183
Egypt, 21–2, 33, 51–2, 102, 108, 110–14, 117–18, 121, 140, 156
Elagabalus, Emperor, 221–2
Elaia, 153
Elephant Victory, 100–102, 104, 109, 124, 127
Eleusis, 41
Emeti, 189
Epeiros, 53
Ephesos, xii, 95, 100, 139, 154, 164
Eposognetos, 157, 159–60, 169
Erythrai, xii, 95–6, 98, 129
Etruscans, 6–7
Eumachos, 207, 212–13
Eumenes I, Attalid king, 142
Eumenes II, Attalid king, 159, 164–6, 168–78, 180
Eurydike, wife of Ptolemy I, 51

France, vi–vii

Gaesatae, 7–8, 26
Gaizatorix, 171, 177
Galatia, vi, *passim*
  kingdom in 198, 212
  massacre of chiefs, 205–208
  and Mithradates VI, 199–210
  Roman province, 215–16
  settlement of, chapter 5
Gallipoli Peninsula
  see Chersonese and
  Thracian Chersonese
Gangra, 168, 177
Gaul, vi, 6, 12, 55, 60–1, 91–3, 155, 174, 190
Gauls, expansion of, vii–viii
Germany, vi, 6, 12, 25, 55, 60, 62, 64
Getai, 17, 194
Gordion, xii, 125, 133–4, 166, 168, 174, 220
Gordios, 199–200
Greece, 12, 16, 20, 38, Chapter 3, 80, 157, 166, 174, 205

Haemos (Balkan) Mountains, 1, 3, 12–13, 15, 55, 66–7
Hallstatt (archaeological period), vi
Harpassos, 144
Halys River, 125–6, 171, 209
Hegesias, 155–6
Hellespont (Dardanelles), 22, 55, 81, 83, 85, 89, 123, 141, 151, 155
Hellespontine Phrygia, 82, 89
Helvetii, 185, 190
Herakleia Pontica, 74, 84, 86, 127, 138, 170
Herakleia Trachinia, 41, 43, 137
Hermos River, 100
Hungary, 7–8, 61, 64
Hylli, 10

Ilion, xii, 90, 97
Illyrians, ix, 9–10, 14, 23, 25, 32, 56, 58, 65, 181, 183, 186
India, 21
Insubres, 6–7
Ionia, 151, 174
Ionian Islands, 16
Ipsos, 16

Iran, 116, 118
Isthmus of Corinth, 40, 47
Italy, vii, 6, 8, 12, 19–20, 23, 25–6, 52, 62, 93, 108, 156–7, 166, 181, 185, 209, 217
Iuventius Thalna, P., 181

Jugurtha, 186
Julia Domna, 223
Julius Caesar, C., 190, 192, 214, 220
Julius Verus, Emperor, 223

Kabyle, 1, 57, 70, 72, 76
Kaikos River, 144
Kalchedon, 84, 86
Kallatis, 156
Kallion, 44–5
Kallippos son of Moirokles, 41, 49
Kambaules, 15–19, 24, 60, 70
Kantares, 145
Kappadokia, 126, 139, 141, 146, 158–9, 163, 167, 175, 177, 179–80, 199–202, 209–10, 215, 217, 218; map 2
Karia, 89, 99, 101, 103, 141–2, 144, 205
Kassandreia, 22, 51, 52
Kassandros, 11, 14–17, 19, 21, 34
Kassignatos, 171–2
Kastor, chief of Tektosages, 208, 213, 215
Kastor II, 219
Kavaros, Tylis king, 72–6
Kavaros, Galatian kidnapper, 93
Kerithrios, 24, 26–7, 29, 31–2, 35, 38, 57, 60, 67; map 1
Kertch, Strait of, 77
Kerkyra, 16
Kiddioukome, 101, 105, 139, 149
Kieros, 137, 170
Klondikos, 122
Koloe, 144
Komboiomais, 160
Komboutis, 44
Kommontorios, 60, 67–71, 81–4, 109
Korupedion, battle, 21
Kos, 48, 50
Kotys II, Thracian king, 27
Kritasos, 190

Kyiv, 10, 77, 86
Kypsela, 139
Kyrrhestai, 118
Kyzikos, 89–90, 92, 96–7, 106, 211; map 2

Lamian War, 49
Lampsakos, 155–7, 164
Laodike, wife of Antiochos II, 115, 138–9, 140
Laodike, wife of Ariarahes VI, 199
Laodikeia-ad-Lykon, 101, 103, 105, 204
La Tene (archaeological period), vi, 10, 66, 77, 132
Leonnorios, 50, 60, 67–70, 80–5, 87–8, 95, 97, 99, 102, 107, 129, 130; map 1
Leosthenes, 49
Lete, Macedon, 184, 188
Libici, 7
Libya, 111
Licinius, P., 172–3
Licinius Crassus, M., 193–5
Licinius Lucullus, L., 210–12
Licinius Murena, L., 209
Limyra, 104
Lingones, 7
Livius Drusus, M., 186
Loutarios, 50, 60, 67–9, 70, 80–3, 85, 88, 90, 97, 107, 130
Lydia, Lydians, 89, 125, 133, 141, 150
Lykaonia, 167, 178–80, 218
Lykia, 101, 103, 205, 218
Lypedon, Mount, battle, 170
Lysimacheia, 23, 82, 107, 109, 139; map 2
Lysimachos, king, 14–15, 17, 19, 21–2, 24, 34, 37, 57, 67, 69, 76, 84, 92, 128, 139, 141, 156
Lysimachos the Galatian, assassin, 119
Lysias (city), 105
Lysias, 148

Macedon, 1–6, 8, 11–12, 14, 16–18, 21–2, 26–39, 40, 50–3, 56, 58–9, 65–7, 80, 81, 83, 107–108, 110, 114, 121, 133, 141, 155–6, 172, 181–2, 193–5, 205

Maedi, 184–5, 187–9
Magaba, Mount, battle, 160, 163, 169, 182
Magas, 102, 110–13
Magnesia, Thessaly, 41–2
Magnesia, Asia, 100, 178
  battle, 118, 120, 158, 161
Maiandros River, 100, 103
Malian Gulf, 41
Malis, 41, 43, 47
Manlius Vulso, C., 124, 137, 157–66, 168–9, 173, 175
Marathon, 49
Marmara, Sea of, 156
  see also Propontis
Massalia, 70–1, 91, 93, 155
Maximinus Thrax, Emperor, 221–2
Megara, 79, 109, 115–16, 118
Meleagros, Macedonian king, 33–5, 37
Melitene, 218
Mesopotamia, 118, 145
Metropolis, 105
Miletos, 93–4, 97, 101, 103
Minucius Rufus, M., 186
Mithradates I, 125–7, 136–7, 139
Mithradates II, 137, 141–3
Mithradates V, 179–80
Mithradates VI, 198–212
Mithradateion, 213
Moesi, Moesia, 12, 15, 64, 66, 187, 190, 194
Moldova, 77
Molon, 117–20
Monunios, 23
Morava River, 14–15, 62–3, 194
Moravia, 77
Morzios, 163, 167
Mysia, 151

Neonteichnos, 101, 105, 139, 149
Nero, Emperor, 219
Nestos River, 59
Nikaia, wife of Lysimachos, 34
Nikomedes I, Bithynian King, 85–7, 91, 107, 117, 123, 127, 135–7, 146, 151
Nikomedes III, Bithynian King, 199–200
Nikomedes IV, Bithynian King, 202–204, 210

Nile, River, 112, 114
Noricum, ix, 25, 64–6, 185, 187, 195, 197
Northern League, 84–5, 87, 92, 99, 106, 190
Noviodunum, 78
Numidia, 223
Nymphis of Herakleia, 137

Octavian, 192–4
  see also Augustus
Octavius, Cn., 210
Odessos, 70–1, 156
Odrysai, 1–2, 13, 76
Oitia, country and mountain, 43–4
Okondiai, 132
Olympichos, 142
Olympus, Mount, Galatia, 160–1, 169, 182
Onomaris, 9
Oppius, Q., 204–205
Orchomenos, battle, 205
Orestis, 184
Orestorios, 44
Ortiagon, 60, 169–70, 176, 208, 214
Ottoman Empire, ix, 63

Paionians, 27, 29, 31, 35, 38, 59–60, 66, 103; map 1
Palestine, 119
Pamphylia, 205, 215, 217; map 2
Panion, battle, 119
Pannonia, 61–2, 64, 77, 78, 185, 187, 191–2, 194, 196
Pantikapaion, 77
Paphlagonia, 163, 171, 177, 199–200, 202, 204
Papirius Carbo, 186
Parthia, 123, 215–18
Patrai, 44, 49
Peion, 213
Peiraios, 41
Pergamon, 83, 96–7, 100, 106, 131, 141, 144, 147, 149, 153, 168, 175, 201, 205–207
Perinthos, 1
Pernik, 14, 27
Perseus, Macedonian king, 122, 172, 174, 181
Perseus, pretender, 181
Persian Empire, Persians, 2, 5, 13, 41, 45, 48, 133

Pessinos, 125, 131, 153–4, 161, 176–7, 214, 217; map 2
Petra, Troad, 97
Pharnakes I, Pontic King, 170–1, 173, 175
Pharnakes II, Pontic King, 214
Pharsalus, battle, 194, 214
Phila, wife of Antigonos II, 52
Philetairos, Lord of Pergamon, 84, 89–90, 141–2
Philip II, Macedonian king, 1–4, 7, 12, 29, 56, 57, 193
Philip V, Macedonian king, 65–6, 121–2, 151, 170
Philip the Arab, Emperor, 223
Philip, pretender, 181
Philippi, battle, 194, 214
Philippopolis, 1, 15, 57
Philomelion, 105
Philomelos, 46
Phokaia, 55; map 2
Phokis, 40, 45, 50
Phrygia, 55, 125, 127, 131–3, 167, 173, 175, 180, 201, 204, 210; map 2
Phthiotis, 41
Pindus Mountains, 19, 59
Pisidia, Pisidians, 103, 105, 178, 212–13, 216–17
Pleistainos son of Antipater, 99
Po River, vii, 6
Poland, vii, ix, 78
Polykritos, 95, 98–9
Pompeius, Sex., 184–5
Pompeius Magnus, Cn. (Pompey), 192, 211, 214
Pontos, 84, 125–8, 136, 138, 141, 167, 180, 190, 200, 203, 209, 212
Porcius Cato, C., 186
Posdala, 212
Priene, 93–5, 97–8, 101, 106
Propontis (Sea of Marmara), 1, 4, 55, 81, 170
Prusias I, Bithynian king, 74, 123, 134, 152, 155, 169–70, 175–77
Ptolemaios, son of Pyrrhos, 108
Ptolemy I, 21–2, 37, 51
Ptolemy II, 22, 24, 33, 51–2, 102, 104, 108, 110–14, 116, 123, 135, 137, 139–40
Ptolemy III, 138, 140–1, 155

Ptolemy IV, 120–1, 157
Ptolemy Keraunos, 22–4, 26, 28–34, 51–2, 88, 96
Ptolemy, son of Lysimachos, 22–3, 30, 36–7, 51–2
Pydna, battle, 122
Pylaemenes, 216, 219
Pyrrhos, king of Epeiros, 17, 22–4, 32, 52–3, 108–10, 115, 118, 121

Raphia, battle, 119–20
Rhodes, 74, 168, 204
Rhodope Mountains, 27, 32
Rigosages, 117–18, 120, 122, 132, 134
Romania, vi
Rome, vi–viii, 10, 20, 58, 60, 63, 65–6, 122, 130, 137, 153, 155–6, 168–9, 172–80
Scordisci, 181–97
Mithradates VI, 198–212

Samnites, vii
Samothrace, 23
Sangarius River, 125
Sardis, 84, 99, 154, 173
Satala, 218
Sava River, ix, 8, 63–6, 182, 187, 192
Scepsis, 97
Scirians, 78
Scopje, 64
Scordisci, ix, 1, 4, 8–11, 14, 18, 25, 48, 50, 55–6, 60, 65–6, 73, 76, 79, 112, 121, 156–7
Rome, 182–98, 211, 215
Scordus, Mount, 9
Scribonius Curio, C., 190
Seleukeia-in-Pieria, 119, 140–1
Seleukid kingdom, 20, 52, 98, 104–105, 107, 138, 141
Seleukos I, King, 21–4, 28, 32, 52, 83, 92–3, 105, 127, 139, 156
Seleukos II, King, 115, 140–3, 148, 150
Seleukos III, King, 116, 119–20, 148
Seleukos IV, King, 158
Sellassia, battle, 121
Sentinum, battle, 19
Senones, vii, 7, 12, 19–20

Sentius, C., 189
Septimius Severus, Emperor, 221
Servilius Vatia, P., 210
Seuthes III, 13–16, 27, 57, 70
Seuthopolis, 15, 27, 57, 70
Sicily, 16, 52, 108
Silius Nerva, P., 197
Singidunum, ix, 8, 15–16, 63, 197; map 1
see also Belgrade
Sinope, 130, 170, 204
Sinorix, 214
Sinti, 189
Siscia, 181, 184–5, 187, 192–4, 196
Skythians, 2
Solovettius, 172, 174, 176
Sosthenes, 36–8, 50–1, 81
Sotas, son of Lykos, 94, 98
Sostratos of Kalchedon, 76
Spain, vi, viii, 12
Sparta, 91, 107, 108, 121
Spercheios River, 41, 42–4, 47–50, 80, 113
Stobi, 62, 66
Stratoike, wife of Ariarathes, 139
Strymon River, 14, 27
Sulpicius Quirinus, P., 217
Synnada, 173
Syracuse, 16, 91, 107
Syria, 21, 22, 98, 105, 110, 117, 139–42, 149, 178
Syrian Wars;
First, 102, 104, 113
Third, 116
Fourth, 116
Syrmos, Triballian king, 3

Taurisci, ix, 4, 185, 187, 190
Taurunum, 64
Taurus Mountains, 16, 19, 144, 146, 167, 174, 210, 213, 216
Tavium, 125, 217; map 2
Tektosages, 7, 50, 60–1, 69, 87–9, 91–3, 97, 99, 101, 103–104, 114, 125–6, 136–9, 141–5, 160, 163, 170–1, 208, 213; map 2
Telamon, battle, 25, 137
Telesarchos, 44
Telmessos, Lykia, 52, 170
Teutoni, 20, 185, 199

Themisonion, 103, 105
Thermopylai, 40–2, 44–5, 47–9, 69, 80–1, 100
Thespiai, 49
Thessaloniki, 52–3, 184
Thessaly, 40–1, 43–4, 47–8, 55, 81, 170, 172
Thracian Chersonese, 16, 22, 51
see also Chersonese
Thrace, Thracians, ix, 1–3, 5, 9, 13–16, 24–6, 31, 50, 55–8, 60, 67–8, 70–7, 80–2, 103, 119–20, 145, 151, 154, 156, 157, 182–3, 185, 189, 191, 193; map 1
Thundza River, 70
Tiberius, Emperor, 197, 219
Tigranes, Armenian king, 200, 208, 211
Teion, 86, 170
Tisza River, ix, 64
Tolistobogii, 85, 88–9, 95, 99–102, 104, 114, 124–6, 135–7, 143–6, 149, 151, 153–7, 159–60, 163, 169, 176, 208, 212; map 2
Tolosa, 50, 55, 60, 91
Trachis, 44
Trade, 13
Triballi, 2–4, 12–13, 15, 26, 28–9, 31, 56–7; map 1
Troad, 12, 89, 123
Trokmoi, 85, 88–9, 104, 125–6, 135, 139, 160, 163, 175, 177, 179, 208, 212; map 2
Tylis, kingdom, 29, 55–6, 60, 66–8, 70–7, 79, 96, 109, 112, 139, 151, 156; map 2
Tyras, 77, 81–2

Ukraine, vii, ix, 10, 76–9, 87
Upper Satrapies, 117, 119

Valley of the Roses, 15, 27
Veneti, 6–7
Vennii, 197
Vespasian, Emperor, 218
Vetren, 14, 27
Voturi, 132

Ziaelas, Bithynia king 131, 136–8, 143, 145–6
Zimnicea (Novae), 3
Zipoetas, 85, 87, 90